THE PENTIUM
CHRONICLES

Published by John Wiley & Sons, Inc., Hoboken, New Jersey.
Published simultaneously in Canada.

For general information on our other products and services or for technical support, please contact our Customer Care Department within the United States at (800) 762-2974, outside the United States at (317) 572-3993 or fax (317) 572-4002.

Wiley also publishes its books in a variety of electronic formats. Some content that appears in print may not be available in electronic format. For information about Wiley products, visit our web site at www.wiley.com.

Library of Congress Cataloging-in-Publication Data is available.

ISBN-13 978-0-471-73617-2
ISBN-10 0-471-73617-1

Printed in the United States of America.

10 9 8 7 6 5 4 3

THE PENTIUM CHRONICLES

The People, Passion, and Politics Behind Intel's Landmark Chips

Robert P. Colwell

A WILEY-INTERSCIENCE PUBLICATION

CONTENTS

v

FOREWORD

This book is simply a treat. Ever since Bob Colwell contacted me about writing the foreword for the book, I have not been able to stop reading the draft. There is something extremely seductive about this book but it took me a while to realize why that is so. Bob is the first person, to my knowledge, who has managed to tell the story of an ambitious engineering project in a way that is truly insightful and funny. With every page I turn, I run into crisp, insightful episodes that can make both engineers and executives smile. Having managed several large projects in a research environment, the chapters take me back to so many stressful moments in my career and provide insights that I was not able to articulate nearly as clearly as Bob has. Bob's insights are by no means limited to microprocessor development projects. They are fundamental to any ambitious undertaking that requires a large team of talented people to accomplish, be it movie making, a political campaign, a military operation, or, yes, an engineering project.

Please bear with me for a moment and allow me to disclose how I came to cross paths with Bob. My professional life began when I decided to work on a superscalar, out-of-order processor design called HPS for my PhD thesis at the University of California at Berkeley in 1984. I was a first-year graduate student who had just read papers on data flow machines, CDC6600, IBM 360/91, and CRAY-1. It was during a time when VLSI technology had just become capable of realizing interesting processor designs. There were several vibrant processor design projects going on in academia and industry. Many of us dreamed of changing the world with great ideas in processor design.

My office mate, Mike Shebanow, my thesis advisor, Yale Patt, and I started to kick around some ideas about using parallel processing techniques to drastically improve the performance of processors. In retrospect, we had an intuition that turned out to be correct: there is tremendous value in using parallel processing techniques to speed up traditional sequential programs. We felt that the parallel processing ideas back then were flawed in that they required programs to be developed as parallel programs. This is like requiring a driver to hand-coordinate the engine combustion, the transmission, the turning of the wheels, and the brake pads while driving down a busy street. Although there may be a small number of race car drivers who really want to explicitly control the activities under the hood, the mass market demands simplicity. Achieving massive speedup that requires explicit parallel programming efforts would not have nearly as much impact as achieving modest speedup for simple programming models. We settled on the concept of designing a dataflow machine whose sole responsibility was to execute instructions in traditional programs with as much parallelism as possible. We envisioned having a piece of hardware to translate traditional instructions into dataflow machine instructions, execute them in parallel, and expose their results in a sequential manner. All parallelism would be "under the hood."

In the summer of 1984, Yale, Mike, and I received an invitation to go to the Eastern Research Lab of Digital Equipment Corporation to try to apply our ideas to VAX designs. We started at the conceptualization phase described by Bob. After a few sessions, we realized that we needed some way to quantify the amount of opportunity we could expect from real code. I ended up developing the equivalent of the data flow analyzer tool Bob describes in "The Right Tool" Section in Chapter 2. Joel Emer and Doug Clark graciously allowed us to access the execution traces they had acquired from real VAX-11/780 workloads. I studied the 780 microcode so that I could write a decoder program that translated the VAX instructions into simple microoperations. The dataflow analysis tool was then used to analyze the amount of intrinsic parallelism available among these operations. From our experience with the dataflow analysis tool, we quickly realized that we would need to be able to overlap the execution of operations that are separated by conditional branches. We would also need to generate these operations and expose their results in a fast enough manner to keep the dataflow execution units busy. We managed to focus much of our work with the help of the analysis tool. We also had a first-hand experience as to how much energy one can waste by trying to convince each other without quantitative results.

Now we are getting to the point of my long-winded story. Between 1984 and 1987, I worked passionately with Yale and my fellow students Mike Shebanow and Steve Melvin on a first design of HPS. I personally experienced the conceptual phase and the refinement phase as part of a four-person team. There were many questions that we tried to address with our limited ability to formulate a potential design and acquire simulation data. In retrospect, we left many issues not addressed; our project generated many more questions than we answered. It was a heroic pioneer-style exploration of designing a speculative out-of-order-execution processor. We presented the core ideas and discussed the design challenges in a pair of 1985 papers (see references [1] and [2] in the Bibliography). We showed a high-level schematic design of a conceptual out-of-order processor in which we described a vision for the branch prediction, speculative execution, instruction scheduling, and memory ordering mechanisms. Variations of these mechanisms have indeed appeared in the industry designs, including Intel's P6. I used to feel that we deserved all of the intellectual credit for the out-of-order execution processors in the marketplace today. As I grew more experienced, I began to see that what we had actually still required a lot of intellectual work to finish. Bob's chapters give great explanations of these intellectual efforts. I have never seen a book that gives such an insightful, comprehensive treatment of the intellectual challenges involved in managing a large-scale project to success.

When I presented my thesis work at major universities in 1987, I received numerous skeptical comments from many prominent computer architecture researchers. Many of them were working on much simpler design styles referred to as RISC [3]. The message that I consistently received was that the HPS style processor design was much too complicated. No one in his or her right mind would build a real machine based on the concept. Even if someone did, the complexity would result in such a slow clock that the processor would not be competitive. Yale and I argued forcefully about the feasibility of the model but had no hard evidence. While Bob and his team created a product that is a great business success, they also created hard evidence that our original vision was on the right track. It takes an extraordinary team to go against so many prominent naysayers to achieve a vision that is considered pie in the sky. Personally, I feel forever indebted to these great individuals for redemption of personal value.

In 1987, I decided to join the faculty of the University of Illinois, Urbana–Champaign. During the second semester of my teaching career, I taught an advanced graduate course in computer design. Naturally, much of the material I covered came from my thesis work, which I taught with great conviction. There was a student in my class named Andy Glew, whom I noticed from day one. At every lecture Andy would ask me extremely probing questions. Sometimes, I had to politely tell him to stop so that I could move on to the next topic. He was especially intrigued by the concept of register renaming and what I did in my PhD thesis. The structure that performs register renaming was one of the trickiest parts of my thesis work. We named the structure Register Alias Table (RAT) in our papers, partly due to the fact that it was such a pain to design. For those of you who are familiar with the P6 microarchitecture [34], the register renaming structure assumes the same name. This should not be a surprise considering the fact that Andy was the architect who did the initial work on the structure. It is also amazing how the real technology transfer always takes place in almost random student placements.

Please do not let me get away with convincing you that this is a book just for computer designers. The real soul of the book is about how to manage intellects in the real world to accomplish incredible goals. In an honest manner, Bob gives the ultimate principles of great project management: acquire the best minds, organize them so that each of them operates within their comfort zone, protect them from the forces of mediocrity, help them to take calculated risks, and motivate them to tie up the loose ends. Mediocrity is the equivalent of gravity in the world of creative projects. Whether you are in the business of making movies, running a presidential campaign, developing a new drug, shooting a spacecraft to Mars, or starting a new chain store, you will find the insights here to be of ultimate value. Buckle up and enjoy the ride.

WEN-MEI HWU

University of Illinois
February 2005

PREFACE

Microprocessor design, on the massive scale on which Intel does it, is like an epic ocean voyage of discovery. The captain and his officers select the crew carefully, so as to represent in depth all the requisite skills. They pick the types, sizes, and numbers of ships. They stock the ships with whatever provisions they think they will need, and then they launch into the unknown. With a seasoned crew, good weather, and a fair amount of luck, most of the voyage will go as expected. But luck is capricious, and the crew must inevitably weather the storms, when everything goes awry at once and they must use all their experience to keep the ships afloat.

Being involved in a major microprocessor design project like the P6 feels exactly like that except for the passage of time. Most ocean voyages do not take the 4+ years we invested in the P6.

From the beginning, my publisher wanted to title this book "The Pentium Chronicles." I was initially skeptical. When I hear "chronicle," I immediately think of a history, and I am no historian. But the second definition of chronicle, "narrative," fits exactly with what I envisioned for the book—a series of events as told by a P6 insider. So, reassured by this definition and the publisher's prediction that *Pentium Chronicles* would have the majestic draw of *Lord of the Rings,* I acquiesced to the title (as long as Orlando Bloom plays me in the movie version).

WHAT YOU WILL FIND HERE

The substance of this book, its heart blood, are the events that taught me something about the craft of computer design in the context of a large company. Most of the narrative centers on events surrounding the P6 project, with some devoted to the Pentium 4 project as well. I had several reasons for focusing on P6, but the main one is that the project is far enough in the past that I can confidently avoid its intellectual property issues. The Pentium 4 project is still too recent; I cannot yet disentangle the general engineering lessons we learned there from the specific product context.

You will find real names in this book, but not in every instance. My policy on real names is simple: I refuse to purposely show any specific engineering colleague in a negative light. My intention is to use real incidents and events to illuminate the general engineering methods; it doesn't matter who made a particular mistake. What matters are the conditions that led up to a particular design or project error, and how someone might prevent a similar occurrence in future designs. We all make mistakes—that's one of the book's major themes. Our designs have to work flawlessly despite us.

But I will use real names in other cases. One major reason is to avoid giving the impression that I was solely responsible for the outstanding engineering being described.

The P6 project had many more than its fair share of brilliant engineers, and credit should go where it's due.

Parts of this book may come across as my personal treatise on how to do technical project management. It is not my intent to compete with the mountain of "how to do project management" tomes in existence. I learned more from my talented and dedicated design manager partner, Randy Steck, than I did from the dozen or so project management books I read along the way. My intent is simply to describe what we did in the P6 project and how it worked out—the bad along with the good.

I believe that in any well-intentioned, well-run engineering endeavor, choices will be made among multiple plausible options, some of which will turn out to be brilliant, others not. We should always learn from our mistakes, but if we are striving for excellence, we should also consider the triumphs and tribulations of others. I sincerely hope that by exploring lessons from the P6 and Pentium 4 projects, this book provides a way to do that.

HOW THE BOOK IS ORGANIZED

I wrestled with the question of how best to present these lessons. I could simply describe what happened in the project and let the reader draw inferences as needed. But then I would be guilty of breaking an important rule I learned as an engineering manager: Never let an engineer get away with simply presenting the data. Always insist that he or she lead off with the conclusion to which the data led. The engineer's job in that presentation is to convince you that he reached the right conclusion. If he or she cannot draw a conclusion, or will not, then either the work or the engineer lacks the maturity to justify making the presentation at all.

I could also write a book that consists only of the lessons learned, with anecdotes provided to buttress the case where necessary. The trouble with that approach is that it might become boring, pedantic, quite possibly pretentious, and would push the book into the already overpopulated camp of how to manage design projects.

I decided to seek a middle ground, one that relies on actual events for its authenticity and immediacy, but is heavily seasoned with what I personally found important and educational about the events' outcomes. My aim is to make that narrative compelling, and if it falls short in places, then at least it will be entertaining.

Readers who know me, who have heard me deliver technical talks, or who have read my columns in *Computer,* the IEEE Computer Society's flagship magazine, know that I hold lots of opinions on pretty much everything, including other projects and product lines within Intel, other microprocessor design firms, the future of the industry, and so on. You won't find me expounding on those topics at great length within these pages. Read the column and go to the talks. A book stretches my plausible deniability safety net just a little too far.

Having arrived at my middle ground, I was then faced with how to build on it. The most natural way was to present the P6 project chronologically, so the book is mostly organized in that sequence, although it is hardly linear. P6 was a big project that started with one person (me), grew over several years to 450+ people, and then eventually decreased to zero staff. In between were waves of concurrent activity. For the first year or two, the project was a handful of chip architects conceiving and documenting a general approach that would realize the project's overall goals. Meanwhile, a design team was being recruited, organized, and trained so that it would be ready to hit the ground running when the architects were ready. Two validation teams, presilicon and postsilicon, were also recruiting, training, and writing tests for the day when they were needed. Other groups were trying to anticipate the requisite manufacturing production challenges and what could be done to ameliorate them. Marketing was preparing their campaign strategies, marketing literature, and promotional materials, and setting up customer visits to validate the architects' design feature choices and to inform potential customers of what lay ahead on Intel's product road map. Try plotting all that on a single line.

At the P6 project outset, we were charged with designing a new microprocessor for Intel. But before we could start thinking about how transistors could be organized, we had to consider how the *project* would be organized. P6's first architecture manager, Fred Pollack, and P6's design manager, Randy Steck, came up with an initial division of labor and made judgment calls about overall team sizes and effort allocations. It's also clear in retrospect that Fred, in particular, was a masterful corporate diplomat, keeping the existing corporate antibodies from killing or damaging our project, back when we were a bunch of unknowns proposing odd plans and slinging scary-sounding phrases like "out-of-order microarchitectures" and "glueless multiprocessing." Even early on, Fred gave us the freedom to roam, and trusted us to come back with something worth keeping.

The basic steps that the P6 project would have to accomplish were reasonably clear: conceive a microarchitecture, do the detailed chip design, debug first silicon, and drive the chip into production. You can map these steps informally into microarchitecture conception, writing the structured register-transfer logic (SRTL) software model, and debugging early silicon. But looking at the project with the benefit of hindsight, I believe it's more useful to view it as four phases: concept, refinement, realization, and production. Consequently, these four phases constitute most of the book and can serve as a kind of framework for any large chip-development project.

Naturally, not every lesson stems directly from the P6 project. Any undertaking is influenced by its environment, and the P6 project was no exception. The book is filled with lessons about how teams, corporate policies, and even location can affect a project's effectiveness.

As a final chapter, I couldn't resist including some of the more interesting questions that I've been asked over the years.

FOR THE RECORD

I dreaded writing the following section. I knew I couldn't do an adequate job of acknowledging the indispensable contributions of hundreds of people, and only a few words to those I explicitly name isn't nearly enough. I cannot do justice to all who contributed to the microprocessor developments outlined here. Just listing all the names would make the book twice as long and still would not be sufficient recognition for the dedication, creativity, enthusiasm, and unstoppable élan of a great design team.

But it would be an even greater injustice to say nothing. So with considerable humility and trepidation, but profound gratitude, I offer the following thanks.

ACKNOWLEDGMENTS

The P6 project was an effort of many people, and, on a smaller scale, so was this book. In a quasirandom order, here is a list of people I must single out for thanks.

Richard Calderwood, for being an outstanding patent attorney, an astute reviewer of partially baked manuscripts, and a reliable friend.

Dave Papworth, Glenn Hinton, Michael Fetterman, and Andy Glew—with you guys on my team, I'd do it all again.

Wen-mei Hwu, for your encouragement, your perspective, your unselfishness, and your foreword to this book.

Readers of my *IEEE Computer Magazine* "At Random" column, for your interest and support. You convinced me there might be a book hiding somewhere in my memories of the P6 project. This book is all your fault.

Dadi Perlmutter, Mike Fister, Will Swope, and Pat Gelsinger, for the opportunities you gave me and the errors you forgave. In your own way, each of you gave me the maneuvering room to try new things and the support I needed when a few of them went awry.

Lew Paceley, Jerry Braun, Richard Dracott, and John Hyde—by your examples, you showed me where my biases were regarding marketing, and the lessons you taught me were among the most important that I learned at Intel. Frank Binns, thanks for proving that marketing people can do real technical work, and for having a twisted sense of humor—balm for tough days. Terry Nefcy, Adrian Carbine, Gary Brown, Jim Hunt, Tom Marchok, John Barton, Donald Parker, Keshavan Tiruvallur ("K7"), Bob Bentley, Ticky Thakkar, Rani Borkar, and Steve Pawlowski—thanks for helping make Intel a great place at which to work. Katie Abela-Gale, thanks for the candy and the smiles.

Dawn Kulesa, Human Resources representative extraordinaire—for me, you were the human face of what sometimes seemed a cold, impersonal corporate machine. Your initiatives on training and mentoring at Intel were exemplary and helped the team enormously.

Mary Kay Havens and Mary Killeen—it wasn't your job, but you showed me the ropes of managing a large group and routinely went well beyond the call of duty. You can be on my design team any day.

Nancy Talbert, this book's editor—thanks for your innumerable improvements to this manuscript. You helped turn a pile of ideas into something approaching coherency.

Joseph Malingowski, for your constant mentoring as I was growing up. It becomes clearer to me with each passing year how uniquely valuable your tutelage in technology really was. The details of how things work, I learned in college and industry; how to organize and think about them, I learned from you.

Scott Hamilton and Judi Prow, *Computer Magazine*'s dynamic duo: I wouldn't have written this book if I hadn't been writing the "At Random" column, and I wouldn't have done that column without your help and encouragement.

Randy Steck, my partner in this enterprise—nobody does it better.

My parents, Bob and Agnes Colwell. I still aspire to the standards that you set, and thank you for that invaluable legacy.

Ellen Colwell, my wife, sounding board, editor-in-chief, and best friend. She wasn't on the payroll, but in a very real sense she was also a member of the P6 team. I couldn't have done that project, nor this book, without her unwavering support. Thanks also to my children Kelly, Ken, and Kristen, who grew up during the P6 and Willamette years and often wondered where Daddy was.

THE JOY OF PURPOSE

I realized early on that it would not be easy to capture the nuances of a project of this magnitude. P6 was a landmark design project and microarchitecture, both for Intel and for the industry. I felt that way during and after the project, and dozens of other project engineers have told me they felt the same. For those very reasons, I felt compelled to record at least some of the vast experience that went into P6 development—insights and vision that might otherwise be lost.

George Bernard Shaw wrote, "This is the true joy in life, the being used for a purpose recognized by yourself as a mighty one . . . the being a force of nature instead of a feverish, selfish little clod of ailments and grievances complaining that the world will not devote itself to making you happy."

Here's to mighty purposes and vicarious educations.

1

INTRODUCTION

God tells me how the music should sound, but you stand in the way.
—Arturo Toscanini, to a trumpet player

In June 1990, I joined Intel Corporation's new Oregon microprocessor design division as a senior computer architect on a new project, the P6. This division would eventually grow to thousands of people but at the moment it had a population of exactly one—me. I spent my first day buried in forms, picking primary health-care providers mostly on the basis of how much I liked their names. The second day, my boss stuck his head in my office and said, "Your job is to beat the P5 chip by a factor of two on the same process technology. Any questions?" I replied, "Three. What's a P5? Can you tell me more about Intel's process technology plans? And where's the bathroom?"

P5, as it turned out, was the chip the Intel Santa Clara design team was developing, the team that had created the very successful 386 and 486 chips. P5 would become the original Pentium processor when it debuted in 1993, but in June 1990, my time frame, P5 was little more than a letter and number.

The P6 project was to follow the P5 by two years. Extrapolating from Moore's Law, it appeared that P6 might have as many as eight to 10 million transistors and could become a product as soon as late 1994. My job and the job of the team I was to help recruit was simply to figure out what to do with those transistors and then do it.

In summer 1992, two years after joining the project, I was promoted to architecture manager and served as Intel's lead IA-32 architect from 1992 through 2000.

Somewhat to my surprise, the P6 design project turned out to be a watershed event in the history of the computer industry and the Internet; it could keep up with the industry's

The Pentium Chronicles. By Robert P. Colwell
© 2006 IEEE Computer Society

fastest chips, especially those from reduced-instruction-set computer (RISC) manufacturers, and it had enough flexibility and headroom to serve as the basis for many future proliferation designs.

It also gave Intel a foothold in the maturing workstation market, and it immediately established them in the server space just as the Internet was driving up demand for inexpensive Web servers.

> *The P6 has become the most successful general-purpose processor ever created.*

The P6 project would eventually grow to over 400 design and validation engineers and take 4.5 years to production. But that huge investment paid off—P6 became the Pentium Pro microprocessor, was adapted to become the Pentium II and then the Pentium III, and, most recently, has evolved into the Centrino mobile line. From the basic design have come numerous Xeon and Celeron variants.

In short, the P6 has become the most successful general-purpose processor ever created, with hundreds of millions of chips being shipped. This book is my personal account of that project, with occasional excursions into Pentium 4.

P6 PROJECT CONTEXT

To fully appreciate where the P6 came from, you must first consider the industry and technology context. The microelectronics industry has been blessed for several decades with an amazing benefaction: The silicon chips on which we place our circuits improve drastically about every two years. New process technology historically provides twice the number of transistors, makes them fundamentally faster, and generally reduces the power requirement as well. If we were to do no engineering other than to simply convert an existing design to the newly developed silicon process, the resulting chip would be faster and cheaper without our having done very much work. That sword has two edges, though. The good news is that if I start designing a new CPU chip today toward a production goal that is, say, three years away, I know I can count on having a new process technology. So I design to that new process technology's particular set of design rules, and I am pretty confident that this better technology plus my design team's clever innovations will give my new chip a clear advantage over what is available today.

But the main reason to go through the expense and effort of designing a new CPU is that it will be substantially better than what exists. For microprocessors, "better" generally means higher overall performance that will enable more interesting software applications, such as operating systems with improved user interfaces and shoot-'em-up games with ever-more-realistically rendered bad guys. My new chip has to deliver higher performance than its predecessors or I have accomplished nothing. My competition will also migrate to the new process technology within my three-year horizon and its existing chip will have become faster. That's the sword's other edge: The target isn't stationary. A new chip has to beat the competition's new design, as well as any process-migration chips from any source, including my own company.

My and my fellow chip architects' job was, therefore, to find ways of organizing the new microprocessor's internal design so that it would clearly be superior to any others. Naturally, the first step was to identify "any others" and thereby establish the focus of our project goals. In 1990, Intel was still developing Intel 486 chips—33 MHz,[1] 50 MHz, and

---

[1]MHz stands for megahertz, or millions of clock cycles per second.

66 MHz, eventually reaching 100 MHz by 1992. P5 was the code name of the design project being done in Santa Clara by (mostly) the same team that had produced the 486 and the 386 before that. Task 1 was, therefore, to scope out the P5, analyze its performance potential, investigate the techniques the Santa Clara team was using, and then come up with something that would be twice as fast.

Betting on CISC

Other Intel chips were not the only competition. Throughout the 1980s, the RISC/CISC debate was boiling. RISC's general premise was that computer instruction sets such as Digital Equipment Corporation's VAX instruction set had become unnecessarily complicated and counterproductively large and arcane. In engineering, all other things being equal, simpler is always better, and sometimes *much* better. All other things are never equal, of course, and commercial designers kept adding to the already large steaming pile of VAX instructions in the hope of continuing to innovate while maintaining backward compatibility with the existing software code base. RISC researchers promised large performance increases, easier engineering, and

> *In engineering, all other things being equal, simpler is always better, and sometimes* much *better.*

many other benefits from their design style. A substantial part of the computer engineering community believed that Complex Instruction Set Computers (CISCs) such as the VAX and Intel's x86s would be pushed aside by sheer force of RISC's technical advantages.

In 1990, it was still not clear how the RISC/CISC battle would end. Some of my engineering friends thought I was either masochistic or irrational. Having just swum ashore from the sinking of the Multiflow ship,[2] I immediately signed on to a "doomed" x86 design project. In their eyes, no matter how clever my design team was, we were inevitably going to be swept aside by superior technology. But my own analysis of the RISC/CISC debates was that we could, in fact, import nearly all of RISC's technical advantages to a CISC design. The rest we could overcome with extra engineering, a somewhat larger die size, and the sheer economics of large product shipment volume. Although larger die sizes are generally not desirable because they typically imply higher production cost and higher power dissipation, in the early 1990s, power dissipation was low enough that fairly easy cooling solutions were adequate. And although production costs were a factor of die size, they were much, much more dependent on volume being shipped, and in that arena, CISCs had an enormous advantage over their RISC challengers. In joining Intel's new x86 design team, I was betting heavily that my understanding was right. P6 would have to beat Intel's previous chips, AMD's best competitive effort, and at least keep the most promising RISC chips within range.

Proliferation Thinking

We quickly realized we were not just "designing a chip" with the P6 project. Intel's modus operandi is for a flagship team (like the P6) to start with a blank sheet, conceive a new microarchitecture, design a chip around it, and produce relatively limited production volumes. Why is that a good plan, in an industry where large economies prevail? There

---

[2]Multiflow was a computer systems startup that folded in 1990.

are several reasons. The first is that the architects must be fairly aggressive in their new design; they will want to spend every transistor they can get, because they know how to translate additional transistors into additional performance, and performance sells. This means that the first instantiation of their concept will fill the die, making it large. The physics of manufacturing silicon chips is such that a larger die is much less economical than a smaller one, since fewer such chips fit onto a silicon wafer, and also because random manufacturing defects are much more likely to ruin a large chip than a small one. Because of this large-die issue, the first version of a new microarchitecture will be expensive, which automatically limits its sales volume.

But the second, third, and nth proliferations of the original chip are the moneymakers. These follow-on designs convert the design to a new silicon process technology, thereby gaining all the traditional Moore's Law benefits. The chip gets smaller because its transistors and wires are smaller. It gets faster because smaller transistors are faster. Smaller is also cheaper—more silicon die fit on a given silicon wafer, and there will be more good die per wafer, with less die area exposed to potential contamination. Moreover, the team is much smaller than the original design team, and it only takes about a year instead of 3 to 5 years for the flagship process. Henry Petroski points out that this flagship/proliferation paradigm is not unique to the microprocessor industry: "All innovative designs can be expected to be somewhat uneconomical in the sense that they require a degree of research, development, demonstration, and conservatism that their technology descendants can take for granted." [7]

When it became clear that P6's real importance to Intel was not so much its first instantiation (which Intel eventually marketed as the Pentium Pro), but in its "proliferability," we began to include proliferation thinking in our design decisions. Early in the project, proliferability figured prominently in discussions about the P6's front-side bus, the interconnect structure by which the CPU and its chip set would communicate. Some of the marketing folks pointed out that if the P6 had the same front-side bus as the P5 (Pentium) project, then our new CPU would have ready-made motherboards when silicon arrived. If the P6's chip set was delayed for some reason, we could debug our new CPU on the P5's chip set.

These arguments were absolutely correct on the surface, but they overlooked the bigger picture: Long-term, the P5 bus was woefully inadequate for the much higher system performance levels we believed we would get from the P6's proliferations. We had also begun considering whether a multiprocessor design was feasible, and the P5 bus was very inappropriate for such systems. We could do a lot better with the new packaging and bus driver circuits that were becoming available.

Another design decision that proliferation thinking heavily influenced was the relative performance of 16- and 32-bit code. 16-bit code was legacy code from the DOS era. We knew P6 would have to run all Intel Architecture x86 code to be considered compatible, but we believed that as the years rolled by, 16-bit code would become increasingly irrelevant.[3] 32-bit code would be the battleground for the RISC/CISC conflict, and also the future of general software development, and we intended to make a good showing there. So we concentrated on designing the P6 core for great 32-bit performance, and with 16-bit performance, it would be "you get what you get." (In the section "Feature Surprises" in Chapter 5, I discuss this particular issue in more detail.)

---

[3]The ascendancy of 32-bit code over 16-bit probably seems perfectly obvious today, and the trend was indeed unmistakable. But as in music, politics, and electronics, timing is everything.

The Gauntlet

That was pretty much the environment of the P6 project. We were designing a product we hoped would be immediately profitable, but we were willing to compromise it to some extent on behalf of future proliferations. P6 would have competition within the company from the P5 chip and outside the company from other x86 vendors and the RISC competitors.

Although some of us were very experienced in computer systems and silicon chip design, a team as large as the one we were envisioning would have to have a large percentage of novice "RCGs" (recent college graduates), and we were still a brand new division, with no x86 track record. Over the next 5 years, Intel would bet several hundred million dollars that we would find answers to these challenges. We not only found the answers, but we also came up with a microarchitecture that propelled Intel into volume servers, fundamentally changing the server space by making servers cheap enough that every business could afford one.[4] Intel also realized a handsome profit from the three million Pentium Pro microprocessors it sold, so we hit that goal too.

But at the beginning of those 5 years, about all we had were some big ideas and a short time in which to cultivate them.

DEVELOPING BIG IDEAS

The first step in growing an idea is not to forget it when it comes to you. Composers, writers, and engineers routinely work hard at simply remembering their glimpses of brilliance as they arise. Then they try to incorporate their brainchild into the current project and move on to the next chal-

> *The first step in growing an idea is not to forget it when it comes to you.*

lenge. For small ideas, those that affect primarily your own work, any number of techniques will allow those good ideas to flourish.

Not so with big ideas. Big ideas involve a lot of people, time, and money, all of which are necessary but not sufficient conditions for success.

Engineering projects begin with a perceived need or opportunity, which spawns an idea, some realizable way to fill that need. Even if your boss just tells you to do something, you still "need" to do it. So ideas start with "Wouldn't it be great if we had a bridge spanning San Francisco harbor to Marin County?"; or, "What if we placed towers every so often along busy highways, and used them to relay radiotelephone traffic?[5]"; or, "We could put up satellites, time their movement and transmissions, and then use them to determine someone's exact position on the earth's surface," and so on.

In 1961, President John F. Kennedy committed the United States to placing a man on the moon by the end of the 1960s and returning him safely to Earth [13]. That was the perceived need or opportunity. NASA engineers had to conceive ways to realize that vision. Could they make booster rockets safe enough to carry humans into space? What were the feasible ways of landing a craft on the lunar surface such that it could later take off again? How could that hardware be transported from Earth to the moon? Should it be launched directly as a straight shot, or should the lunar attempt launch from the Earth's orbit?

---

[4]Such servers were, of course, essential for the explosive growth of the worldwide Web in the mid 1990s, but we hesitate to take credit for the Internet. That goes to Al Gore. Ask him. He'll tell you.
[5]I know! We could call them "cell phones"!

The process NASA followed was to identify several promising ideas and then attack each one to see if they could find a showstopper flaw in it. They systematically eliminated the plans that would not work, and increased their focus on the ones that survived. In the end, they settled on a compound plan that included the orbit around Earth, the trip to the moon, a lunar orbit, and a landing craft with two pieces, one for landing (which would be left behind) and one for takeoff and return to lunar orbit.

At every step of the Apollo program, this overall concept determined the engineering and research. The two-stage lunar lander could be accurately estimated as to weight and size, which set the thrust requirement for the lander's engines. The overall thrust required to get the rocket, its fuel, and the lander into Earth orbit in turn guided the development of the huge Saturn V booster. The various docking and undocking maneuvers implied a need for airtight docking seals and maneuvering thrusters.

Our approach to the P6 project was a lot like NASA's approach to the moon shot. We tried as much as possible to reuse existing solutions, tools, and methods, but we knew at the outset that existing technology, tools, and project management methods would not suffice to get our project where we wanted it to go. So we purposefully arranged the design team to address special technology challenges in circuits, buses, validation, and multiprocessing.

Defining Success and Failure

Engineers generally recognize the validity of the saying, "Creativity is a poor substitute for knowing what you're doing." (Ignore what Albert Einstein is reputed to have said: "Imagination is more important than knowledge." That might be valid for a scientist, but as an engineer, I *know* that I can't simply *imagine* my bridge tolerating a certain load.) Good engineers would much rather use a known-good method to accomplish some task than reinvent everything. In this way, they are free to concentrate their creativity on the parts of the design that really need it, and they reduce overall risk.

On the other hand, if we apply this thinking to overall engineering project management, we are in trouble. Our instinct to exhaustively research project management methods, pick the best one, and implement it will lead us to an infinite loop because new project management methods are being written faster than we can read them. Worse, there's no apparent consensus among these learned treatises, so there's no easy way to synthesize a "best-of" project management methodology. Moreover, methods that work on one project may fail badly on the next because the reward for succeeding on one design project is that you get to do it again, except that the next project will be at least twice as difficult. That's the dark cloud around the Moore's Law silver lining.

The P6 project was blessed with a team whose members either had never worked on Intel's x86 chips or had never worked at Intel.

Large, successful engineering companies must constantly struggle to balance their corporate learning (as embodied in their codex of Best Known Methods) against the need of each new project to innovate around problems that no one has faced before. In a very important sense, the P6 project was blessed with a team whose members either had never worked on Intel's x86 chips or had never worked at Intel. This helped enormously in getting the right balance of historical answers and new challenges.

Senior Wisdom

In most cases, a company will present the "new project" need or opportunity to a few senior engineers who then have the daunting job of thoroughly evaluating project requirements and answering a two-pronged question: What constitutes success for this project and what constitutes failure? They must identify possible avenues for the project to pursue that will lead to the promised land. The path is not easily recognizable. Nature is biased against success: For every plan that works, thousands fail, many of them initially quite plausible. And the success criteria are not simply the logical converse of failure conditions. For the P6, success criteria included performance above a certain level and failure criteria included power dissipation above some threshold.

In essence, a few senior people are making choices that will implicitly or explicitly guide the efforts of hundreds (or in NASA's case, tens of thousands) of others over the project's life. It is, therefore, crucial that project leadership be staffed correctly and get this phase right, or it will be extremely hard for the project to recover. Do not begin the project until the right leadership is in place.

Occasionally, you will see articles about computer programmers who are wildly talented at cranking out good code. Such people do exist. We don't really know where they come from, and we don't know how to make more of them, but we know them when we see them. To try to put these superprogrammers into perspective, their output is usually compared to that of their less sensational compatriots—"one superprogrammer can turn out as much code in a day as three of her coworkers could in a week." As with senior project leadership, this kind of comparison misses the point: You can't substitute higher numbers of less gifted people for the efforts of these chosen few. Quantity cannot replace quality. Guard these folks when you find them, because you cannot replace them, and their intuitions and insights are essential to getting a project onto the right track and keeping it there through production.

FOUR PROJECT PHASES

Small projects involving only a few engineers can succeed on a seat-of-the-pants, just-do-whatever-needs-doing basis. As long as an experienced engineer is in charge—one who can recognize when the team has found a workable product concept and when to drive the project forward—the project can succeed. But large projects suffer from this ad hoc treatment. Large projects can be outrageously inefficient if not managed properly and might even implode if allowed to stall long enough. Large projects require structure and scheduling.

Although we certainly had structure and a schedule, we did not start with the conceptual framework that forms the backbone of this book. Rather, the framework presented is a product of my attempt to impose order and labels on what we *actually* did, with the benefit of hindsight and the passage of time.

The four major phases I've been able to distill are

1. Concept
2. Refinement
3. Realization
4. Production

In the *concept* phase, senior engineers consider the request or opportunity and try to brainstorm ways to satisfy it. If the need was "a better way to get from downtown San Francisco to Marin County," they would create a set of possible solutions that might include ferries, tunnels, bridges, trained dolphins, blimps, water wings, submarines, inflated inner tubes, human cannonballs, and jet-skis. (Remember, this is the anything-goes brainstorming phase.)

The *refinement* phase weeds out the implausible solutions and prioritizes the rest so that the project's limited engineering effort concentrates on the ideas that are most likely to pan out. Of the initial set of, say, 10 or 20 ideas that exit the concept phase, only two or three are likely to survive the refinement phase. One of these will be designated the *plan-of-record* and will receive the most attention at the beginning of the realization phase.

Realization is the actual engineering process. The design team takes the best idea that has emerged from the refinement phase (and may even have been the instrument by which refinement occurs) and implements the prototype product.

The last phase of the engineering process—*production,* driving what you've created into solid high volume—is often overlooked by design teams. Design teams must shepherd their creation all the way through volume production, not simply transfer responsibility to some production engineering group at the first sale.

As in any project framework, the four project phases overlap. The project as a whole may be transitioning from concept to refinement over a few weeks or months. Any design engineer in the project might be at some point in this transition, substantially lagging or leading the rest of the project. One part of a design team might be finishing a previous design and thus be unable to join a new effort until most of the concept phase is over.

This four-stage model can be extremely useful as a management tool, as well as a way to coordinate the design team. (I wish *we* had recognized it as such.) The team should superimpose the four stages on the overall project schedule, as in Figure 1.1, so that everybody knows how to best make their local decisions. Ideas that are worth chasing down when the project is in the concept phase might have to be triaged at later phases, for example.

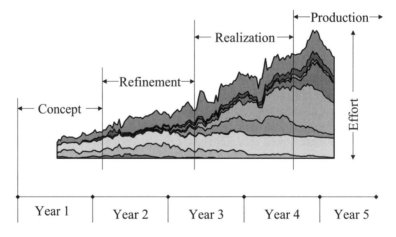

Figure 1.1. Concept, refinement, realization, production, and team size. Different shades of gray indicate staffing of various design activities such as circuit design, validation, layout, RTL development, project overhead, and so on.

THE BUSINESS OF EXCELLENCE

I would be remiss if I did not emphasize the role of the P6 *team*. In the 1970s, the Pittsburgh Steelers football team won four Super Bowls. It wasn't just that the Steelers had dominating players at so many positions. It wasn't just that they were well trained and executed brilliantly much of the time and at least competently the rest. It wasn't even that the Steelers were underdogs for the first half of the 1970s. It was that the Steelers were *determined to win*. There was a palpable sense about that team that they would face and subdue any challenge that turned up. They would do whatever it took to succeed, and their definition of success was to be the best in the world at what they did.

The P6 team had those qualities. We relied heavily on Randy Steck's excellent innate managerial instincts and constant drive to improve and a very experienced senior technical leadership who didn't have to be told what to do next. We also had an entrepreneurial slay-the-dragons-as-they-appear resilience and a willingness to try new things. In the end, P6 turned out the way it did because an incredibly talented design and architecture team was fervently committed to making it a success.

I am not implying that we necessarily knew more than other project managers, nor am I suggesting that ours was a better approach than any project management book would propose (although I *am* sure it was better than some). I simply want to relate what we did, why we did it that way, and how it turned out.

The P6 team is on every page here, either directly in an anecdote or as the substance of a lesson learned—a lesson that can be passed to other determined project engineers. In the chapters that follow, I hope to show that an amazing combination of intelligence, wisdom, stubbornness, and ambition made P6 what it is, and in the computer business, or any business for that matter, excellence is a critical prerequisite to success.

2

THE CONCEPT PHASE

"On the hardware side, it's nearly a science. . . . You can almost predict the timetable by which you can do developments. But on the software side, there's so much genius and creativity that you can't predict when it's going to happen."
— *TV announcer, introducing Intel's new P6 chip*

The concept phase is the quintessential architect's phase of a project. Get it right and the rest of the project has a good chance of flowing smoothly. Get it wrong in any number of ways and the project is in big trouble (and you probably won't find that out until it's much too late to recover in any graceful way).

Many people imagine the concept phase to be a group of brilliant people sitting around a small circular table, intently watching each other's faces. "Did you think of anything yet? No? Neither did I. . . . How about *now*?"

This is *not* how it's done.

On the other hand, people have plenty of room for pure inspiration and opportunities to simply enumerate all the ways a given task could be accomplished and hypothesize which is best. Intense brainstorming can last from days to months. Of course, not all the possibilities from a properly run brainstorm will be equally plausible, and the weeding-out process will begin immediately.

OF IMMEDIATE CONCERN

Senior engineers have very high leverage during this phase and must be careful not to accidentally or arbitrarily constrain the project's "solution space." They can commit any number of grievous errors, such as doing the mathematical equivalent of choosing a local optimum instead of the global one their competitor found. In the worst case, they could choose an overall product approach that two years later turns out to be technically infeasible, forcing a major reset to the project and wrecking its schedule and morale. In *It Sounded Good When We Started* [4], Dwayne Phillips and Roy O'Bryan relate a story of an engineer who became so infatuated with using a particular handheld computer as an input device that he stuck with it tenaciously for the real product through several distinct phases:

1. It's a cool gadget. It adds panache as a controller for the product and nobody minds the serial cable required.
2. The gadget is not as cool as new laptops that are coming out, but it's still usable.
3. Producer switches from original handheld to new laptop, but sticks with the old MS-DOS environment because of earlier handheld choice. The cable is becoming a real hindrance.
4. The engineer is gone, the handheld is gone, and the now-hated cable is the only thing remaining.

Another error is to overlook something in the competitive landscape. Some product feature that used to be minor could now be a primary selling point, but the current design choices hinders its use. In *Small Things Considered* [6], Henry Petroski describes how Volvo learned that the rules concerning cupholders in cars had changed. In only a few years, cupholders went from being irrelevant curiosities to absolute requirements, and to the consternation of auto designers everywhere, their placement and usability have become important factors in the buying decision.

Fortunately, what conceptual errors we made in the P6 project turned out to be of the nongrievous variety. But we did make choices that had implications we did not fully understand at the time. For example, we chose to put the L2 cache[1] into the same physical package as the P6 microprocessor itself because of the substantial performance advantage this arrangement provided. That expected performance advantage turned out to be real and was a major factor in P6's suitability for servers and workstations, which were new markets for Intel in 1995. But at the time we chose to pursue this "two-die-in-package" strategy, we did not fully realize how difficult it would be for Intel's manufacturing plants to build this way. It turned out that the usual automated machinery that places bare silicon die into ceramic packages could not be used with the dual-die scheme, and human thumbs had to do the job. This would have severely limited production capacity had it become necessary for the original Pentium Pro to be shipped to volume desktops. As things turned out, we were okay—the Pentium processor held the desktop market long enough for the single-die follow-on part, the Pentium II, to become available.

SUCCESS FACTORS

There are no guarantees, but the chance of a successful concept phase is much higher if you start with clear goals, choose the project team wisely, and pay attention to the mechanics.

---

[1]Cache is a fast memory array that the processor uses as a temporary scratchpad. For implementation reasons, it's often efficacious to design not one large cache memory, but a hierarchy of caches: a small but fast L1, then a bigger but slower L2, and so on.

Clear Goals

If a project does not have crystal-clear goals, under no conditions should the team begin anyway in the hope that "someone will come up with something." A team launched into the void with no compass and no map will succeed only at floundering and wasting time. To the uninitiated, the ensuing blur of activity might appear to be what a competent team does as it churns successfully toward its goal. Don't be fooled. What you are really seeing is money being turned into useless Brownian motion at a macroscopic level.

Architects pointed toward an agreed-on goal are far more likely to get a lucrative idea. They must be able to answer these questions above all others: What constitutes project success, and what constitutes failure? The art of all engineering is compromise, trading one thing for another. Such trades can be intelligently made only according to some weighted scoring of all major project goals. For P6, we had a schedule, target die size, target performance (on many benchmarks), and power dissipation budget. Later, we developed a clock frequency target as well.

> *Architects must be able to answer these questions above all others: What constitutes project success, and what constitutes failure?*

When we started the P6 project, performance was our primary target. We wanted to double the P5's performance. We guessed (correctly, as it turned out) that if we found a way to hit that target, we could engineer solutions to other targets along the way. Conversely, if we did not have enough performance to constitute a viable product, then merely hitting the schedule, power, or die size targets would not be enough.

Never assume that all team members have the same implicit goals. If there is a chance for any two people to miscommunicate, assume that they will find it. Write the goals on a giant poster in order of priority and have all team members walk past it to get to their meetings. Projects that don't know what their goals are have no chance of hitting them. Intel general manager Pat Gelsinger believed in this so strongly that he had a habit of walking up to design team members and saying "Quick! What constitutes success for this project?" If they couldn't simply rattle off a coherent answer, it meant they hadn't completely internalized the project goals.

> *Never assume that all team members have the same implicit goals.*

You might feel safe in assuming that at least corporate management understands the project and its major product goals. After all, they initiated the project, they staffed its leadership positions, they established the schedule and budgets, and they have responsibility for other corporate projects that this one might affect. Besides, they hold a highly visible position in the company, which they would not have if they had not had some amount of competence, right? Right, but these assumptions can lead you to wrong conclusions. Executives have a lot on their minds, and things change rapidly across the corporate landscape as well as the competitive arena. Just as they tell you what to do, they may have their bosses telling *them* what to do. And the advice they're getting and giving may be mutually inconsistent. Consider this actual dialogue: "Now that the chip performance appears to be among the best in the world, it's time to make the chip consume the lowest power as well." At this point, you might be tempted to reply sarcastically, "Why not a cure for cancer?" Resist, or they will add that to your list of deliverables.

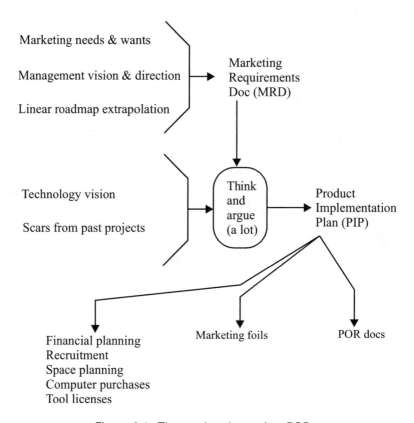

Figure 2.1. The road to the project POR.

Our solution was to establish a formal project document, a project-wide plan-of-record (POR), which was our official response to what upper management and marketing were requesting of our new design. In past projects, upper management blessed the marketing document (actually a set of Powerpoint slides) and simply expected that to be the new plan-of-record. But as technology became more complicated and the trade-offs more subtle, we found it necessary to write our own document, containing our best estimates of feasible schedules, required headcount, new tools, the competition's likely offerings, the general direction of the project design, and so on. Some of the project-level interactions associated with POR are shown in Figure 2.1.

Marketing and management will not usually ask for a combination of features, cost, and schedule that are simultaneously realizable—count on that. They will reliably ask for the impossible. They do this for several reasons. In a business as lucrative and fast-moving as microprocessor design, aggressive risk-taking is a given, virtually a requirement.[2] Moore's Law was once a far-sighted prediction, but by the 1990s it had become a self-fulfilling prophecy. It's a very short step from using Moore's Law to *check* your road map to using it to *dictate* the road map. There are also subtle interplays between the vari-

---

[2] I often felt that if Intel and its competitors would all slow down simultaneously, they and we would be a lot better off. Until that day comes, though, the only rational strategy is to push the technology as hard and fast as you possibly can.

ous project goals (performance, power, thermals, schedule, cost), which may not be entirely obvious even to the design team, let alone marketing or upper management.

Marketing and management will not usually ask for a combination of features, cost, and schedule that are simultaneously realizable.

So our Product Implementation Plan was essentially our proposal of the best compromise that we thought was feasible. After several negotiation rounds with both marketing and management, this document became the project POR, and was signed by all concerned, especially design management. The POR changed throughout the project, but it was much better to have an established, agreed-on starting point for such changes. (How to control changes to the POR is an important topic in the "Engineering Change Orders" section in Chapter 3.)

The Right People

The senior leadership of any design project is the single most important predictor of project success, bar none. These are the people the project will count on to keep it on track. They must routinely select a workable path from among a forest of alternatives, most of which eventually turn out to be untenable. Project leadership must constantly check the project's progress and goals against the competition, monitor the effects of previous decisions, make repairs as necessary, and directly intervene in the actual design when only supreme technical wizardry can transcend the next roadblock.

The senior project leaders must not concern themselves only with technical issues. When they propose a block diagram at the beginning of a project, they are writing a check that the designers must be able to cash in the time allotted to the overall project. Therefore, the senior leaders ask not only, "Is this approach technically feasible? Can it be built?" but also, "Can this particular team build it?" while avoiding the trap of imagining that the whole team operates at the same intellectual and experience level as they do.

P6 Senior Leadership. The concept phase for Intel's P6 microprocessor lasted approximately six months, from November 1990 through March 1991. Five architects drove this phase: Dave Papworth, Glenn Hinton, Michael Fetterman, Andy Glew, and I. Dave was a senior hardware architect with whom I had worked at Multiflow Computer from 1985 to 1990 and is probably the most brilliant design engineer with whom I've ever had the pleasure to work. Dave has an uncanny gift for identifying (frequently on the basis of scant clues) which of many possible avenues for solving a given problem are most likely to pay off. This gives a design project an enormous mechanical advantage over the possibility space, in that the team can quickly abandon less-promising choices so as to concentrate on the one that will eventually become the POR. Glenn is a genius at creating his way out of whatever corner the project has inadvertently painted itself into, a role he fulfills with aplomb and abundant good humor; he is a joy to work with. Michael was a recent college graduate (RCG, in Intel-speak), but had some industry experience and was so bright and unafraid to speak his mind in any engineering context that he fit into our team immediately. Michael also had the charming and absolutely essential ability to gracefully give suggestions to his boss (me) on how to improve my software without covert snickering or outright laughter in the process. Andy was an idea fountain; mention a problem and he'd instantly recite the seven known ways to solve it and then invent four more spontaneously (at least two of which would actually work). His intellectual energy was extremely valuable to our conceptualizing.

The composition of the concept phase team was crucial to P6's success. The three senior engineers (Dave, Glenn, and I) kept the project pointed in promising directions and retained the confidence of Intel's upper management so we could make the right decisions without undue corporate overhead. We also worked hard to prevent oversubscription. We wanted to push the technology as far as it could reasonably be pushed, but without burning out the design team, missing schedule deadlines, or sacrificing any success-critical features.

We CPU architects also benefited tremendously by having Gurbir Singh, who had designed the system bus for Intel's i960 chip. We gladly delegated essentially all the systems considerations for P6 to him. While we focused on getting the out-of-order core right, Gurbir and his team handled our chip's interface to the rest of the world. (Although this worked wonderfully at a technical level, our belief that we had the right to design our own chip interface led to later political problems. See "Another One Rides the Bus" in Chapter 3.)

The senior leadership steered an aggressive path, but also purposely worked to keep the project out of trouble. The two junior engineers (Michael and Andy) brought new insights and the latest thinking from elsewhere. Their constant questioning of the senior engineers spurred us to higher and better planning throughput and generally kept us from thinking too much inside old boxes.

Setting the Leadership Tone. Nothing is more corrosive to overall design team morale than perceived disarray in the senior project leadership. What engineers do is hard work and their intellect is generally well above average. From there, it is but a short step to an unrealistic self-image. For senior leaders to work together without debilitating ego clashes, they must strive for mutual respect. If they respect each other, they will find a workable arrangement among themselves. If they do not, the VP responsible for the project must take action because the senior leaders will not remain in a project in which they are not getting the respect they require to succeed.

Project leaders must be both resilient and resourceful and they must recognize that they are not going to be given the easy questions—the ones that get answered at lower levels in the project hierarchy. Most or all decisions made at the leadership level will threaten one or more key project goals. There will be no reliable data on the possible avenues for resolution and little time to collect much more. As the project progresses, the choices get tougher, because time is shorter and the degrees of freedom are fewer. All this argues for good judgment up front. The project leaders must reserve enough design margin (but not so much that they are "sandbagging," which can also kill a project) in the early stages that they have room to maneuver when the surprises appear later.

> *Most or all decisions made at the leadership level will threaten one or more key project goals.*

One of the main reasons I enjoyed the P6 project so much was precisely because the architects naturally avoided ego clashes. I can remember only three cases in which even trivial friction arose between us. The first was very early in the project, when it became clear that a prospective senior architect was coming up short in the teamwork department and, fortunately for all of us, decided to pursue other activities. Another was when a fellow architect chose a particularly unfortunate time to stick his head in my cubicle and opine that I was driving the team too hard. He may have been right, but I had just stayed up all night working on the design and was not in the mood to consider whether it had been a pointless sacrifice. I kicked him out of my cubicle and asked him to come back when I could be rational about the issue, a process that took about a week. The other time was when our manager, for reasons I never did understand, dragged Glenn, Dave, and me into a conference room to inform us that if we ever reached an impasse on a technical issue, Dave's vote would prevail. We all just looked at each other, shrugged our shoulders, wondered what management book had prescribed this intervention, and went back to work. The feared impasse never did arise.

Managing Mechanics

The concept phase could also be called the "blue sky" phase because all things seem feasible, the horizons are very far away, and the possibilities are infinite. Many system architects enjoy this phase of a project so much that they are loathe to leave it. After all, the crystal castle they're building in the clouds of their gray matter has only good features, unsullied by compromises, physics, economics, road-map choices, customer preferences, and schedule pressures. Every university has some PhD students who enjoy the process so much that they never feel compelled to actually finish the work, and these people could eventually find themselves on concept phase architecture teams. The project leader must be able to sense when the project's concept phase is nearing the end of its usefulness and have the fortitude to push the team to the next phase. (Conversely, project leaders must also be able to accurately discern when the project has not yet come up with ideas strong enough, and prevent the project from committing to a plan that cannot produce a successful product.)

Paying attention to some basic mechanics can make it easier to manage this phase and its transitions.

Physical Context Matters. When we first began working out the fundamentals of P6's microarchitecture, we met informally in each other's cubicles and quit each day when we were too tired to think straight. Unfortunately, we were also disturbing neighboring cubicles, so we started using conference rooms. But that didn't work well, either; the whiteboards were cleaned nightly, and every time we met, we felt as if we were starting over rather than picking up where we left off. More to the point, other people *knew* we were in the conference room, which meant we could be interrupted. We discovered by trial and error that it usually took us about an hour to reliably get back to the point where we had left off the previous day. As Figure 2.2 shows, we also found that our period of peak brainstorming efficiency was about two hours, so it took about half of each brainstorm session just to reconstruct what we had done the day before. If we were interrupted, the one-hour start-up transient would begin again, causing a severe loss in efficiency.

The start-up transient was a function of several things. Which decisions had we tentatively made? Which open issues had we chosen to be in the "must attack this immediately" versus "probably has a workable solution, so leave until later" category? Which previously open ideas had we suddenly realized were probably not going to work and should be permanently abandoned? We were chagrined at how often we found ourselves groupthinking through an extremely complicated design scenario, only to suddenly realize that

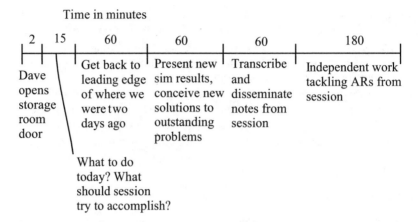

<u>Figure 2.2.</u> Brainstorming time segments and sequence.

we'd already had this exact discussion two weeks ago, concluded it was all a dead end, and agreed not to revisit it.

When we did manage to get the same conference room, and the janitorial staff had observed our request to not clean the whiteboards (at least this time), we discovered that we could get back to our previous conceptual point much more quickly, because all our prior scribblings were still on the wall in our own handwriting. That context was invaluable in reminding us of the twists and turns of our previous meeting.

The Storage Room Solution. On one memorable day, when we again found our conference room unavailable, we solved all three problems—disturbing others, loss of context, and interruptions—simultaneously. Dave demonstrated one of his many surprising skills by using his Intel badge to jimmy open a nearby storage room, which happened to be fairly large with lots of unused wall space. On the grounds that it's easier to ask forgiveness than permission and with the same authorization that Dave used to get in the room, we procured lots of whiteboard units and installed them into our new meeting space. We were ecstatic! Nobody ever cleaned the storage room, nobody else could preempt us from using it, and we were never interrupted because no one knew where we were. Several months later, the room's owner stumbled across our think session and evicted us, but by then the project was well on its way and we didn't really need it anymore.

The idea that physical context matters is hardly new. When musicians are trying to combat the debilitating effects of nervousness on their virtuosity, they often practice in the same venue in which they will deliver their recital. Likewise, students who are anxious about performing well on a test may benefit from studying in the same room in which the test will be administered.

> *Sometimes, just meeting temporarily in a different room can break the logjam.*

The converse of this idea is also valuable. If a particular physical context has contributed to the current project state, it makes sense to change that context when the project occasionally stalls and needs a really good new idea. Sometimes, just meeting temporarily in a different room can break the logjam.

Beyond the Whiteboard. Although no one can dispute the usefulness of whiteboards, no matter how many you have, you will run out of space and have to erase some of your ideas to make room for new ones. Our solution to whiteboard limitations was to create a meeting record, or log, that captured our key decisions as we made them. The honor of record keeping fell to a designated "scribe," whose job was to notice ideas and decisions worth writing down. The scribe would then circulate the meeting minutes among the rest of the concept phase team for error-checking as soon as possible after the meeting. The scribe not only captured decisions made and directions set, but also tried to document roads not taken and why. Brainstorming in the meetings commonly ended with an Aha! moment, in which everyone suddenly realized why an idea we had all thought had some potential would in fact not work. Or we might come upon a related idea that we all felt was a good one but not appropriate for our project. If no one had documented such moments as they occurred, they might have been lost forever.

Recording the roads not taken turned out to be particularly valuable for another critical concept phase task: accurately transferring the project plan into the design team's many heads (an art form in its own right, as I describe later). Transferring the roads not taken helps the designers understand the project direction, since they then have a clearer picture of what it is not. It also helps them avoid making lower-level design decisions later that might not be congruent with the project direction.

"Kooshing" the Talkers. You want doers, not talkers, on a concept phase team. Doers write programs, run experiments, look up half-remembered papers, ask expert friends, and come up with boundary-case questions to help illuminate the issue. Talkers generate endless streams of rhetoric that seem to enumerate every possibility in the neighboring technical space. When you become exasperated and cut them off, however, you will discover that this long list has brought you no closer to resolving anything.

> *You want doers, not talkers, on a concept phase team.*

With dozens of complex concepts being invoked or invented, and a few overall project directions still on the table, the possibility space becomes enormous. Each choice you tentatively make generates five new issues, each of which embodies some number of knowns and unknowns. The team will not have much data to guide them in this phase. They must find their way through these choices with a combination of

1. *Knowledge* (what is in the literature or was proven at last week's conference)
2. *Experience* (we did it this way eight years ago, and it worked or didn't work)
3. *Intuition* (this way looks promising to me; that way looks scary)

Talkers monopolize the room's extremely limited bandwidth. We had natural or rapidly converted doers on the P6 project, but if we had had a talker, there would have been one person expounding on every idea that popped into his head, while four others frantically wrote down the ideas that were flashing through their minds before they were forgotten or steamrollered by the next conceptual bit of flotsam bobbing along on the audible stream of consciousness. One technique we stumbled onto quite by accident was the Koosh-ball gambit. When brainstorming, many engineers like to have something to play with in their hands: a pen, keys, their cell phone. One of us brought a Koosh ball to a meeting, a small rubber ball with colorful rubber-band-hair sticking out in all directions, and absentmindedly tossed it up and down throughout the meeting. Within a week, we all had Koosh balls, and a new phenomenon emerged: If someone threatened to monopolize the discussion, the others had the right to register their displeasure by tossing their Koosh ball at the offender. Before long, all someone had to do was pick up the Koosh ball and look menacingly at the speaker for that person to realize it was time to let others speak.

A DATA-DRIVEN CULTURE

An important part of the concept phase is to establish the project's technical roots. For P6, we had to choose some basic project directions such as 32-bit virtual addressing versus 64-bit, 16-bit performance, front-side bus architecture, and out-of-order microarchitecture versus the P5's in-order architecture. Somewhat later in the project, we faced similar questions about clock frequency, superpipelining, and multiple processors on a bus.

These directions might not have come as quickly (or at all) had we not had a team of doers who actively sought project-wide, high-level decisions, the points of highest leverage in a project. We knew from the beginning that deciding on an out-of-order microarchitecture was the number one conceptual priority, since that choice would drive most of the other questions. An out-of-order core would imply a much more complicated engine, which would tend to increase the number of pipeline stages, which would impact the clock frequency (making it either higher or lower, we were not entirely sure which), and so on.

In our early concept phase discussions, we briefly considered all the ways that we knew might give us the required performance, including a very long instruction word (VLIW) approach, since Dave and I had worked on VLIW designs while at Multiflow. But we kept coming back to out-of-order, despite the dearth of successful out-of-order designs before P6. Glenn felt that there were solutions to the obvious problems of an out-of-order Intel Architecture chip, and Andy had worked on out-of-order ideas in his master's thesis and was enthusiastic about the concept's performance potential. Dave and I knew from our VLIW experience that the implicit code reordering of an out-of-order engine had real potential, but also substantial complexity, and it was not out of the question for an out-of-order engine to lose more performance to overhead than it gained in cleverness. We also knew how easy it was to make global performance-driven decisions early in a project that would later turn out to have spawned whole colonies of product bugs.

Despite these drawbacks, we settled on out-of-order as the POR in only a few days. After a few hours of discussion, we had generated a list of open items, things we knew were important and could make or break the project, but we did not yet know how to resolve them. Again, had our team been talker-dominated, we would have spent the next several months debating every issue without a single resolution, because there is no religious demagogue worse than an engineer arguing from intuition instead of data. If any two concept phase engineers have opposing intuitions, and neither collects data sufficient to convince the other, the debate cannot be resolved and quickly degenerates into a loud, destructive ego contest.

We avoided most such encounters in the P6 by allocating the list of open items to the five participants and then requiring that the item be argued at the next meeting on the basis of data to be collected by then. In this way, we established the project's data-driven culture.

Each person had to think of and then execute an experiment to help resolve a technical issue or unknown in sufficient detail and veracity to convince the rest of us that his conclusion had merit. The lack of time and resources actually worked mostly to our advantage. You might think that there was not enough time to do a really good experiment between Tuesday noon and Thursday 8 A.M., but the short deadlines forced us to think carefully about exactly what was being asked. The thinking was the important part; if we got that part right, then writing up some code or researching the literature was usually simple. And the focus it provided our answer tended to make that answer right, or at least useful.

Not being able to quantify the answer to a particular issue was sometimes the first indication that we were not chasing some technical corner case but, in fact, had possibly stumbled onto an important, potentially difficult problem that might need everyone's immediate, concerted attention. I knew very little in those days about the Intel Architecture, and was acutely sensitive to signs that something fundamental in the instruction-set architecture would prevent any reasonable out-of-order implementations. My nightmare was that we would build a very fast computer that could not, no matter how clever we were, run all x86 code properly. I knew, for example, that to ensure high performance, we had to be able to service loads in a temporal order other than what the program code implied.

> *My nightmare was that we would build a very fast computer that could not, no matter how clever we were, run all x86 code properly.*

Would any examples of Intel Architecture code break if some loads were executed out-of-order?

We eventually invented some mechanisms by which loads that needed strict sequentiality could be identified by hardware and handled separately, but early in the project there were dozens of such worries. Those that we could not quickly dispatch via experiment, we added to a watch list for further scrutiny, and in some cases initiated longer exploratory work.

Of course, insisting on data for *all* decisions will lead to analysis paralysis. In this case, schedule pressure and proactive leadership are the antidotes. Legendary NASA designer Bill Layman said

> If you force people to take bigger intuitive leaps, and their intuition is sound, then you can get more and more efficient as you force larger and larger leaps. There's some optimum point where they succeed with ninety percent of their leaps. For the ten percent they don't make, there's time to remake that leap or go a more meticulous route to the solution of that particular problem. . . . There's an optimal level of stress. [15]

> *There's an optimal level of stress.*

The Right Tool

Very early on in P6 development, when only Dave, Glenn, and I were on the project, we had noticed that all out-of-order performance results in the literature were RISC-based. Was there something about the x86 architecture that obviated those results and would not let us achieve the performance predicted? Dave and I wrote the dataflow analyzer, or DFA, to get a quick answer to this important question.

We purposely called this tool a dataflow "analyzer" because it was most emphatically not a simulator of any kind. DFA was aimed solely at answering the question of how much parallelism was intrinsic to general x86 code, and it operated from execution traces. An execution trace is a record of exactly how a processor executed a program, instruction by instruction, including memory addresses generated and branches taken. After DFA had walked over the entire trace, we could compare how many clock cycles DFA's rescheduling would have taken to how many instructions were executed (again, assuming one clock cycle per instruction for ease of analysis). We would then know the theoretical speedup limit.

In a few weeks, results from DFA confirmed that the published results should apply quite well to x86. Glenn added a graphical interface and DFA became a mainstay tool for the rest of the P6 project. It also helped define the project's data-driven culture because it was general and open source. Thus, we could use it to attack a wide variety of questions and any of us could modify it as needed.

Dave, Glenn, and I were hardware engineers, not professional programmers. We could write code, and it would work when we were finished, but it never surprised us when others would later point out better ways to do things. (Andy and Michael were outstanding programmers, but they didn't join the project until a few months after DFA's creation.) As an example of Michael's diplomacy in the face of egregious overstimulation, he once pointed out to me that a set of command line parsing routines were available in the standard library, so I had not had to write my own. He didn't even crack a smile, even though outright guffaws would have been warranted. In my defense, I hasten to point out my command line parsing routines *worked,* and nobody ever found a bug in them.

The lesson for all chip architects at this phase is to get your hands dirty.

The important thing was not how pretty the DFA code was; it was what we learned in creating and using it. The lesson for all chip architects at this phase is to get your hands dirty. What you learn now will pay off later when all the decisions become painful trade-offs among must-have's.

The "What Would Happen If" Game. Having a data-driven culture in a design organization is always a good idea, but never more so than when the team's leaders are learning new technology. When you have spent 10 or 15 years designing computers, as Glenn, Dave, and I had, you will have absorbed a subliminal set of intuitions about what seems reasonable. For example, *this* size for an L2 cache should mean that the L1 cache is *that* size; if the CPU is *this* fast, then the frontside bus must have at least *that* bandwidth. This kind of experience base can be immensely valuable to a design team, since it focuses the team's efforts on the few solution sets that might actually work, instead of allowing them to wander in the much larger general possibility space.

But DFA quickly taught us that much of what we had subconsciously learned was wrong; it just didn't apply to out-of-order engines. Undiscouraged, Dave and I started a little prediction game that went something like this: I would show up at my office and start work. Within the hour, Dave would arrive, sporting an "I know something you don't" grin, and say, "What do you suppose would happen if you had an out-of-order x86 engine with 300 arithmetic pipelines that could do 200 simultaneous loads but only one store per clock?" Now, Dave didn't just make up that question on the spot, and he wasn't asking because he hoped I would know the answer. He was asking because, just last night, *he* didn't know, and he stayed up all night experimenting until he found the answer—an answer that apparently delighted him with its unexpected nature, and taught him something worth knowing about this strange out-of-order universe. He could just tell me the answer, but where was the fun in that?

My part of the game was to think through the conditions he specified, and let my intuition provide my best guess (which is exactly what he had done the previous night). Of course, I would cheat a little bit, because I knew that if the answer were obvious, Dave wouldn't be smiling, so I offered him the most extreme among the possibilities my intuition said were at all feasible. Then, when he told me what he had found, I would realize how far my experience had led me astray, which then motivated me to apply the right amount of corrective mental pressure. Consequently, the next time we played this game, I would get closer on my first try. Occasionally, my intuition even turned out to be right, but many times that meant I had just found a bug in DFA.

This DFA-induced intuition retuning was key to P6's overall success in the concept phase. Data has a way of making you ask the right questions.

> *Data has a way of making you ask the right questions.*

DFA Frontiers

DFA was a great success. It was a conceptual flashlight that we used to illuminate many dark corners of the design space, where lurked subtle interactions among multiple design choices. It allowed us to quantify our ideas, to show which ideas were better than others and by how much. DFA guided us to places where performance was being lost so that we could concentrate our creativity on those areas.

One of our more interesting forays was a pursuit we dubbed "walking the rim of the known universe." If DFA was not constrained, the results it returned essentially answered the question, "How much intrinsic instruction-level parallelism is in this program?" For certain programs, such as vectorized, floating-point codes, intrinsic program parallelism is known to be essentially unbounded. But for most programs, the academic literature varies wildly in its estimates, from numbers as low as 2 to as high as 100. If intrinsic parallelism really was only 2, then investing a huge amount of design time and die space on an out-of-order microarchitecture would never be repaid in performance. It would be like drilling a deep well somewhere you knew had no water.

DFA quickly resolved the theoretical limits for x86 parallelism. While touring the galaxy with it, however, it dawned on us that it would be straightforward to also make it answer an important follow-on question, "How much of the theoretical maximum parallelism is still available when running on hardware with real constraints on functional unit numbers, bus bandwidth, memory bandwidth, branch prediction, and instruction decoder width?" Within a few weeks, we had rigged DFA with default values for a representative hardware configuration, with command-line options to override them. This arrangement let us identify out-of-order-isms, areas where this still-new out-of-order universe collided with our intuitions. We ran a series of experiments with DFA set to assume an infinitely capable microarchitecture, except for one important subsystem that was constrained by reality.

The first thing these experiments showed us is that the weakest-link-in-a-chain model still applied: An infinitely capable machine might show that intrinsic parallelism on a given program would be, say, 35x, but constrain anything in the machine, and even if 90% of the engine is still infinitely capable, the overall performance will slow drastically. Constrain any two things, and performance falls even more, although not as precipitously. Constrain *everything*, as in a real machine, and DFA's results begin approaching reality.

By its very nature, however, DFA would tend to overstate parallelism because anything left out of the run would tend to unconstrain it, thus (artificially) boosting parallelism. Much of DFA's subsequent development over the next several years was devoted to installing ever more accurate constraints.

DFA had one other major limitation. Besides being out-of-order and superscalar, P6 performed speculative execution. The "hello world" example given in "Out-of-Order, Superscalar Microarchitecture: A Primer" in the Appendix is contrived, but it demonstrates a realistic effect: A conditional branch occurs every few program instructions. If a microarchitecture cannot reorder code beyond a conditional branch, the supply of available work will dry up to the point where even designing a superscalar engine would be moot. If the engine does permit code to be reorganized around conditional branches, the supply of concurrent work is much bigger. This larger supply comes at the price of much bookkeeping hardware, however, which must notice when a branch did not go the expected way, repair the damage to machine state, and restart from that point. DFA had a built-in weakness with respect to speculative execution. Because it could see only the trace of what an actual program *did,* it did not have any way to go down the wrong path occasionally and then have to recover from that, as a real speculative engine would.

We could have addressed this shortcoming by giving DFA access to the program object code and datasets, as well as the execution trace, but it seemed too much work for the improvement we could expect. We ended up collecting enough heuristics to reliably cover the tool's shortcomings, but even so, under certain conditions, it was relatively easy to fool ourselves.

A subtle benefit of a handcrafted tool such as DFA is that it is written directly by the architects themselves. The act of codifying one's thinking unfailingly reveals conceptual holes, mental vagueness, and outright errors that would otherwise infest the project for a much longer time, thus driving up the cost of finding and fixing them later. Having the architects write the tool also forces them to work together in a very close way, which pushes them toward a common understanding of the machine they are creating.

> *The act of codifying one's thinking unfailingly reveals conceptual holes, mental vagueness, and outright errors.*

We probably got too enamored of this tool, however. As we finished P6 and were beginning the Willamette project (which would eventually become known as the Pentium 4 microprocessor) we once again needed an early behavioral model. We could start from scratch, buy something off-the-shelf, or stretch DFA (despite some misgivings that DFA did not appear to be a great fit for the Willamette machine). Sticking with what worked in the past, we chose to extend DFA, and quickly found that it was taking exponentially more work to get marginal increments in usefulness out of it. The moral of the story is, don't fall in love with your tools but rather use or make the right tool for the job.

PERFORMANCE

As I described earlier, our immutable concept phase goal was performance. Doubling the P5's performance was a simple, straightforward mission, exactly the kind you could rally the troops around.

Benchmark Selection

It didn't end up being that simple. The troops had a lot of questions. Performance on which of the dozen important benchmarks? Did we have to get 2× performance or more on *all* of them? Or did the global average have to be 2×, with some benchmarks substantially better than that, and perhaps a few that were much slower? And if some programs could be less than 2×, how much less could they be? Was it okay for the slowest chip of the P6 generation to be slightly slower than the fastest chip of the previous generation? Were some benchmarks more important than others, and therefore to be weighted more heavily?

We also had to determine what methods we would use to predict P6 performance. Would benchmark comparisons be made against the best of the current generation, or today's best extrapolated out a few years? In some cases, such as transactions processing, actual measurements are extremely difficult to make, and theoretical predictions are even harder. Yet that type of programming is important in servers, and you cannot just ignore it.

Avoiding Myopic Do-Loops. It is dangerous to use benchmarks in designing new machines, but not as dangerous as *not* using them, since the best you can say about computer systems designed solely according to qualitative precepts instead of data is that they are slow and unsuccessful. But relying too heavily on a benchmark has its own pitfalls. The most serious is myopia: forgetting that it is, after all, just a benchmark, and therefore represents only one kind of programming and only to some limited degree.

> *It is dangerous to use benchmarks in designing new machines, but not as dangerous as* **not** *using them.*

Myopia develops in a manner something like this. After driving DFA all night, an architect announces that benchmark X is showing a performance improvement of only 1.6× over P5 instead of the targeted 2×, and the reason is a combination of memory stack references, which are inherently sequential and thus resistant to some kinds of out-of-order improvements. The architect proposes that to fix this problem, the microarchitecture must now include heroic measures associated with stacks. After several days of intense effort, the architects believe they may have a palliative measure that they can actually implement and this should help benchmark X. They modify DFA to include the new design and reanalyze the benchmark. Not wanting to seem ungrateful for everyone's hard work, DFA reports that benchmark X is now 1.93×, which the happy architects agree is close enough for now.

The next night, however, when the same architects run another performance regression (which they do because the project is so well managed) they are not as happy. DFA reports that the new changes have helped 70% of all benchmarks, some a little, some a lot, but the new changes have also slowed the other 30%, and in benchmark Y's case the slowdown is rather alarming. Now what? The architects have several choices. They could

1. Back out the heroic measures and try to fix benchmark X some other way
2. Leave the heroic measures in and try to fix only the worst of the collateral damage
3. Reconsider their benchmark suite and ask how important benchmark X is versus benchmark Y
4. Intensively analyze benchmark Y to find out why a seemingly innocuous change

like the fix for X should have had such a surprising impact on Y (a choice that invariably leads to back to choice 1 or 2)

Such do-loops can rapidly become demoralizing, as architects spend all their time pleasing the benchmark and lose sight of the project goal: how to achieve true doubled performance over the previous generation. Moreover, given the difficulty and intellectual immersion the do-loop demands, architects must make superhuman efforts to rise above it and ascertain that project performance is really still on track.

Floating-Point Chickens and Eggs. Intel Architecture x86 chips had not been known for industry-leading floating-point performance in the 1980s and early 1990s. In fact, their relative anemia on floating-point code was a major reason that RISC vendors had the engineering workstation market to themselves at that time. But because of that history, we were not being asked for much floating-point performance from the original P6 chip. Essentially, two times the P5's floating-point performance was not very hard to achieve, and because the x86 floating point had been slow for so long, no x86 applications needed fast floating point.

This was a classic chicken-and-egg scenario. Nonetheless, we believed that the P6 family would find a ready home in workstation and server markets if it had competitive floating-point performance, so we included it in our design decisions even though normal benchmarking would have excluded it.

Floating-point performance also raises some subtle issues in project goal setting. Intel had a large market share in the 1990s; it supplied the microprocessors for over 80% of all desktops. Knowing this, an insidious mental distortion can easily set in. One could start thinking that whatever Intel does is de facto good enough, and whatever floating-point performance our chips supplied, the industry would simply adjust their software demands accordingly.

> *Seek a balance between what the technology makes possible, the cost of various design options, and what buyers can afford.*

But that is no way to keep an architectural franchise healthy. It is a much better idea to seek a balance between what the technology makes possible, the cost of various design options, and what buyers can afford. If one makes that trade-off optimally, one's products will be competitive independent of existing market share. That is what we tried to achieve with P6.

Legacy Code Performance

The hardware design community is often guilty of overlooking a glaringly obvious market truth: Buyers spend their money to run software; hardware is only a necessary means to that end. Yes, some people do buy computers (or at least they did at one time) just to have bragging rights to the fastest machine on their block. And some have bought computers just to run some new application, not much caring about the existing software legacy base. In the late 1990s, about one to three million new microprocessors could be expected to be sold at an exciting markup to people playing leading-edge games. For these users, the additional performance edge was tangible and valuable.

But the economics of microprocessors reward much higher volumes. Mainstream x86 designs can expect to ship upward of 100 million units, which is where their true return-on-investment lies. For P6, this meant we had to pay attention to the existing code base during the concept phase, not just new benchmarks.

In many ways, legacy code is a more difficult target for a new microarchitecture. A mountain of x86 code has accumulated since the 1970s. Designing an engine to correctly run both legacy code and modern compiled code at world-class performance levels is like designing a new jet fighter to run on anything from jet-A fuel to whale blubber and coal.

The compiler group could not help us here. The legacy code was compiled some indeterminate number of years earlier, and its target machine was now considered thoroughly obsolete. The compiler probably optimized for all the wrong things compared with more modern designs.

For us, the most difficult aspect of legacy code was judging how important relative performance would be. Would this software continue to be heavily used? Would anyone run it on the new platform? If the new microprocessor sped up this code, would anybody care or even notice? Even if our best judgment said that existing code was in heavy use and would be used on our new machine, and that performance was potentially important, we still had to contend with the expense of accommodating changes aimed specifically at the legacy code.

Early in P6's microarchitecture development, for example, we realized that general computing's future would be 32 bits, not the 16-bit code characteristic of the i386 and i486 era. Eventually, it would migrate to 64 bits, but our collective best judgment in 1991 was that the final move to 64 bits would not impact the P6 family, so we decided to focus our efforts on 32-bit performance. We checked with Microsoft about their plans for migrating Windows operating systems and were assured that their "Chicago" release (eventually renamed

> *Our collective best judgment in 1991 was to focus our efforts on 32-bit performance.*

Windows 95) would be 32 bits only, all legacy 16-bit code having been excised. That was great news for us, until late in 1993, when Microsoft admitted that they had been unable to replace the old 16-bit graphics display drivers with the new 32-bit versions they had created for Windows NT and would have to retain the old code to maximize hardware compatibility with old monitors and video cards. I describe the scramble that ensued in "Performance Surprises" in Chapter 5.

Intelligent Projections

Performance projections are extremely important to a design project, and no less so to the corporation itself. Big design companies such as Intel will usually have several CPU design projects going at any time, plus their associated chip-set developments, and many other related projects, such as new bus standard developments, electrical signaling research efforts, compiler development, performance and system monitoring tools, marketing initiatives, market branding development, and corporate strategic direction setting.

All these must be coordinated. It is hard enough to convey information accurately to a customer about a new design's schedule, performance, power dissipation, and electrical characteristics, without also having to explain why the design appears to compete with another of your company's products. Customers have the right to assume (and they will) that their vendor has its act together and is actively coordinating its internal development projects so as to achieve a seamless, comprehensive product line that makes sense to the customer and is something the customer can rely on in making their own product road maps. That customer's customer will assume the same thing of them, after all.

This is a challenge in any venue. Have you ever watched a duck languidly gliding across a pond? That placid appearance doesn't come without furious churning below the surface. A seamless product line is no different, except for the feathers and webbed feet.

All Design Teams Are Not Equal. Many executives approach the task of managing multiple design teams by reasoning that if all design projects do things the same way and use the same tools to do their performance projections, comparing their expected outcomes should be rather trivial. When such grand unification attempts inevitably fall short, they blame "not invented here" and interproject rivalries. Those can be major influences to be sure, but a more important reason all projects can't do things the same way is that they aren't designing the same things, and the teams do not comprise the same designers.

Sports teams provide a persuasive analogy. One basketball team might have two very tall players, and base their game strategies on getting the ball to them. Another might have fine outside shooters. A third could be exceptional at passing and running. Design teams, too, are a collection of all the individual talents and abilities of their members, amplified (or diminished) by interpersonal team dynamics and overall management skill. To treat all teams the same is to cripple the exceptional teams while implicitly insisting that the weaker design teams somehow perform above their capability.

> *To treat all teams the same is to cripple the exceptional teams while implicitly insisting that the weaker design teams somehow perform above their capability.*

I believe a company's strongest design team must be allowed to do what its leaders believe is necessary to achieve the finest possible results. Other teams in the company may find it helpful to follow their lead, or may themselves be strong enough to strike out in new directions. Upper management must make this judgment call; if they refuse, and instead end up with a one-size-fits-all direction, it's almost certainly wrong.

In this context, a project's official performance projections are not just the output of a standard company simulator. Performance projections are project leadership judgments that have four critical bases:

1. A deep knowledge of what is being designed
2. Risks that important as-yet-unresolved issues will be settled favorably
3. Composition of the performance benchmark suite
4. Most important, the particular design team's culture as modulated by the corporate culture

Overpromise or Overdeliver? To put this relationship of design team to performance projection in a more familiar context, consider this cultural/philosophical question: Is it better for a design project to overpromise and underdeliver, or to underpromise and overdeliver?[3] There are rational arguments to be made for both choices, but the point is

---

[3]Yes, there is theoretically a third alternative: deliver exactly what you promised. But if that is your team's aim, then they are probably underpromising so as to increase their chances of hitting the real target.

that each design team will have its own ideas. Moreover, they must pick one and studiously avoid the other, generally making their selection a point of pride for them and justification to ridicule those who picked the other.

Table 2.1 shows the various dimensions of the tension between the choices. The overpromising team will take fierce pride in the awesome performance numbers they've established as their target, and will consider all other teams to be either timid or simply underperforming. The overdelivering side will see the other teams as untrustworthy, promising the moon and stars while delivering at best a micrometeorite.

Thus, what appears to be a simple technical determination—establishing a realistic performance target for a new design—is in fact a deep statement of how a design team sees itself and to what heights that team aspires.

The overpromise side will argue that there are uncertainty bands in any simulation, measurement, or projection. If you always pick the most pessimistic edge of the uncertainty band, then you are seriously sandbagging your performance projection, and it may not be meaningful or useful. It's

> *What appears to be a simple technical determination is in fact a deep statement of how a design team sees itself and to what heights that team aspires.*

a competitive world, and if you can reasonably argue that your project might be able to hit a certain performance target, then by all means make that your project goal and tell everyone about it. Trying to achieve a high target and if necessary falling slightly short might, in fact, yield the best possible final result. Besides, customers have heard unrealistic promises for so long that they routinely downgrade whatever you tell them, and if you give them a realistic performance number, it could well be noncompetitive after being judged down. It's best to take the complete context into account when projecting performance.

I have two words for those arguments: Get real. If I'm going to surprise a customer, I want it to be accompanied with delight, not dismay. I believe in the think-straight, talk-

Table 2.1. Project Target Philosophies

	Rationale	Early results	Final results	Side effects
Overpromise and underdeliver	Optimism spawns creativity	High performance numbers make management very happy	Management very angry because the team can't produce the promised moon and stars	Project won't notice trouble in time to fix it
	Might as well judge unknowns in your favor	Troop morale high	Disappointed customers	Team loses credibility with management and customers
Underpromise and overdeliver	Realism yields best products	Management stays concerned	Management happy	Issues dealt with openly, early, honestly
	Unknowns won't all be in your favor	Troops know distance to finish line	Product hits project goals	Customers can make credible plans

straight school of engineering. Set a clear goal, get the design team's buy-in on the goal, and then tell the company and the customers where you are going and how you will get there. Do performance projections knowing that the project is in an early state, that surprises are inevitable, and that they are virtually never in your favor. Allow for that by judiciously moderating any preliminary rosier-than-reality performance numbers. Don't make official performance targets that are so low you can't possibly miss them, but do pick targets that you have reasonable confidence you will hit. As the project proceeds and confidence grows in the numbers, adjust upward as necessary. And watch out for more aggressive projections from other teams being used to shame you into raising yours. Practice diplomatic ways of saying, "I'm sure that other project had some valid technical basis for making their ludicrous performance claims, but I do not think it's in the company's best interest for me to join them in their delusions." But after all is said and done, *hit your targets.* The overpromise camp is expected to miss, but the overdeliver side cannot fall short if they hope to retain their credibility for the next project. With P6, we chose underpromise and overdeliver—when we committed to project targets, it was because we had high confidence we could meet or exceed them.

As with any other areas of disagreement between projects, the coexistence of these diametrically opposite viewpoints causes serious friction at the executive levels (and therefore among project engineers). A senior vice president will always have two or more project reports on his desk simultaneously, and if he cannot be reconciled to the teams' cultural differences, he will deem the reports inconsistent and irreconcilable. The judgment and experience required to look behind the numbers and see where the judgments are being applied is exquisitely rare. Worse, the microprocessor design business moves so fast that the conservatism or aggressiveness of a design team becomes apparent just after the team has disbanded, been decommissioned, or split apart.

The best you can do is purposely adopt the philosophy that matches a team and its leadership, make it clear to management and other projects what that philosophy is, and remind them of it at all opportunities. And then *execute* to it.

CUSTOMER VISITS

While we were working through the concepts that would underlie the P6 family, our new marketing organization was catching up on our plans, and making the right contacts in the industry so that we could get useful feedback. They scheduled customer visits with all Intel's "tier one" customers and many of the tier two and three customers and software vendors. Typically, customer visits consisted of one or two field sales engineers, a couple of marketing people from our design division, and an architect from the design team.

Loose Lips

When I was first asked to go on these visits, I assumed that the field sales engineers would be delighted to have someone from the actual design team accompany them. We didn't know all the answers to every question that might come up, but we could quickly judge the implications of a customer's concerns or requests, and we could accurately convey that information to the design team. It turned out, however, that field sales engineers are leery of what they call "factory personnel," and they are not at all inhibited about informing said factory personnel of their reservations.

Field engineers have reason to worry about designers talking directly to customers because these meetings require a certain protocol. Egos are involved, as are corporate rivalries and interpersonal histories among the participants. An overriding factor is that the field sales engineer makes his living by keeping the relationship between the two companies healthy. Design engineers can damage that relationship pretty fast just by being themselves, which means blurting out what they believe is the technical truth[4] and then letting the facts lead them to the right course of action. But very often what designers find in their truth trunk is really a combination of objective technical facts combined with things they happen to believe with high enough confidence to qualify as a reliable basis for conjecturing or analyzing (i.e., opinions). Worse, engineers enjoy what they do. They find technical discussions with razor smart people to be first-rate intellectual stimulation, and in the ensuing verbal meltdown they can say many things that would have been better left unsaid. So these designers can be loose cannons in meetings with their technical counterparts from other companies and can innocently say things that will take the field engineers weeks of counterspin to undo.

Memorable Moments

I could fill this book with accounts of customer visits, but this chapter is already on the long side, so I'll limit myself to three standouts.

Microsoft. It amazed me how uniformly short the planning horizons of the companies we visited seemed to be. We were talking to them in 1991 to 1992 about a microprocessor that would be in volume production by 1995, so Intel had to have at least a five-year planning horizon for its microprocessor road maps. This meant we had to at least try to look into the future that far. Initially, I had hoped that we could compare and contrast our vision for that time frame with various customers' plans and visions, to the benefit of both. But what we found was that almost no companies even tried to see out beyond two years, let alone four or five, and they were not all that interested in the topic.

Microsoft was an exception. Their developments were as long-lived as Intel's and like Intel they were very sensitive to the long-term implications of establishing standards and precedents. At one classic meeting with them, a few of us Intel engineers found ourselves at one end of a long table. On one side sat the Chicago (Windows 95) development team. On the other was the Windows NT team. We had hoped to present the general ideas behind the P6 design and our performance targets, and then spend the rest of the meeting getting both teams' inputs on our proposed physical address extensions.

It was not to be. As we were presenting the preliminary P6 material, we became uncomfortably aware of a strong undercurrent in the room, some dynamic that was keeping us from getting complete mindshare from the Microsoft folks. I don't remember what set it off, but all too soon the Windows NT team members were shouting at the Windows 95 engineers about their poor reliability and lack of understanding of their legacy code, and the Windows 95 engineers were equally loud about which team was earning money and which team was just spending it. I'm not sure they even noticed when we left the room.

Novell. In 1992, networking had not yet been built into the operating system, so if you wanted to interconnect PCs back then, Novell was the answer. All of us sensed that net-

---

[4]Richard Feynman noticed this during his investigation of the Challenger disaster, and believed he got much more accurate information "from the bottom," directly from the engineers [19].

The Lost Art of Roadmapping

Our customers' inability to see beyond two or three years shocked me, because tactics must reflect strategy, and strategy must be aligned with the global trends that regularly sweep across the computing industry. Operating systems with graphical user interfaces demanded more DRAM and removable storage capacity; CD-ROMs answered that challenge but needed better buses; PCI was the 1990s answer to that.

Taken as a group, those things formed a very capable computing platform, and together with compelling games, drove demand for better audio and graphics. And when those building blocks were in place, and CPUs had gotten fast enough and modems cheap enough, the Internet was born, the implications of which are still filtering through every corner of the computing universe.

You don't have to see every turn coming, but you have to try to form a general map and plot your company's best path through it. Very few companies we visited seemed able to do that.

---

working was going to become much more important (although few of us, including me, were able to make the conceptual leap to today's Internet), and we thought that talking to Novell might be a way to see more clearly what was ahead. Our standard pitch was to explain what out-of-order was, the general methods we were using to achieve it, and the high performance we expected. Usually, the performance numbers would elicit at least some interest and excitement as the listener pondered, "What could I do with a machine that fast!?"

But the reaction we got was very different from what we expected. The Novell personnel actually yawned, and one said, "We don't need faster computers. The ones we have now are fast enough."

Staggered by this attitude, I invoked Moore's Law. "It's real," I explained. "Computers are going to get orders of magnitude faster for the same or lower cost over the next 10 to 15 years. If you have no way to take advantage of that, you're going to lose to whomever does." They remained unimpressed. One very senior person asked to talk to me afterward, but my remaining illusions about that company were dashed when all he wanted to know about was some obscure corner case of a complicated x86 instruction.

Compaq. Visiting Compaq was always interesting. In our first encounters, they expressed dismay over our plans to incorporate the L2 cache into the CPU package via the two-die-in-package scheme. They pointed out that, unlike most of their competitors, they could engineer buses and cache designs in ways that gave their systems a performance edge. What Intel thought of as a boon to the OEMs, designing the L2 cache and providing it in the package, Compaq thought of as a lost opportunity to differentiate themselves from their competition. They were even more unhappy, at least initially, about our proposal for P6 to feature glueless multiprocessing.[5] They correctly saw that this would lead to multiprocessing systems assembled by OEMs with much less engineering ability than historically required.

As far as they could see, we were lowering the bar, and forcing them into new positions on the technological ladder. I replied that we were following where the fundamental

---

[5]Glueless, as in no extra chips, all necessary bus logic contained on the CPU chips; multiprocessing as in more than one CPU on the frontside bus.

silicon technology was going. The P6 generation was the first with enough transistors to do a credible multiprocessor design, and when we combined that with our two-die-in-package approach and a new frontside bus, our best POR was clear. Compaq eventually turned its attention to designing very high performance servers and was quite successful in that market.

Insights from Input

The customer visit phase was enlightening on many fronts. I was amazed, horrified, and indebted by turns.

Not So Secret Instructions. Every CPU architect has heard this request at least once from people who should have known better: "Would you please put a few special instructions in there, just for us? That way, our code will run faster than our competitor's." I learned not to roll my eyes when I heard this, but it is so wrongheaded about something so basic that I had to wonder what else they probably didn't understand. The reality is that most code is not heavily performance-bound by the lack of one instruction. Yes, you can find some encryption software that may spend 80% of its time in a tight inner loop that wants a "find-first-one rotate through hyperspace inverse square root twice on Tuesdays" instruction that you somehow neglected to provide, but most code won't notice that instruction or any other simple fix. So the belief that the microprocessor is but one or two instructions away from blindingly higher speed is almost always wrong.

> *Yes, you can find some software that wants a "find-first-one rotate through hyperspace inverse square root twice on Tuesdays" instruction, but most code won't notice.*

Worse, however, is the idea that if someone could provide such instructions, somehow competitors wouldn't notice. Not in *this* architecture; code is too easy to disassemble. The time lag between "What is this opcode I've never seen before?" and "Oh, *that's* what this does" is measured in hours or minutes, not years.

Help from the Software World. By far the shortest planning-time horizons we saw on customer visits were at the software vendors. Those folks behaved at all times like the world would end 18 months from today and there wasn't much point in pretending time existed beyond that. Some of them were helpful, anyway. John Carmack of ID Software comes to mind. He had some deep, useful insights about when and why a software vendor would ever use instruction subsets such as MMX, SSE, and SSE II. He also knew more than anyone else about the difficulties of writing software that would deliver a compelling gaming experience while remaining compatible with dozens of sound and video cards, on top of choosing between the then-competing Open-GL and DirectX standards. John was one of the few people we encountered who really understood the systems and CPU issues and how those would translate into the gaming experience for his Doom and Quake games. [12]

The Truth about Hardware and Software. I rapidly discovered that software vendors and hardware vendors are not completely aligned. Hardware vendors traditionally earn their best profits on their latest, fastest, and best hardware, and that is what they normally promote most zealously in marketing programs. A few years later, the magic of cleverness, hard work, big investment, and Moore's Law enables them to produce something even better, and the cycle repeats. Hardware vendors want the buyer to be so dissatisfied with their current products that they will replace them with the latest and greatest. They want software vendors to produce programs that are so demanding of the hardware, yet compelling to the buyers, that buyers will upgrade their systems so that they can run them.

Software vendors, on the other hand, want to sell as many copies of their new title as possible. If they write the code so that it requires leading-edge hardware, they will drastically limit their immediate market. There may be at most a few million computing platforms with the fastest CPUs, but there are hundreds of millions of computing platforms running older operating systems and hardware. Software vendors must try to ensure that their code runs acceptably on these legacy systems, and even better on newer machines.

Put in directional terms, hardware vendors are looking forward, trying to make today's computing platforms obsolete, whereas software vendors are often looking sideways or backward, trying to sell their newest wares to those same platforms.

ESTABLISHING THE DESIGN TEAM

Toward the end of P6's concept phase, we felt confident that some parts of the overall design were mature enough for design staff to begin working on them. Integer ALUs, floating-point functional units, the instruction decoder, the frontside bus, and the register alias tables were candidates, since they seemed unlikely to need major reworking before the project's end. We had less experience with the out-of-order core, including the reservation stations (which began as split-integer/floating-point reservation stations but were later combined into one), the reorder buffer, and much of the memory subsystem.

At this point, Randy Steck, P6's design manager, began organizing the design troops with a secret map we had provided that detailed our best estimates of how complex the various units would ultimately be. Randy needed to put his best, most experienced engineers on the hardest parts of the design so that these units would not end up unduly stretching the schedule. At the same time, he had to integrate over 100 new college graduates, and he could not leave any of them leaderless. He also had to convince a significant number of his experienced engineers that managing these new engineers was a good thing. It is a tribute to Randy's effectiveness as a project manager that he succeeded in extending many design engineers' effectiveness into first-line supervisory duties while they remained the design's principal technical drivers.[6]

Teams are assemblages of individuals, each of whom has unique physical and intellectual capabilities, as well as individual circumstances in their personal lives that will impact their effectiveness.

Randy understood deeply that a design team is no less a team than a group of professional basketball players who must be assigned their roles for maximum aggregate effectiveness. Teams are assemblages of individuals, each of whom has unique physical and intellectual capabilities, as well as individual circumstances in their personal lives that will impact their effectiveness throughout the game, project, or whatever other goal they must accomplish together. With basketball teams, it is easy to remember that players are not equally capable at every task. Clearly, the really tall players should be centers, and the short players who are good shooters should play the outside and handle the ball. If the coach botches these assignments, the same set of players will deliver a much different result because there's a reason those really tall players seldom try to dribble the ball very far.

Design team members need the same kind of careful positioning—a reality that technical design managers often forget. They see a baccalaureate degree, coupled with hiring (passing the firm's sanity check), which they take to mean that someone is at least minimally competent at some set of engineering or programming tasks and can learn more on the job.

But really good teams go way beyond this job assignment level, actively judging each design engineer so as to give her or him the best possible point of leverage on the project. Some engineers thrive in an assignment with high uncertainty and high pressure; they enjoy the challenge and feeling of being the first to wrestle with the concepts that must coalesce if the project is to succeed. These folks tend to gravitate toward architectural and performance analysis assignments. Others like the logic and stability of a design assignment. You tell them exactly what a unit has to do, give them constraints for die space, power dissipation, clock rates, connections to other units, and schedule, and they will apply their ingenuity to solving that N-dimensional problem. Still others live for technical arcana; they get an intellectual thrill out of knowing how many open page table entries any single x86 instruction can possibly touch, and the attendant implication for how the microprocessor must handle page misses in general. These folks are the microcoders.

Place people where they can excel at what they're gifted at doing and you are on your way to a winning team. This seems obvious enough, but it's surprising how many managers act as if they don't get this. Treating engineers as if they are all alike, the human equivalent of field-replaceable units, is a sure recipe for mediocrity.

> *Treating engineers as if they are all alike is a sure recipe for mediocrity.*

Roles and Responsibilities

After a few weeks of intense deliberation, we had a preliminary allocation of design engineering heads to known tasks. And we had also turned up some new and interesting issues about the relationship between design and architecture. Who did presilicon validation? Who did microcode development? Where was performance analysis to be performed? What was this new "MP" group and who owned it? Who owned the process to develop the register-transfer logic (RTL) model?

There were no useful corporate precedents. Previous projects like the 486 were so small (by P6 standards) that for them, any of several organizing methods would work equally well. The concurrent P5 project being developed in Santa Clara had separate architecture and design organizations, as we did with P6, but they arrived at that organizational structure too late for us to learn much from it. So we worked through the issues with a week of focused, daily meetings.

We ended up with an overall organization similar to that in Figure 2.3. The general manager of this division was originally Randy Young, who recruited me to this project.

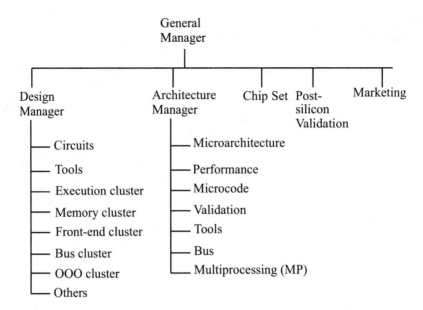

Figure 2.3. MD6 (Microprocessor Division 6) basic organizational chart.

Within six months, however, he was replaced by Pat Gelsinger. A couple of years later, Will Swope and Dadi Perlmutter took over, then Dadi and Randy Steck, and then Randy Steck and Mike Fister. The general manager position has a great deal of authority and responsibility; thousands of engineers report to these folks, and they are the primary voice of a project to upper management, as well as the executives' main communication channel back to the project.

The general managers had other projects beside P6, but P6 was their main focus and where most of their headcount resided. The P6 design manager had groups devoted to design tools and circuit libraries and expertise, but most of the design group was partitioned into clusters, with each cluster further subdivided into functional units.

The architecture organization consisted of microcode development, performance analysis, presilicon validation, frontside bus design, the microarchitects, and a group devoted to getting our multiprocessing story straight.

Other groups at the divisional staff level included the P6 chip-set development team, a postsilicon validation organization, a marketing group, a finance group, and several others.

Presilicon Validation. The two basic types of validation for microprocessors occur before and after silicon. The presilicon validation tests the register-transfer logic (RTL) model as it becomes available, and is aimed at preventing design errata from ever appearing in the actual chip. Postsilicon validation, a combination of two Intel groups, Compatibility Validation and System Validation, tests the actual CPU silicon against its specifications and ensures that the new CPU successfully runs all legacy software.

I felt strongly that presilicon validation had to be separate from, but embedded within, the design team. Design engineers often have invaluable knowledge of the corner cases of their unit, the places where they made the most complex trade-offs or where the most confusion was present during design. For experienced validation engineers, such knowledge is extremely useful, because they know that where complexity and confusion reign, design errata follow. Dedicating validation engineers to the units they are testing also helps the validators overcome any us-against-them thinking on the part of the design engineers. Validators can more easily learn the design engineers' lingo and become accepted team members. So it may seem logical to embed validators into the design team itself.

Offsetting those advantages are the simple design logistics. Design projects are always late or under extreme schedule pressure. Surprises come along as the design progresses, unanticipated events that are never in the designer's favor. If you ever do get close to hitting your schedule, the odds increase that your unit will be asked to contribute one of its design engineers to some other unit in worse trouble. This pressure gives rise to a tempting but self-defeating strategy: After accepting the validators onto a design team, absorb them as "temporary" extra design heads until the next schedule crunch has been averted. This syndrome seems very logical because, after all, you cannot test something until it has been designed. Also, the looming schedule crunch is not an isolated event (more are behind the one that is visible), and skimping on validation does not seem to hurt right away. Poor validation becomes painfully evident only much later in the design project.

Our final answer to organizing presilicon validation was to require that unit owners, the designers who actually wrote the RTL code, write sanity-check regression tests for their own code. Before the designer officially released a new, latest-and-greatest version of his unit's code for use by other designers or validators, he had to have tested it to at least some minimal level. This turned out to be a really good idea. Full-chip models comprised several dozen units, and even a minor typo in any of them could result in a full-chip model that would not compile or run any useful code. Having a high-level wizard (more on wizards next) debug such problems at the full-chip level is possible[7] and sometimes necessary, but it is never as efficient as having the unit owners do some testing before release.

We also reallocated a small fraction of the expected presilicon validation headcount to the various units, with the proviso that some unit testing would now be required. This requirement for at least minimal self-testing helped interpersonal relationships, too. Few things are as annoying to a too-busy design engineer as the feeling that someone else saved himself a little work at that engineer's expense.

We slotted the rest of the presilicon validation heads into a team under the architecture organization. From that vantage point, validators could get the technical help they needed to track down malfunctions and could muster the authority needed to get always-overloaded unit owners or design engineers to fix things properly before moving on. Being officially in another organization inoculated the validators from possible conscription or from being sacrificed to the schedule gods.

Wizard Problem Solving. We ran the P6 project primarily with the "bigger wizard" stratagem. If a designer at a project "leaf node" had the wherewithal to resolve a problem, then she was expected and empowered to do so. If she could not, she would discuss the issue with her technical supervisor and often they would come up with an answer. If that did not resolve the problem, they went in search of a bigger wizard. This process would repeat until the issue ended up on the desk of the biggest wizards in the project, those who *had* to resolve the problem. Watching brilliant people like Dave,

---

[7]We eventually realized we had to require release testing because Michael Fetterman's outstanding technical acumen was allowing him to successfully hand-debug many full-chip models in a row, but the process was grinding him and his family down.

Glenn, Michael, Andy, and circuits wizard Paul Madland pull technical rabbits out of hats was always a thrill, and they came through for the project again and again. I was always left with the impression that when confronted by a really sticky technical problem, they would somehow mentally leave this galaxy, go check around in some other one, find the answer, and return home with the solution in tow.

Paul Madland deserves a special mention here. In the early concept days of the project, the basic structures we were considering for the microarchitecture were changing radically on almost a weekly basis. Paul had an uncanny ability to guess which structures were likely to survive our ruminations, and he would proactively design circuits that would be needed for such structures, so that the project would not get inadvertently oversubscribed. Paul's creativity and eye for circuit detail were major reasons that P6 (and its progeny) hit their clock targets.

Making Microcode a Special Case. As Figure 2.3 shows, we kept the multiprocessor (MP) group under architecture, since it was clearly an architectural task to get all the corner cases of cache coherence straight and to figure out how to start up four CPUs with indeterminate amounts of time for each to race through its power-on self-test and become ready to run the operating system.

We also kept the microcode group under architecture organization, but that decision was not as clear-cut as the MP group placement. Conceptually, microcode really is another design unit, just like the instruction decoder or the branch predictor, but it is special in many ways. In a chip-design sense, I think of x86 microcode as being similar to the "default" case in a C program switch statement:

```
switch (design problem) {
      case Integer: integer ALU; break;
      case Memory: loads, stores, cache coherence; break;
      . . .
      default: microcode
}
```

Other units are explicitly called out in the switch statement; they know where their locus of complexity lies. It's not that those units are simple or easy to design; it's only that their unit's job has some identifiable boundaries, and it's reasonable to assume that ignoring what lies beyond will be a safe tactic.

Microcode cannot assume *anything*. When the chip powers up, it starts executing code that is in the microcode ROM. Complex instructions, of which the x86 has many, rely on microcode for their implementation. Faulting instructions will end up in microcode. Floating point has an extensive footprint in x86 microcode.

> *As the project progresses, various units become silicon-area landlocked or power constrained.*

Most insidious of all, however, is that as the project progresses, various units become silicon-area landlocked or power constrained. With the passage of project time, designers lose degrees of freedom in handling surprises—they don't have the die space to include new circuitry, or they require the cooperation of neighboring units that lack space. Microcode, on the other hand, is a combination of a ROM storage area and the programming it contains. Experienced designers know to always leave themselves room to maneuver whenever possible and as they use up their margin, they look outside their local "box" for solutions. Microcode is so flexible that you can often use it to solve problems in surprising ways. Perhaps a design error is discovered late in the project in which unit X is not properly handling corner case Y. It is entirely possible that sufficiently clever microcode can prevent corner case Y from ever happening.

Exquisite judgment is required to play the microcode card properly. Used judiciously, microcode fixes can keep a project on track; used profligately, the microcode space will fill up, or the complexity injected by all those unrelated and unexpected fixes will cause more bugs in the microcode itself. It is also possible that a microcode fix could cause an unacceptable performance slowdown. It was primarily to help modulate this process that we kept microcode development on the architecture side of the project organization chart.

Cubicle Floorplanning

We quickly discovered that the design engineers' physical proximity profoundly affected their mutual communication bandwidth. "Out of sight, out of mind" comes close but doesn't quite capture the problem. It is certainly possible to design complex software or hardware in a geographically distributed way, as the Gnu Freeware development efforts demonstrated, but it is not optimal. After many years of designing and leading designs, I am convinced that all the same tribal inclinations that drive wars are present in any endeavor that involves multiple humans, including chip design. Simply put, people you see often are much less likely to end up on your subconscious us-versus-them list.

> *The design engineers' physical proximity profoundly affected their mutual communication bandwidth.*

When I was a graduate student at Carnegie Mellon in the late 1970s, computing consisted of sitting in a room full of timeshare terminals connected to centralized minicomputers. I literally sat elbow-to-elbow with my fellow students. All of us grumbled about needing to walk to that room to use computers, but looking back, the proximity was extremely beneficial. If you had any questions about how things worked or what some error message meant, all you had to do was say it out loud. Brian Reid, creator of the Scribe word formatting system, or James Gosling, creator of the Unix Emacs editor and the Java programming language, or a dozen other computer science luminaries would immediately provide both the answer to your question and (intuiting what you were *really* trying to do) a better way to tackle your problem in the first place. They not only answered your question authoritatively, they solved your real problem, and they did so in such a way that you and everyone else in the room benefited.

The same kind of high-bandwidth communication is achievable in a design project for the same reason: carefully wrought physical proximity.

As part of organizing the P6 project, I had helped Randy figure out who would do what, at least initially. We took as a given that designers working in a single unit would have adjacent cubicles. But what would be the best cubicle floor plan for architecture as opposed to design? And where should we place the unit groups?

Coincidental to our cubicle floorplanning was the first cut at a P6 die layout that aimed to minimize long wiring so as to decrease die size and power dissipation and increase the clock rate. It occurred to me that a cubicle layout fashioned after the chip layout could achieve the same result. After all, units are made adjacent neighbors because they must have many interconnections to work properly. Likewise, placing the designers' cubicles next to each other would tend to facilitate the one-on-one communication needed to get the chip's interconnections right. This stratagem worked well for a few months, until we hired so many new people that we had to choose between neighbor and intraunit communication. But by then we had worked out the interfaces.

We chose to put the relatively small (60 person) architecture team in the middle of the design cubicles specifically to avoid the us-versus-them psychology and to make sure the architects felt the designers' pain. Performance maximizing always comes at a cost. Balancing the win against that cost is the very essence of engineering, and architects must thoroughly understand both ends of the trade-off before they make it. Architects who always try to resolve design issues with whatever alternative maximizes performance are not doing their jobs properly.

Architects, Engineers, and Schedules

Projects that require hundreds of people and last more than four years are extremely expensive. Corporate executives tend to notice this and consequently exert constant pressure on project leaders to find ways to shrink the overall schedule. Better tools, better methods, more engineers, more vehement tongue-lashings—no means to this end seem unreasonable. I cannot fault the executives for their basic motivations.

> *The more distant production is, the more far-sighted the architects must be and the higher the risk the project must bear.*

Long projects *are* expensive, and the more distant production is, the more far-sighted the architects must be and the higher the risk the project must bear.

The concept phase itself is an obvious point of high leverage on the schedule in at least two ways. In drawing up their plans and specifications for the overall design, architects are essentially writing checks that the design engineers must later cash. Any mistakes the architects make will eventually translate into schedule slips. On any given issue, the time spent getting the design right up front will typically more than offset the time required for a diving save to fix a conceptual error later.

> *In drawing up their plans and specifications for the overall design, architects are essentially writing checks that the design engineers must later cash.*

But it is also true that a four-year project may spend a third of its overall schedule leveraging the efforts of only a few people, the architects. Improving their efficiency and shortening this time will have an immediate impact on overall project schedule.

The question is how to speed up the project's conceptual phase while attaining the same goals as before. One proposal that just won't stay dead is to have a specialized team of researchers and architects, whose sole job is to anticipate the microarchitecture and feature set that some future chip will require, and have that design ready by the time the design team becomes available.

I hate this idea.

Who *are* these people who can see even further out than the usual chip architects? They are the same chip architects, who, much to their dismay, have been unceremoniously yanked from another design project. How does that simple reassignment help anything? It certainly cuts the close ties to the design team that might otherwise have been possible. Granted, this estrangement could, at least in principle, help some architect see something promising he might have overlooked, but it's also highly likely that architects, working alone and without designers to keep them honest, will make some fundamental assumptions about die size, power, circuit speeds, or design effort that will force a restart to the architecture work anyway.

While these architects are off working on basic research for a future chip, who is finishing the existing designs? The temptation is always strong to pull the architects themselves off a project once it has taped out, but I think that is a mistake. They can productively spend part of their time on current designs, and part in concept development meetings. Many architects would rather spend their time dreaming up new ideas for future chips than facing daily reminders that not all their previous ideas worked out the way they had hoped (which is a really good reason to keep them engaged with the current design).

Another reason advance development does not work is that these teams tend to be like the United Nations. Everybody wants their interests represented or, better yet, unfairly biased toward them if possible, and researchers quickly find that they have many masters. In a short while, realizing that no single solution will satisfy the logical union of all requests, they begin to examine the politics. If they can't satisfy all their masters, it is prudent to identify the most important ones and at least make *them* happy. Even this is problematic, however, because the folks with the power today might not be the ones who have it in five years.

Advance development thus produces imponderables that require leadership to define a useful path. And where will that leadership come from? From one of the masters, of course. Under these conditions, the advance development team can easily spend lots of time employing high-powered engineers and yield essentially nothing, doomed from the start by the lack of clear mission and goals.

Not that *all* research efforts must have this gloomy end. Advanced development *can* productively investigate new features that require specialized knowledge of the field, such as security or encryption engines. Requiring chip architects to do this investigating is inefficient, at least with the intense schedule of a chip development. If done properly, the advance development team can draw a map of the technical possibilities, indicating which feasible points match the requirements for that feature. With this expert tutelage, the architects can quickly and with low risk incorporate new features into their products.

Coding, Egos, Subterfuge

One thing that attracts certain people to engineering is that they can objectively evaluate a healthy fraction of everyday ideas. These are issues with concrete answers, and people *agree* that they have concrete answers. They are not a matter of opinion, personal philosophy, or religious faith.

Many of the same people who insist on objectively provable answers will engage with apparently unlimited fervor in topics for which there are multiple feasible approaches with no commonly accepted means for numerically resolving them. Typically, two or more camps will emerge, both of which believe the issue at hand really can be resolved objectively if only the other side were not so illogical and obtuse.

Old-timers will recognize the choice of Unix editor as being one of these topics. To some, the simplicity and unpretentiousness of the vi editor was the only right choice; to others, it made sense to enter the emacs universe and never leave it. PCs or Macs, Intel or AMD, Windows or Unix—all attract the unresolvable fury that intuitive certainty engenders.

Coding standards is another such topic. Professional programmers who collaborate on a design project must at some point reach a working consensus on languages, interfaces, overall product architecture, and so on. Because they know that achieving such a consensus is essential to the product's success, they push to find a useful common ground.

Early in the P6 project, several of us set out to write a simulator that would validate some of the key microarchitectural concepts we were considering. On day two of this effort, we discovered that we had five (or possibly six) different ideas of what constituted readable, maintainable C code. One person had been trained to make his code look like Kernighan and Ritchie's classic C book [30]. Another believed white space was a resource to be rationed and that indenting was worth at most one space on the next line, and sometimes the next line part was optional.

Some of us realized it would be better to try to converge on a viewpoint at the beginning of code development, not after writing lots of widely disparate code. So we convened one of the more rancorous meetings it was ever my misfortune to attend. The size of the indignation evinced by nearly every attendee was obviously out of proportion to the gravity of the issue. Eventually, it became clear that the problem was not a technical or even a rational one. In effect, we were not really trying to mutually determine the best compromise between our differing ideas on what constituted good-looking C code. The issue, clearly (albeit subconsciously) perceived by all, was that in the absence of data, opinion and intuition would decide, and nobody wanted to defer to anyone else on that basis.

> *The issue was that in the absence of data, opinion and intuition would decide, and nobody wanted to defer to anyone else on that basis.*

Then I had an inspiration. We all go through stages of computer maturity when learning computer science and programming. At first, the computer strikes us as really obtuse and stupidly designed, and then positively malevolent, as though it is actually sentient and working very hard to make our lives miserable. Eventually, the student outgrows this feeling and no longer takes it personally when an attempted compile generates a long list of error messages. In effect, the student learns that the computer is simply following its internal rules and has no opinion about that student whatsoever, so it is clearly a waste of indignation to react to it emotionally.

I decided to use this learned behavior to help channel coding conventions toward an acceptable common ground, while also defusing the personality conflicts that were fueling useless style debates. I proposed that all coders had to filter their code through the Unix "lint" tool before it would be accepted. If the filter did not modify the code, then the coding convention was being adhered to. If the tool complained, the coder was required to alter his code accordingly. Even though the particular flags that governed the lint tool's scrutiny were themselves selected by one of us (me), the coders did not feel devalued, because they were conditioned to resignedly accept what the computer wanted.

Why did this subterfuge work so well? All the participants had well above average intelligence; they knew the scam that I was perpetrating. It worked anyway because it allowed all egos to back out of the conflict without visible loss of face. It moved the conflict from "who knows best," which can be resolved only by anointing one coder above all others, to a mechanical means for homogenizing the code to a mutually acceptable level. Paying attention to this kind of human dynamic has many other applications in a long, large design project.

3

THE REFINEMENT PHASE

The Pentium Pro, launched by Intel Wednesday, is now the world's fastest. But apart from sheer speed, it offers nothing that isn't already available.
—A TV anchor introducing P6

"Apart from sheer speed . . . ?" What did that TV anchor want his microprocessor to do, tap dance while juggling spinning plates and singing "Georgia on My Mind"? A computer's processing speed is its raison d'être. With few exceptions, it is the additional computational "horsepower" of each new generation that allows new usage models and system features. The TV anchor in question was betraying his near-total lack of understanding of what computers are and how they do what they do.

But he was also inadvertently revealing how buyers view our products. It's easy to get so wrapped up in the technology that you lose sight of how buyers will eventually judge your efforts. Few buyers will be motivated by your slick design. Most care only that the product adds value to their lives. It is extremely difficult to make a chip design run faster, so difficult that you become fixated on the task and forget that speed must translate into tangible benefits to the buyers or the chips will not sell.

This is perhaps the main difference between the concept and refinement phases. The concept phase has generated a few ideas that look promising. The refinement phase must now evaluate them against the project goals, including their appeal to potential buyers.

In that respect, the refinement phase is a bridge between the concept phase's blue-sky, anything-goes brainstorms and the realization phase's nuts-and-bolts schedule pressure. During this phase, architects are still happily juggling several castles in the air, but they are no longer trying to invent new ones. The point of the refinement phase is to settle on

The Pentium Chronicles. By Robert P. Colwell
© 2006 IEEE Computer Society

the most promising idea that appears to meet the project goals and make it the project's formal plan-of-record (POR).

It is not easy to choose from among possibilities that the team has spent months identifying. Senior technical leadership has weighed each proposed direction carefully for its ability to create products that satisfy the major project goals. If all have passed this level of scrutiny, how do you refine the selection further?

There is also the matter of ramping up from the very few concept phase engineers to the team of hundreds who will realize the design after refinement. Finally, to help design team management, the refinement phase should identify which parts of the skeletal design are likely to be the most difficult and which might be easy (perhaps borrowed wholesale from a previous design). The design manager can then assign the best or most experienced designers where expertise is most needed.

OF IMMEDIATE CONCERN

For P6, the identification and assignment process worked reasonably well. On the basis of what we found difficult in the concept phase, we architects guessed what would be most difficult in the logic and circuits, and the best designers found themselves assigned accordingly.

This assignment is not static, however. For many reasons, some parts of the overall design reach maturity before others. Project management must then borrow engineers from the leading units and reassign them to the laggards, because the project is not over until the last unit is finished. This can feel to the leading unit owners like punishment for doing their jobs well, which is likely to damage morale. Who wants to work over the weekend if it means losing 20% of your engineering troops to those who cannot seem to keep up? Project management must keep a constant focus on the "leading edge of the wave" so as to reward and recognize units that are out front. Units that have fallen behind can then measure the lag and plan ways to catch up.

> *Who wants to work over the weekend if it means losing 20% of your engineering troops to those who cannot seem to keep up?*

It is also crucial for project managers to correctly identify *why* units have fallen behind. The reasons are not always strictly technical. For example, late in the P6 development, the validation manager and I were analyzing the latest validation results and were discussing why one unit seemed to be generating the most design errors when a neighboring unit that we had worried about seemed to be doing fine. We had not expected the unit in question to be so complex as to generate such results. After investigating the engineering-change-order (ECO) trail, the validation bug pattern, and the intrinsic microarchitectural complexity, the answer began to crystallize: The leader of the unit that was doing fine was a conservative, down-to-earth engineer who did not hesitate to ask for help from an architect when he was not sure exactly how his unit should behave under all corner conditions. At the head of the unit in trouble was an engineer determined to make his mark on the project and show that there wasn't any level of intellectual complexity he couldn't handle; he never once asked for help. Given enough time, he probably could have succeeded on his own, but there wasn't enough time. We imported a set of experts into that unit, fixed some things, removed some complexity, and got things back on track.

The concept-to-refinement project transition is a subtle one. It's not like throwing a switch. One day you're dreaming up new ideas, and the next you've picked one and tossed the rest out. It's more of a gradual zooming in on the ideas that look most promising so that the ensuing, more intense focus can identify the one idea that will carry the project to victory.

SUCCESS FACTORS

As I described in the previous chapter, quantifying opinions with data is vital to this process. Project leadership must acquire or develop tools and teach the team members how to use them. In this way, a common language and a common data-driven culture evolve, in which to test the team's ideas and absorb the best ones into the project's POR.

On the other hand, you cannot resolve everything with data. Some issues might require too much time, programming, risk, or more market data than is reasonably available, so to be successful a project must rely on intuition as well. Multiple perspectives are also key to success in this phase, and during this time validation and product engineering can provide useful insights. Finally, complexity on the scale of P6 requires both planning and careful modeling if the design is to avoid constant rework.

Handling the Nonquantifiable

Multiprocessing (MP) capability was not in the original P6 project goals, but the original P6 architecture manager, Fred Pollack, had an MP background from previous projects and once we had some promising directions from the concept phase, he urged us to consider what it would take to make P6 an MP design. Senior architect Glenn Hinton realized that one outcome of our performance-driven choice to put the L2 cache on the CPU's backside (not connected directly to the frontside bus) was that the CPU had become self-contained enough that making it an MP design was now feasible. We then took it upon ourselves to investigate what an MP design would mean to the frontside bus, concluded that it looked doable within project schedule and die-size constraints, and adopted MP as a new project goal.

Changing a project's goal in midstream is a delicate matter. On the one hand, there's a strong argument not to. It's much simpler to identify the right project targets early and permit no distractions while the project is en route. On the other hand, there's also a strong argument for being flexible. Design projects are long, with enough time for exigencies to arise and for the team to learn things midway through the

Changing a project's goal in midstream is a delicate matter.

project that they did not know at the outset. If you resolutely ignore such discoveries, but your competition finds a way not to, their product may turn out to be considerably more compelling than yours. With MP, I believe we did exactly this to AMD, for example.

How do you decide whether somebody's midstream brainchild is worth the risk and additional effort? It's a judgment call that must be made with the cooperation of management (who must sign off on the extra schedule pressure and die size), marketing (who must estimate the size of the additional market made available by the new feature), and, most important, the design team. If the project leadership can sell the new idea to the design team and get them excited about it, that new idea is off to a great start. If the design team feels that the new feature is being imposed on them against their will, its odds of working as envisioned are considerably reduced. Team morale will suffer, as well as their confidence in their leadership.

Design teams like data. If they can see why the new feature will make a more profitable product, their assessment of its implementation difficulty will be noticeably more optimistic. Unfortunately, many such decisions must be made when there really is no data to support the vision.

Adding instruction sets is another area that is hard to resolve with data alone because data is hard to get or only partially useful. Company engineers (not those of us on P6, although we contributed) proposed the original MMX instructions because they understood that certain programs would benefit from instructions that performed simultaneous parallel operations on related data. They also knew that implementing these instructions would cost considerable die area, so their task was to convince the powers-that-be that the trade-off was worth it. Their first two attempts to get this new set of instructions into the x86 architecture were denied on three grounds: no user demand; too much heavy lifting would be required of marketing, compiler, and tools efforts by Intel and the industry; and the die-size increase, however tiny, was unacceptable.

What compelling data could they use to refute these allegations? *Of course* there was no user demand; the proposed instructions weren't there yet. The question really was, "If we build them, will users come?" To answer this, the engineers could easily gather some data about applications rewritten to use the new instructions, and the performance advantages quantified and considered in the decision to use them. Naively, we pointed out that the MMX instructions would substantially speed up certain voice recognition algorithms. Unfortunately, the executives had grown irremediably jaded with regard to the speech recognition promise, having heard for years that this technology was almost ready (and would spark a huge uptick in demand for fast CPUs). In the end, however, the engineers prevailed with assurances that no one would perceive the x86 instruction set as dead, but the competition certainly might drive a new set of instructions first and then we would have to follow. On the basis of these inherently unquantifiable concerns, the executives finally accepted MMX.

My point is that a design project will always have unquantifiable issues. To resolve them, about the best you can do is go with the intuition of your best experts. Don't let them off the hook too easily, though. Pure intuition should be a last resort, after the experts have tried to find ways to first quantify that intuition. For P6's technical issues that resisted quantification, we found that even a failed effort to quantify them was invariably instructive in its own right and well worth attempting. It also helped cement the data-driven culture we wanted.

> *A design project will always have unquantifiable issues.*

Managing New Perspectives

Validation is not an active part of the concept phase, generally because validators are still immersed in testing the previous project. It should, however, be included in the refinement phase, partly to improve the validation team's morale and partly to help spot the cases in which seemingly innocuous choices made now will have major validation impact later. Among the hundreds, sometimes thousands, of major unknowns still in this phase, the only difference between two workable approaches might be that one makes validation much easier.

Product engineering must also start to get involved in the refinement phase. In P6, we had been tantalized by a packaging engineer's offhand comment that "if we wanted it, they could actually stick two silicon dies into the same package and run bond wires between them." This looked like a great solution to the problem of keeping the L2 cache close to the CPU. At that time, process technology was not advanced enough to put the cache onto the CPU die itself. But if the L2 cache were a separate chip on the motherboard, electrical signaling would be too difficult to run at the full CPU speed, substantially cutting overall system performance. We took the two-die-in-package approach and got the performance we wanted, as well as the desired MP capability. Years later, we were told that production of these two-die-in-package parts required manual intervention, which was fine for the limited volumes of servers and workstations, but would have been a crippling constraint on desktop volumes.

Architects must constantly fight the urge to put both hands in the cookie jar. If they can resist, they'll see great benefit in keeping production engineering in the loop, starting with the refinement phase, which is the perfect time to bring them up to speed on general project directions. Do not be surprised if what they say has a measurable impact on the project. As with validation, product engineering knows things that the technical development leadership needs to learn.

> *Architects must constantly fight the urge to put both hands in the cookie jar.*

For example, having decided that P6 would be capable of multiprocessor operation, the obvious question was how many microprocessors could be on the same bus. Simulations would readily tell us how much bus bandwidth we needed to reasonably support four CPUs on a bus, and accurate simulations would even illustrate the effects of bus protocol overhead. But bus bandwidth cannot be increased without limit because fast buses are expensive. The architects knew how much bandwidth a four-CPU system needed, the circuit designers knew how longer wires on the motherboard would affect the bus clock frequency (which is a first-order determinant of the bus bandwidth), but only the product engineering team knew how large the CPU packaging had to be. They also knew how many layers of signals would be available in the motherboard, the impedance and variability of each, the stub lengths to the CPU sockets, and the relative costs of the alternatives being considered.

Planning for Complexity. It is important to plan ahead for the complex issues that will become part of the POR. When we chose to make P6 an MP design, I realized that, as a team, we were not deep in expertise on that topic, so I did some checking around. It was time well spent, because I found that all the CPUs reported in the industry that had attempted this feat had had major problems. Either they were late or they had design errata that prevented initial production from being usable in a multiprocessing mode.

I proposed to the division's general manager that the project should bring in new engineers, whose job would be to get P6's MP story right on the first try. We recruited and hired a team of five, led by Shreekant (Ticky) Thakkar, an ex–Sequent Computer architect, to make sure that our CPU cache coherence schemes, our system boot-up plan, our frontside bus architecture, and our chip set would work together properly in an MP mode.

BEHAVIORAL MODELS. Prior to the P6, Intel did not model its microarchitectures before building them. These earlier efforts began with block diagrams on whiteboards and left-over unit designs from previous projects. Some of the design team would start working on circuits, some would write a register-transfer logic (RTL) description, and the rest would devote themselves to tools, microcode, placement, routing, and physical design. Before joining Intel, I was one of seven engineers who designed the entire Very Long Instruction Word (VLIW) minisupercomputer at Multiflow Computer, a mid-1980s startup that went out of business in 1990 after shipping over 100 machines. At Multiflow, we didn't even have units to borrow from, but we still didn't do any modeling. We designed straight to hardware and did our testing and learning from the circuit boards themselves. If you saw one of our early memory controller boards, you would immediately grasp the dark side of that strategy—the early boards were festooned with over 300 "blue-wire" modifications, the fallout of a design oversight.

The oversight was pretty fundamental and likely something that modeling would have revealed. Multiflow's main memory incorporated error-correction coding (ECC). Along with the data being fetched, a set of syndrome bits were accessed, which could identify a single bit as being erroneous. ECC bit flips are rare, and when one was detected, the machine required three more clock cycles to do the ECC check and correction. To maintain performance, we did not want to routinely run all memory accesses through the ECC circuits; instead, our plan was to stall the entire machine during the rare times an ECC flip had to be corrected. Unfortunately, we forgot to provide a way to stall everything and steer the data through the ECC circuit on a bit-flip detection. Oops!

For the most part, seat-of-the-pants computer design seemed to be extremely efficient, especially given an experienced team with high odds of making compatible implicit assumptions. But there are limits to how much complexity can or should be tackled that way. For an in-order, two-way superscalar design such as the original P5, seat-of-the-pants was doable, especially since the P5 design team had just completed what amounted to a one-pipeline version of the same chip, the Intel 486. (I'm not advocating this design approach, mind you; I'm just relaying history and explaining why the P5 design team succeeded despite the lack of performance or behavioral models to guide their decisions.)

We could *not* have done P6 this way. In a section of the previous chapter (The "What Would Happen If" Game in Chapter 2), I described the process we followed in recalibrating our intuitions about out-of-order microarchitectures. Without a performance model to keep us honest and expose where our intuitions were wrong, we could have easily created a P6 with all the complexity and none of the performance advantage we had envisioned.

> *Without a performance model to keep us honest and expose where our intuitions were wrong, we could have easily created a P6 with all the complexity and none of the performance advantage we had envisioned.*

In the same section, I also said that DFA was a peculiar model. Wielded properly, it could tell you the performance impact of various microarchitectural choices, but because it was arriving at its answers via a path other than mimicking the actual design, there were limits to how deeply it could help you peer into a design's inner workings.

So, somehow, we had to get the project from a DFA basis to a structured RTL (SRTL) model, because SRTL is the model all downstream design tools use and the one that is eventually taped out. In some form, nearly all design activities of a microprocessor development are aimed at getting the SRTL model right. The question was how to translate our general DFA-inspired ideas for the design into the mountains of detail that comprised an SRTL model.

It seemed to me that we needed a way to describe, at a high level, what any given unit actually did, without having to worry too much about how that unit would be implemented. In other words, we wanted a behavioral model that would be a stepping stone to the SRTL model. This behavioral model would be easy to write, since most of the difficult choices surrounding the detailed design would be elided, yet the model would still account for performance-related interactions among units. Rather than describe a 32-bit adder in terms of dozens of two-input logic gates, for example, we could write a placeholder model for that unit with code like OUT := IN1 + IN2. Because we could create such behavioral code quickly, we could build a working performance model without having to delay all performance testing until the most difficult unit worked through all its design conundrums.

Just to get our ideas onto firmer footing, we started writing a C program to model the essentials of the P6 engine we had conceived. We called this program the grassman, because it wasn't mature enough even for a strawman. After a few weeks, we had coded the basics, as well as realized that coding would take several months to complete and would not easily translate to SRTL.

While reading the SRTL manual one day, I noticed that Intel's hardware description language (iHDL) referred to a behavioral capability. I checked around and found that the language designers had anticipated our quick prototyping needs and had made provision for behavioral code. "Just what we need!" I thought, and went about collecting enough RTL coders to begin the P6 behavioral model development. Equally exciting was the prospect that we would not have to translate our behavioral model into SRTL when we completed it. We would write everything behaviorally at first, and then gradually substitute the SRTL versions in whatever order they became available. This process also promised to free the project of the "last unit" effect on performance testing I described earlier.

The only problem was that we were the first to ever try using iHDL's behavioral mode. Undaunted (no one had ever tried to do an out-of-order x86 engine, either), we launched into creating the behavioral model with a few designers and five architects. I estimated to my management that we would have it running code within six months—Christmas or bust. I wrote three quick C programs, carefully tailored to need only what would be running by then, and posted them as the immediate targets.

On the second day of the behavioral RTL (BRTL) effort, it was clear we were months off the schedule I had conceived only yesterday. The behavioral mode of iHDL had major shortcomings. Some were built into the language, some were the growth pains of any new tool technology, and some were just the inevitable surprises that are always present at the meeting of reality and ideas. But the main reason my schedule was so far off was that I had built it assuming that 100% of the BRTL effort would go into coding. I had not accounted for so many unresolved microarchitectural issues, some of which were quite substantial. In my defense, I wanted to begin the BRTL in part to force our microarchitectural unknowns to the surface. I had just grossly underestimated how many unknowns there were. I wasn't even close.

I sidled abashedly into my boss's office and told him it was already clear that yesterday's schedule estimate had been wildly off, and please could I have a few dozen really bright design engineers to help me write the BRTL. After an obligatory and well-deserved upbraiding, Fred Pollack and design manager Randy Steck agreed to commit the core of the design team to helping create the behavioral model.

There ensued an interesting symbiotic (and unanticipated) connection between the newly deputized BRTL coders and the microarchitectural focus groups in which they were already working. Looking back, the pattern is much clearer than it seemed when we stumbled into this arrangement. Writing a computer program to model something will always reveal areas of uncertainty and issues with no clear answers. Likewise, writing a model forces subtle problems into the open. A common syndrome when working in abstract conceptual space is to believe that you have a solution for issue A, another for issue B, and so on. When you look at each solution in isolation, it seems feasible, but writing a model forces you to consider solutions A, B, and so on *together*. Only then do you realize that the workable solutions are mutually exclusive at a deep, irreconcilable level. Writing the behavioral model raised questions, and the focus groups set about resolving them. This virtuous loop continued throughout the behavioral model coding, for approximately 18 months.

We ended up meeting our Christmas goal by sprinting from Thanksgiving on. The core BRTL team worked essentially continuously for six weeks on nights, weekends, and holidays. Two things became clear during this time. First, iHDL's behavioral mode was only marginally higher in abstraction than the usual structural iHDL. Second, because we were committed to our initial concept of how P6's out-of-order engine would work, we would not have enough schedule slack to make any substantial changes to that concept.

In other words, we were stuck. So much for risk-reducing, quick performance models. Even with BRTL, we still had to identify every signal in and out of any given unit with proper unit pipelining and staging. That level of detail implies the same detailed designing required for SRTL, and that process takes time. Luckily (both in the sense of capricious luck and in the sense of luck related to hard work), our initial concepts proved to be workable and the BRTL helped us iron out the details.

When we started the BRTL effort, we had hoped that having the BRTL as an intermediate project milestone would make it easier to get the SRTL going later. Having now complained that the abstraction level of iHDL's behavioral mode was too low, it's only fair to add that this made conversion to SRTL vastly simpler. And since the same designers who wrote the behavioral description of their unit were responsible for writing the SRTL, we avoided an entire class of potential translation errors. In essence, BRTL took too long, but SRTL was shortened and was of much higher quality in terms of functional validation.

We purposely limited these new BRTL teams to fewer than ten people each, and through Randy's customary foresight, we "rolled them up" through the lead architects, not their usual management chains.[1] This combination of organizational tactics meant that the architects were firmly and visibly ensconced as intellectual leaders of the various refinement efforts, thus encouraging them to lead their new subteams directly (and quickly).

I had hoped to keep the behavioral model up to date as project emphasis shifted to SRTL, but that wasn't practical. The BRTL gradually morphed into the SRTL, and asking every designer to maintain both models would have cost too much project effort and time for the return on that investment. We now had the butterfly, but sadly, the caterpillar was gone.

For years after the P6 had gone into production, I would occasionally hear comments from BRTL participants that the "behavioral model wasn't worth it." I think they are wrong. They are remembering only the price paid, without carefully considering what

---

[1]In effect, Randy inserted the lead architects into the BRTL developers' technical management reporting chains, thus ensuring the architects would get the necessary mindshare.

was achieved or what the alternative would have been without the behavioral model. The P6's BRTL *was* expensive to create, and there is still much room to improve the language and how we used it, but it still taught us that computer design has moved far past the point where people can keep complex microarchitectures in their heads. Behavioral modeling is mandatory. The only question is how best to accomplish it.

> *Behavioral modeling is mandatory. The only question is how best to accomplish it.*

MANAGING A CHANGING POR

The only constant in life is change, and this rule is omnipresent in an engineering project. At any moment, a project's state comprises a vast amount of information, opinions, decisions made, decisions pending, the history of previous changes to the POR, and so on. One day, the project's official plan might be to implement the reorder buffer as two separate integer and floating-point sections; the next day, it might be to combine the two sections. (For the Pentium Pro, that very decision was made over a napkin in a Chinese restaurant in Santa Clara, where General Tso's chicken was the computer architect's sustenance of choice.) It is imperative that projects have a means for unequivocally establishing the POR, as well as an organized, well-understood method for changing it.

In the early 1990s, during P6 development, Web sites or browsers didn't exist. Files could be shared, and we briefly entertained the idea that the project POR would be kept in a file that all project members could access. Regrettably, we reverted to the familiarity of classical engineering practice. We kept the POR in a red-cover document, so it was sure to become dated within days of its release and none of the current document holders could ever be sure they had the latest-and-greatest version.

Some projects deal with this version problem by collecting all old documents and issuing the new one to the list of previous recipients. Ugh! A more reliable solution involving far less labor is to keep the POR online and rigorously control the means by which people can change it or access it.

Humans are supposed to learn from their mistakes. If the project POR isn't rigorously maintained in a place all design team members can access, they quickly learn that the only way to be sure of its present status is to go ask the person responsible for it. In the P6 project, I was that person, and it often felt as though the project POR was an amorphous cloud floating above my cubicle. I was determined to do better on the Pentium 4 project, but I don't think I succeeded, and for a very dubious reason: an intra-project political power struggle, which was so unnecessary that the account deserves its own subsection ("ECO Control and the Project POR" on page 57).

The Wrong Way to Plan

While it seemed very large at the time, the P6 was a much smaller project than the Pentium 4 (Willamette) development, in every respect. It had far fewer designers and architects and had to satisfy only a handful of marketing engineers. (The P6 POR had to be acceptable to the project's general manager and chief marketing engineer, as well as to the designers and architects.) The Willamette POR was an unstable compromise between mutually exclusive requests from mobile, desktop, workstation, server, and Itanium Processor Family proponents. Early in the Willamette project, our general manager appointed marketing as the POR's owner, and marketing did what marketers always do: They called a series of meetings to discuss the issues. Have Powerpoint, will travel.

These meetings continued through all four years of the project. Every Thursday morning at 7 A.M., the supplicants would timidly enter the great hall, kneel before the king, and present their petitions. About the only thing missing from the general ambiance was a booming voice, bursts of flame, and the man behind the curtain. After due deliberation, which somehow always took exactly two hours no matter how simple or complicated the issue, the court would inform the petitioner that his or her issue had been duly considered and dismiss the hapless party. Sometimes, attendees actually got to see the meeting's minutes, and even less frequently, the minutes indicated what, if any, decision the court had made.

All in all, this is not a good way to run a design project. I can think of at least four major problems.

> *A meeting-based product planning process does not gracefully accommodate the reality that engineers travel—a lot.*

First, a meeting-based product planning process does not gracefully accommodate the reality that engineers travel—a lot. It is true that coordinating meetings with multiple diverse attendees is extremely difficult, and the usual practice is to send a representative if you can't attend. But some of these decisions required an extensive context that a representative could not be expected to bring.

Second, given that virtually all the proposals being considered for POR change will affect the silicon, it is clearly imperative that the design team consider the proposal for feasibility before anyone decides anything. Forcing a design team leader to make a snap judgment that the team is then expected to implement is dangerous. At the very least, the design representative should

> *It is clearly imperative that the design team consider the proposal for feasibility before anyone decides anything.*

be able to request a one-week postponement on any issue so that she can consult the rest of the team. Such a time lag may also help throttle the rate at which project changes are made, and that is a good thing. It is very easy to generate project change requests at rates far higher than the design team can actually absorb, let alone implement.

Third, at least in Willamette, only the meeting attendees of the meeting were informed of the meeting, and even these were not always informed of its outcome (if there was one). The meeting chair was reputed to have kept a red-cover POR document up to date, but to get such a document, you had to formally request it from document control and then surrender the old one. No one was willing to do this every week.

Fourth, meeting-based product planning does not allow time to deeply consider how a decision will impact the design itself. Changes appear easier, more enticing, more feasible, and less threatening than they really are. Many proposed changes were, in isolation, fairly simple and low-impact. But a substantial number interacted in subtle, entertaining ways with other requested changes or previously accepted features. Only a design team representative fully conversant with all these interactions could be expected to spot such problems, and possibly not even such an expert could.

The irony was that the design team had its own POR, and a means to carefully change it: our engineering change order (ECO) process. Modern microprocessor design teams make hundreds of important daily decisions, day after day, week after week, year after year. Each decision is a careful trade-off between die real estate, power consumption, complexity, performance, schedule, design and project margin, risk, and the user-visible feature set. Each decision helps set the context for future choices—good prior decisions will afford the project good options when new issues arise. Conversely, cutting corners early or naively attempting to incorporate conflicting ideas will eventually lead to a day of reckoning that will at best severely damage the schedule. Our internal POR was the mechanism by which we kept score of project decisions made and those pending, and by which project designers were informed of the same.

> *Naively attempting to incorporate conflicting ideas will eventually lead to a day of reckoning that will at best severely damage the schedule.*

Engineering Change Orders

ECOs have been around as long as engineering itself, but they used to be a piece of paper with a sign-off list, rather than today's e-mail or Web-based mechanisms. Each signatory would sign a line to accept or reject it and route the document to the next signatory. It was mandatory to explain any rejection.

Some people believe that if you "properly" plan a project from the beginning, you will never need to change it en route. I have had the misfortune of working closely with such people, and a good time was had by none. Their (partly correct) argument is that most ECOs end up costing the design team more work and, therefore, negatively impact the project schedule. But just because ECOs are not free does not necessarily imply that all ECOs are bad. Nor do ECOs constitute tacit proof that the architects have no discipline. Some ECOs fix errors, others simplify the design, and still others simply reflect mid-course corrections that are reactions to new information about the competition or the customers. Some pushback on ECOs, and more as the project nears its end, is probably healthy for the project. Generalized antipathy toward the entire change process is not.

> *ECOs do not constitute tacit proof that architects have no discipline.*

The Origin of Change. In Willamette, ECOs often came from the project's general management and marketing meeting series and were aimed at managing POR changes. These were primarily ECOs for the design team, since the architects were expected to convert feature ideas from the great hall to implementable ideas. The P6 project did not suffer from this change stream because marketing did not own the POR then, and even if they had, their cubicles were only a few feet away from the design team. This proximity is important to nurture the feelings of being on the same side. Having marketing physically removed from the Willamette team led, I believe, to an almost automatic us-versus-them psychology on nearly all issues affecting the design.

Another stream of design changes on both Willamette and P6 stemmed from performance analysis. As the project design progresses, the performance analysis engineers gradually turn their attention from the abstract performance models on which the project design is based, to the RTL itself. Early RTL is useless for performance studies because it simply lacks the design detail to make performance analysis interesting and may not even implement enough of the instruction set to run the benchmark code. But the RTL gets more capable every day, and eventually becomes mature enough for the analysts to draw useful inferences. Typically, they find that many benchmarks run within the performance envelope as expected, which is great news. They will also find some benchmarks that run outside the envelope and will then work with a team of architects and design engineers to track down the performance shortfall's root cause and propose design changes via an ECO to fix it.

Functional validation also generates a stream of high-priority ECOs to fix design errors that are causing incompatibility or wrong answers.

Finally, changes can occur just because the design is so complex. Architects are monitoring the project status, watching for design areas that are generating more than their share of errata—a sign that often means too much complexity has been assigned to that area. Architects must translate marketing POR changes into practical ECOs, watch the competition, and think about ideas that might have barely missed the cut for this chip but that could still be implemented. Any or all of these may be a source of additional design changes.

So given that there *will* be ECOs, despite best efforts, best intentions, and unenlightened attitudes to the contrary, the issue becomes how to handle them. Difficult questions and trade-offs abound:

1. When does the project go "under ECO control"?
2. What parts of the design effort require ECOs?
3. Whose signatures are on the ECO sign-off list?
4. How can the process be kept timely, especially for controversial ECOs?
5. How do resolved (accepted or rejected) ECOs become visible to the project?
6. Given that other related projects such as tool development or chip-set design need to know about some ECOs or even have signatory input, who decides on the need to know and what process ensures necessary inclusion and notification?

When, Where, Who.   As I mentioned at the beginning of this chapter, the refinement phase has a natural tension between the free-wheeling, all-things-considered mindset and the need to converge on select workable ideas in a timely way. Typically, the project architects will supply the force pointing toward new ideas and away from schedule, and the project managers and designers will provide the countervailing force to rein the architects back in. The project leadership must make a judgment call as to when the architects have done enough exploration. In the P6 project, we architects informed our management that we had arrived at a workable idea (out-of-order), but this was atypical. In general, the architects and project management must negotiate direction convergence.

The initial project direction is the concept phase's output, and the team should formally document ideas that come from that phase to help synchronize and educate the project's growing design team. This document should be available to all team members, as well as to select people outside the team, such as upper management and project leaders for related developments (tools, chip sets, and so on). As I argue in "ECO Control and the Project POR" on page 57, I believe this newly minted POR should go under ECO control for the rest of the project.

At this stage, the design itself is not under any ECO control. There is a point at which the amount of intellectual property that ECO control guards is worth the overhead of the ECO mechanism; before that, ECOs are worse than useless. Until the behavioral model has been designed and is returning useful results, the project is better off without ECOs. The program source codes, on the other hand, should still be kept under revision control,

just to maintain sanity in a programming environment in which many people are contributing code, checking
out and building models, and filing
bug reports.

Eventually, the project will migrate
from a basis that is mostly behavioral
modeling to one that is mostly struc-

> *There is a point at which the amount of
> intellectual property that ECO control
> guards is worth the overhead of the ECO
> mechanism; before that, ECOs are worse
> than useless.*

tural. That migration point is approximately the right time to consider placing the RTL
model itself under ECO control.

As the project gains momentum and the tapeout deadline begins to tower menacingly
over the team, the team's engineers find themselves working longer and longer hours. A
growing sense of fatigue combined with an emotional determination to succeed at this
project can lead to a tendency to grab a broadsword and stride into the midst of the enemy, flailing wildly in all directions. But as project time remaining grows ever shorter, so
does the risk that a change will inject an unnoticed functional or performance bug into the
chip. Project leadership must continually tighten the screws on the project as time goes
on. The ECO process becomes the tiller by which they steer the ship, so its importance
grows as the project proceeds.

All ECOs will have a signature list on their front page. This list will typically have 10
to 20 names. Every ECO will have the ECO Czar's (see "The ECO Czar" on page 57)
name as a signatory so that he or she can begin tracking that ECO for timely disposition,
and ensure that the ECO as submitted contains the necessary information for the other
signatories to reasonably deal with it.

The ECO Czar also tries to make sure that the signature list is appropriate for each
ECO. Most ECOs have a limited scope. If a design engineer realizes that there is a simpler way to achieve some function in her part of the design without compromising anything else, and her peers and supervisor agree, higher-level signatories need not be involved.

Some ECOs have obvious project-level impact, and must be considered by many
people besides the engineer initiating the ECO. Suppose the project POR calls for the
chip's frontside bus to run at 1 GHz, but several months into the design, the bus designer realizes that this target is unattainable. The ECO he files requesting that the project POR be adjusted from 1 GHz down to, say, 500 MHz will require concurrence from
project leaders, upper management, marketing, the chip-set team, performance analysts,
and many others.

Communicating Change. The list of people who need to know what ECOs are
under consideration, which have been accepted, and which have been rejected is much
longer than the list of signatories. In our ECO system, e-mail was generated automatically
whenever a new signature had been obtained (both acceptance and rejection requires a
signature), which helped prompt the next signatory to spend some time on a particular
ECO, and also informed the larger audience of what was being considered and how earlier ECOs had fared.

Because the system was automatic, it was a reliable and timely way to collect signatures. For informing a list of final disposition, however, we probably could have used a
few human comments about the motivation for the ECO, the reasons it was accepted or
rejected, and the implications of that action. Assiduous ECO readers could infer most of
that information by carefully reading the ECO itself, but miscommunications are among

> *Miscommunications are among the biggest time-wasters in a development project.*

the biggest time-wasters in a development project. Avoiding them is well worth the trouble.

TIMELY RESOLUTION, NO POCKET VETOES. Occasionally, when someone proposes a bad idea in the form of an ECO, simply ignoring it for awhile causes the right thing to happen. Given time to consider the idea, its submitter comes to realize that it won't work, logs onto his computer, and retracts the ECO. Problem solved. This does not mean that routinely ignoring an ECO is a good tactic.

ECO signatories must typically grapple with submitted ECOs directly, not just hope they will go away. Politicians can use a pocket veto to "assertively ignore" an issue. The politician has to deal with some popular legislation he would like to reject and would like it to die without having to go on record as formally being against it. So he sends it to an obscure committee that sits on the bill beyond some deadline that automatically kills it.

But although the pocket veto might be popular in politics, it has no place in engineering. Doing nothing inevitably hurts the project because it can derail a change and set off a domino effect of missed errata. If the ECO is a paper document and each signatory on a sequential list of, say, 15 names took an extra week to sign an ECO, the proposed change would not be part of the project for nearly four months. (With Web-based ECO tracking, all signatories can see who has accepted or rejected the ECO and can participate in any order—another reason for having e-tracking.) If the requested change was intended to fix a compatibility design error, whatever code had originally failed is still failing four months later, obscuring whatever other design errors are hiding behind the one that was found.

A rejection, on the other hand, can actually help the project focus attention where it might be most needed. By reading the accompanying explanation, the ECO submitter might gain insights into alternative ECOs or perhaps want to contact the rejecting party and clarify wording or address issues that person raised. Sometimes, signatories simply do not understand the ECO, or they have some other agenda. A rejection brings to light any misunderstandings or differing directions.

The Folly of the Preemptive Signature

Ironically, I was often the final ECO sign-off and, consequently, the ECO Czar's frequent target. For a time, he attempted preemptive strikes by getting me to sign off before all the other signatories had weighed in. The folly of this approach became clear when the engineer who had submitted the ECO *rejected* it after I had signed it, a juxtaposition that he gleefully made certain I knew about. Apparently, the ECO submitter realized he had made a blunder that rendered the ECO clearly unworkable. By signing it, I had proven that either I had a remedial-level understanding of the issue or had barely read what I signed. I threw various objects at my heckler until he went away, and then resolved never to sign another ECO until the submitter, the implementer, and the implementer's supervisor had already signed. Keeping the ECO stream moving is important, but keeping a design team's confidence in its leadership is even more so, second only to maintaining your self-confidence as that leader.

THE ECO CZAR. Project leaders immediately and emphatically agree when you point out that no one should sit on an ECO and that signatories must either accept or reject it. But their good intentions do not automatically translate into the necessary actions. In the Willamette project, getting even noncontroversial ECOs through the sign-off loop was taking so long that designers had begun speculatively implementing them, thus subverting the entire process. To combat this, I appointed an ECO Czar, Warren Morrow, whose job was to prod extremely busy people by asking them to replace whatever they had thought was their highest priority with the ECO sign-off task. Keeping the ECO process moving along took a high degree of indefatigability and an uncommonly diplomatic touch. Warren could often be found waiting patiently in the offender's cubicle until that person pondered the ECO and signed off on it. The embarrassment factor usually worked in Warren's favor, as did the reality that sooner or later, any laggard's refusal to sign an ECO for or against could and would be overridden by the laggard's boss, who was sure to remember the episode at the next employee performance review.

In general, the surest way to prevent a task from falling into the cracks of a large project is to assign someone reliable to that task, and check on their progress every now and then. In the ECO Czar's case, that meant asking if the task was getting done and if the Czar was going crazy. If I got a yes and no, or at least a yes and not quite yet, then all was well. Thank you, Warren.

ECO Control and the Project POR. During one of the infamous Willamette project POR meetings, it occurred to me that some of the overhead and friction that the architecture team was experiencing on the Pentium 4 was due to our need to reconcile decisions at the marketing/general manager level with those at the implementation/ECO level. With rare exceptions, our general manager and our marketing organization were not required signatories on our implementation ECOs, yet some of those design changes impacted project-level goals such as die size, power dissipation, performance, and schedule. The way to reduce the friction between these two parallel streams of project perturbation was to put the project POR on its own ECO control. The engineers would have to approve all changes to a POR regardless of the source.

I was proud of this insight. It seemed such an obviously good idea that I relished presenting it at the next staff meeting.

When staffers really like an idea, it is obvious: They tear their eyes away from the e-mail on the laptop they always bring to the staff meeting, vigorously nod their heads, and share their enthusiasm with the staffers on either side of them.[2] When staffers really hate an idea, it is not as clear, but still readable, because they keep looking at their laptop screens, but they make a face as though something they ate is winning a debate with their stomach. After hearing my POR-under-ECO-control idea, the staffers gave no reaction at all. It was as though Bob-canceling headphones had temporarily appeared on all their heads and my words had been erased from the room's airwaves.

Not understanding their reaction, I tried again a week later. And then again. After a few weeks of this, it dawned on me that I was seeing a form of collective pocket veto. The rest of the staff did not have to debate me on this topic; they had only to do nothing to keep the status quo. In effect, they were voting me down without having to explain their reasons. Once I realized that, I began to wonder why they considered the status quo better than putting the project POR under ECO control.

---

[2]Then they go right back to their e-mail. Enthusiasm has its limits.

One of the silent status quo proponents finally took pity on me and explained what I had been missing. With the Thursday meeting project-planning scheme, the general manager felt he could directly make crisp, clear, timely decisions about the project. (I'm not saying he *had* that ability; he only *felt* he had it.) Because marketing ran these meetings, set their agendas, and circulated the results via meeting minutes, they, too, felt they already had a direct say in the project POR. Both the general manager and his marketing organization viewed my proposal as a threat because now the design team would have to agree to all proposed changes before those changes became the official project POR.

I couldn't blame them. From their viewpoint, the status quo model was perfect: Simply dictate to the design team what you want, and they implement it, no questions asked. Why would considering the design team's feedback before adopting the desired changes result in a better product? To the general manager and marketing, my proposal would result in an unnecessary power struggle. The prospect that someone several organizational levels below them could veto their pet feature was unthinkable.

I consider that kind of reasoning and the attendant project structure paving stones on the road to disaster. Design teams that feel no tangible sense of ownership over what they design could, in principle, create a credible product, if they were exceptionally professional and skillful, but they are much more likely to yield an uninspired, insipid, loser product. Design teams that are emotionally engaged in their work and people who have committed themselves to making the world's best product, no matter what it takes, will turn out a world-class product every time. Conversely, by treating a team like a job shop or guns

> *People who have committed themselves to making the world's best product, no matter what it takes, will turn out a world-class product every time.*

Avoiding Mediocrity

All large companies have at least a few burnouts, folks who simply no longer engage in their work with the same passion and commitment they once did. Burned-out engineers resign themselves to simply accepting whatever requirements are imposed on them from above, knowing that, in the end, if things fall apart, they can always say, "Well, at least it wasn't my fault" and shuffle over to another project to repeat the performance. With big projects, these people can still make a contribution because of the sheer workload to be distributed. But the people who really make the difference between a design that merely works and one that is truly stellar are those willing to defend the project against mediocrity.

Mediocrity can be imposed from above, by management that simply will not allow enough time to do the project right. It can arise from the design team's poor execution. It can be preordained if the project's goals are set too high or too low or the feature set is too timid or aggressive. Mediocrity is the default outcome of any project that does not value people with a total commitment to what they are designing. Management must do its part, but only the architects and design engineers who are actively involved in the project can accurately judge where mediocrity lies, and they must be given an opportunity to speak out whenever necessary to avoid its strong pull.

for hire, project management removes the single best weapon any design project has—pride of ownership by the people in the best position to improve the design. There is a reason Steve Jobs' phrase "insanely great products" resonates in the hearts of good designers.

All electrical engineers are taught communications theory. When digitizing a signal stream, there is a critical sampling rate above which the digitized output can theoretically be used to perfectly reconstruct the original signal. But below that rate, some really ugly distortions arise. One way to think of this is that once you have sampled a signal, that signal had better not do anything very interesting before the next sampling time because your digital stream will not reflect it. The signal is simply changing faster than your digitization process can accommodate. It often struck me while struggling with the ECO-project–POR issue that this is exactly what was happening—the project planning process was sending continuous project-change signals to a design team that could not sample them fast enough.

Put your project POR under ECO control. It will not make your general manager cede any authority, and it does not cut marketing out of product planning. It just enforces the proper lines of communication and makes visible what should have been obvious anyway: The design team must be part of the planning process in guiding a product development to a successful conclusion.

THE BRIDGE FROM ARCHITECTURE TO DESIGN

The essential challenge in bringing a project into the refinement phase is to transfer the core ideas from the heads of the architects into the heads of the design team without serious distortion. This transference involves far more than block diagrams and pipeline drawings; the architects must pass on the overarching *philosophy* of the approach they have conceived. It is not enough to convey to the design team what you think is needed; it is essential to also impart *why* you think that.

> *It is not enough to convey to the design team what you think is needed; it is essential to also impart* **why** *you think that.*

After the P6 project had been underway for several months, and the architects had settled on an out-of-order speculative engine design, it was time to bring the design team core up to speed. We had written a preliminary document that at least superficially covered all the key ideas, but the design was still changing a lot nearly every week. We decided to host a series of luncheons at which the architects would give a live overview of various microarchitecture parts, and the designers would ask questions between mouthfuls.

Our initial attempt at this was a fiasco. I spoke first and gave an overview of the entire microarchitecture as we then conceived of it, pointing out where we were confident and what we were most worried about. The material was challenging, which taxed my memory, my understanding, and my ability to communicate to their limits, so I spent most of the first half hour facing the board, drawing diagrams. When I finally turned around to entertain questions, I was shocked at the sea of horrified faces. After lunch, a design engineer confided that my overview had not quite met his expectations. Someone who called himself an architect ought to have answers, he explained. Instead, I seemed to be content merely to point out the questions, and what had he gotten himself into with this crazy project?

Over the next few months, we architects had to find ways to establish a useful working relationship with the design team, as well as keep the technical momentum going. We knew very well that architects could not be the repository of all knowledge. Our job was to conceive and maintain the project's overall vision, incomplete and flawed as it was at times, and to earn the trust of the design team we were leading by exhibiting a willingness to do whatever it took for the project to succeed.

Meanwhile, the design team was growing, from the original 30 or so, to the eventual 200+. We quickly realized that luncheons would not suffice as the architecture/design communications channel because the next day, three new designers would appear, all of whom should have attended yesterday's lunch.

We had to capture these sessions permanently without requiring the architects to spend the next several months writing. We chose to present the information as a series of video-taped lectures, including an extensive Q&A session with the audience at the end. Apart from my own introductory lecture, which we had to do twice because our professional camera crew failed to record any audio the first time,[3] these videotape sessions went smoothly and the tapes became hot commodities within the project. Upon joining the P6 team, new designers would spend several days watching television, but after this intensive ramp-up, they knew the names of the chip's various units, had at least a vague idea of what the units did, and had faces and names to which they could address their detailed questions.

For mainstream projects like P6 and Pentium 4, groups outside the main project have to understand the project's direction as well as the microprocessor's feature set, projected performance, and other development aspects. For the Pentium 4, that meant any groups designing related chip sets had to develop their products synergistically with the CPU. Compiler, operating system, and tools groups also had to understand the new micro-processor, sometimes in nearly as much detail as the designers. Such related groups found the videotaped lecture series extremely useful.

The videotapes were a record of important intellectual property, so we had to carefully control them. Although most groups requesting the tapes had a clear need to know, we encountered more than a few requests from the merely curious. Our rule was simple: If you would not have had access to the paper equivalent of the tapes' contents, the request was denied.

Focus Groups

A project's concept phase must be driven by a very small group of people but, typically, that small group cannot finish the project by themselves because there is too little time and too much to do. The exception is a startup company, in which the entire technical staff might be that small group. In those circumstances (in which Dave Papworth and I had previously found ourselves while at Multiflow Computer in the 1980s), the team must automate the design process wherever possible, give up all semblance of a life outside work, and cut whatever corners look nonfatal, so as to hit the competitive market window.

Intel cannot approach product design that way and does not need to. The schedule pressure still feels brutal (although readers who are not engineers might find that hard to believe, given that both P6 and Willamette took more than four years from start to pro-

---

[3] I thought it would be cool to ask Mike Meyers, who did the voice of Shrek, to do a voice-over, but I was alone in that opinion.

duction), but there are a lot of engineers available. The difficulty lies in teaching them what they need to know to help realize the design.

If the concept phase is too early to engage the design engineers, then when? We were not sure of the answer to this question as we architects emerged from the concept phase, but opportunity came knocking when Randy Steck pointed out that while we were conceptualizing, he had built the nucleus of the design team, and they were ready to go. Could we use them?

Well, sure, but not in the sense of "Here's what we want, please go build us one." Far from supplying the answers, which some design team members believed was our job as architects, we were mostly arming them with a long list of questions and nudging them in the general direction of a solution. Worse, Dave Papworth and I had only recently joined Intel, so we had neither a track record nor personal relationship with the designers. Luckily, Glenn Hinton had both, and his well-earned and well-deserved personal credibility went a long way toward assuaging the design team's early worries over our general trustworthiness. At any rate, no one quit over the temporary loss of confidence. (They probably couldn't resist sticking around to see where these clowns would take them next.)

We deputized about 30 design engineers as junior architects and split them into teams of five to seven. To each group, we assigned one concept architect who was commissioned to solve some subset of important questions. We then assigned the groups to respective functional subsets of the overall design, such as out-of-order core, frontside bus, and branch prediction. We found this group-to-subset mapping convenient because we were then assured of having at least one expert in key chip areas.

Having a concept architect in each group was critical because the architect could ensure that the focus group observed the fundamental assumptions built into the overall design. If pipeline stalls were to be handled in only one way, then each focus group had to assume that method in all they did.

Careful intergroup coordination was also critical. Focus groups are investigating and resolving open technical issues, and their results must be communicated to any focus groups the resolution would affect. Otherwise, a focus group could claim that its "solution" to a hard problem is to move it to some other group (where that problem might be even *more* difficult to resolve). This is not an unreasonable temptation. A complex design has many overarching problems that several focus groups could reasonably own. In the same sense that design errors tend to flourish between engineers, the big issues can fall into the cracks between groups that assume another unit will "take care of that."

Finally, focus groups must have some global pacing mechanism because the project cannot tape out until the last unit is ready. Pacing is the fine art of ensuring that no group dives too deeply into an issue while still providing the necessary rigor so that decisions made will not have to be repealed and repaired later in the project, when the cost of change is much higher.

PRODUCT QUALITY

Humans make mistakes. Even well-trained, highly motivated engineers, working at the top of their games, make mistakes—big ones, small ones, funny ones, subtle ones, and bonehead ones. Some design errors are so subtle that even when revealed, they generate no reaction from other designers except sympathetic acknowledgment that they would have made the same mistake. Other errors are so blatant that even the design engineer in

> *Even well-trained, highly motivated engineers, working at the top of their games, make mistakes—big ones, small ones, funny ones, subtle ones, and bonehead ones.*

question cannot explain why they occurred. In 1987, I was working at Multiflow and had just completed the design for the floating-point divide/square-root unit. Because I had designed it, I knew where the design's corner cases were, and my initial test suite made sure the unit got the right answers for those cases. I released the design for limited preproduction and made plans to take the weekend off for a short vacation. A few hours before I was to take my well-earned break, a performance analyst appeared in my office. With a puzzled look, he told me that his program appeared to be getting a wrong answer and that he had tracked it to the square-root unit. The unit got exactly the right answer unless the result was a perfect power of two, in which case it yielded a result that was exactly half the right answer. I pondered this for all of about 45 seconds before realizing that perfect-power-of-two answers are precisely those for which the accumulated mantissa bit pattern was all ones, including the rounding and guard bits. And when the mantissa overflows, you must adjust the exponent upward. If you do not adjust the exponent, you know what happens [22].

Another example of a classic bonehead error, and this one wasn't my fault, caused NASA's Mars Explorer spacecraft to crash into the planet instead of orbiting it. Embedded in its navigation sequence was confusion between metric and English units [10]. Oops!

Mismanaging Design Errors

It is a regrettable characteristic of human nature that we often learn what to do by first learning what not to do, sometimes by being extraordinarily counterproductive. Dealing with design errors seems destined to be one of these learn-by-not-doing areas. The following three strategies, in particular, almost never work.

Make an Example of the Offender. In this method, the engineer responsible is put in the corporate equivalent of stocks for public display and humiliation. All the other project engineers are sure to pay attention, which the boss wants them to do, but they will also do two things the boss *does not* want them to do. First, they will take no more risks, no matter how valuable the potential payoff. Second, they will waste intellectual energy hiding their tracks so that no one can trace any project issue that arises to their personal decisions or designs.

Hire Only Geniuses. Some companies simply do not hire any engineers who do not have a certified genius license. This strategy fails because a company should always strive to hire smart engineers anyway, and there is no such thing as a genius license. If there were, geniuses would probably make mistakes anyway, because they are the ones who would be most willing to take risks. If some of the things they try do not fail, they are probably not trying hard enough. It is not a risk if it cannot fail, and those who do not take risks will generally lose in the marketplace to those who do.

Flog Validation. When all else fails, blame it on validation. They let the bug get by them, didn't they? And isn't it their job to prevent that by looking carefully at the validation plan and its execution for holes?

This strategy has the same flaw as "hire only geniuses." Smart validators will take risks to ensure product quality and, being human, they will make mistakes. In the end, a validation team motivated by the final product quality is much more productive than a team simply trying to avoid the boss's tongue-lashing.

Avoid/Find/Survive

I believe that nature has a set of immutable laws wired directly into its fabric, and engineers must observe those laws or suffer the consequences. One of these laws is that no matter how assiduously we work, no matter how motivated and inspired our validation effort, design errors will appear in the final product. This suggests three things:

1. Design errors will appear in a design by default, and we must strive mightily to prevent them.
2. Some errata will elude us and we must find them in the design before they "get out the door."
3. Some errata will hide so well that they *will* make it into production and be found by a paying customer.

If part of a system architecture has a high probability of incurring errors, design and production processes must take that into account. When NASA sends a deep-space probe that can transmit with only a few watts of power, it knows that digging the signal out of the noise will be a challenge, and the radio protocols it adopts reflect that error tolerance. Likewise, CD-ROMs and DVDs, as well as hard drives, incorporate extensive error detection and recovery, because in any storage media (including the brain) errors will naturally arise during access.

Similarly, project managers have to know that mistakes will end up in their design and take appropriate measures before, during, and after they have manifested. A defense-in-depth strategy is the best approach to design flaws I have found: avoid, find, survive.

Design to Avoid Bugs. Design engineers must constantly juggle many conflicting demands: schedule, performance, power dissipation, features, testing, documentation, training, and hiring. They may intuitively know that if they spent the next two weeks simply thinking long and hard about their design, they would produce a far better design with fewer errors than if they had spent the two weeks coding. But their reality is a project manager who must ensure that the project stays on track and on schedule and whose favorite way to do that is to measure everything. It is hard to quantify the project benefits of meditation, but a manager *can* tally how many lines of RTL the designer could have generated had she not spent two weeks simply thinking. This translates into subtle pressure to favor immediate schedule deadlines now, and if more design errors creep in as a result, then so be it. Someone can attend to those later. For now, the project is measurably on schedule and tomorrow may never come.

Management must undo this mindset by emphasizing how much less expensive it is to get a design right in the first place than to have to create a test, debug it when it fails, and then fix the design without breaking something else in the process. Managers can also help by being sensitive to the huge array of issues designers face. Balancing schedule pressure is tricky. Too little, and the project might slip irreparably. Too much, and the pending trouble moves off the schedule, where it is visible, and into some other area, where it becomes design errata, eventually becomes visible, and wreaks havoc on the project schedule anyway.

When I think about finding this balance, I look at what scientists have found in dealing with natural phenomena. The point of an oil pipeline's maximal throughput is the amount and velocity of oil that flows fast, but smoothly, just before the point where a little more liquid in the pipe would cause turbulence to occur. If that turbulence does occur, the overall flow does not just diminish slightly; it falls a *lot*.

Likewise, the efficiency of an airfoil (as well as the generated lift) depends critically on its angle of attack. And the point of highest efficiency is that angle just before the onset of turbulence. A little beyond that, turbulence occurs, and lift falls drastically. (When this happens to one wing of an airplane but not the other, it can cause a flat spin from which recovery is very difficult.) As with the oil pipeline, the optimal policy is probably to carefully edge the project up to the onset of turbulence, where efficiency is at its peak, and then back off a little, on the grounds that going any further gains only a little and risks a lot.

Astute project leaders such as Randy Steck were particularly adept at finding this balance point, especially when accumulated project slippage was pointing toward a formal schedule slip. Few tasks are more unpleasant than having to officially request your boss's approval on a schedule slip. And the boss likes it that way; part of his effectiveness is to motivate you to do everything in your power to avoid this eventuality. But in that exact sense, a project manager who pushes back hard on her subordinates' requests for more time must still be sensitive to the possibility that unless more time is granted, the project's quality will slip below acceptable levels.

> *Few tasks are more unpleasant than having to officially request your boss's approval on a schedule slip.*

Architects have a first-order impact on design errata because they are the ones who imbued the design with its intrinsic complexity. They have ameliorated (or exacerbated) this complexity by clearly (or not clearly) communicating their design to the engineers who are reducing it to practice. Architects write the checks that the design engineers have to cash. If the amount is too high, the whole project goes bankrupt.

> *Architects have a first-order impact on design errata because they are the ones who imbued the design with its intrinsic complexity.*

One day during the P6 project, the three of us who had already designed substantial machines—Dave Papworth, Glenn Hinton, and I—were comparing notes on where design errata tended to appear. We realized that even though the three of us had worked on far different machines, the errata had followed similar patterns. Datapath design tended to just work, for example, probably because datapath patterns repeat everywhere and so lend themselves to a mechanical treatment at a higher abstraction level. If I refer to a bus as Utility_Bus[31:0], I don't have to tell you what hardware description language I am using. You know immediately how wide the bus is and that no bits of that bus have inadvertently been left out.

Control paths are where the system complexity lives. Bugs spawned from control path design errors reside in the microcode flows, the finite-state machines, and all the special exceptions that inevitably spring up in a machine design like thistles in a flower garden. Insidiously, the most complex bugs, which therefore have a higher likelihood of remaining undetected until they inflict real damage, live mostly "between" finite-state machines. Thus, anyone studying an isolated finite-state machine will likely see a clean, self-consistent design. Only analysts well versed in studying several finite-state machines operating simultaneously have any chance of noticing a joint malfunction. And even then it would be an intellectual feat of the first order.

In light of our discovery, we surmised that by careful architecting, we might be able to rule out a whole class of potential design errata. We began looking for ways to simplify the P6 core's exception handling. We noticed that we could implement many of these exceptions on top of the branch misprediction mechanism, which was complicated itself, but so intrinsic to the machine's basic operation that it got a huge amount of exercise and testing.

For the first time in our collective experience, we ended up with a machine that had essentially no important errata associated with traps, faults, and breakpoints.

Our strategy worked, and for the first time in our collective experience, we ended up with a machine that had essentially no important errata associated with traps, faults, and breakpoints. We also found that ruling out a class of design errata this way was by far the most cost-effective strategy for realizing a high-quality machine.

This strategy also makes sense in light of the design's complexity. Complexity breeds design errata like stagnant pond water breeds mosquitoes. Some bugs on the original P6 chip, for example, required many clock cycles and the complex interactions of six major functional units to manifest. In such cases, it is not reasonable to blame any of the six functional unit designers, and it will probably be unavailing to ask why validation did not catch the error. Such bugs lie squarely with the architects, who need to think through every corner case and make sure their basic design precludes such problems. We should have applied our good idea everywhere in the design, not just to those items that were already on our worry list.

When Bugs Get In Anyway, Find Them Before Production. No amount of management attention to presilicon testing and no degree of designer diligence and dedication will avoid all mistakes. Design and validation errors are inevitable (even if you still harbor some hope that perhaps there might be a way to avoid them, however theoretical, it's still better to plan and execute your project as if there weren't). It falls to the validation crew to find these mistakes before production and to work with the designers to fix them without breaking anything else.

Validation teams have the same kinds of crushing pressure as the design teams, and then some. Validators must perform their task without noticeably changing the tapeout schedule, but until the RTL model is reasonably mature, they are limited to trivial tests. The design team typically has several months' head start, but from that time to tapeout, validation is supposed to identify every design flaw and verify that their remedies are correct.

By the very nature of validation, that expectation is doomed to nonfulfillment. The validation plan may be thorough, but it is of necessity incomplete. How can validation test everything with finite time and finite simulation cycles? Given the combinatorial-state explosion that today's complex machines imply, they cannot even get close.

The testing team also learns as it goes along. If a chip unit is behaving in stellar fashion and yielding almost no bugs, while another unit is behaving very badly across a range of tests, the validation team will shift resources to the flaky unit. Some handwritten tests may be finding no bugs, while others find one after another. The testers will do the obvious: Extend the use of the efficacious test, and if they are really on the ball, at least inspect the no-bugs-found test to see if the test itself could be defective. (Yes, it happens. I have personally written at least one validation test that saw routine use for quite some time before I noticed that it would indicate success no matter how broken the machine it was supposedly testing actually was. This kind of revelation severely taxes your confidence in the overall project, not to mention in your own skills!)

IDENTIFYING BUGS. Design errata, bugs, errors, mistakes—whatever you call them, they are exasperatingly elusive because they can come from just about anywhere. Some are caused by miscommunication: inaccuracies in documentation, design changes that were not fully disseminated, and misunderstandings about when mutually dependent design changes were to be made. Others are caused by the designer's muddy thinking, often exacerbated by short schedules or management pressure. Sometimes, a designer simply did not think through all circumstances under which his design must correctly operate or did not identify what actually constituted correct operation in every possible situation. And there are always the "oops" bugs that engineers and nonengineers alike instantly recognize: "I have no idea why I did that. What was I *thinking?*"

> *"I have no idea why I did that. What was I* thinking?*"*

I do not know any comprehensive, useful theory that consistently helps identify any type of bug, but I can offer some rules of thumb.

First, *be careful how you measure bugs if you want to know about them.* Well-run projects are tracked by data the project managers collect. We managers have a good feel for when the project will tape out, its expected performance, and for how much power the chip will dissipate, because we collect a lot of data on those items and track their trends carefully each week.

But the measure-and-extrapolate managerial instinct can backfire when applied to design errata. Many bugs are found close to home by the designers themselves. If designers sense even the tiniest amount of pressure to minimize design errata or to reward those with fewer bugs, they will instantly and directly translate that into "Quietly fix the bug and don't tell anyone else about it." And you will not know they did it. In fact, for a while it will seem as though the project is doing better than before, with less effort going to fix errata.

The same concern applies to validation, in which test coverage is every bit as important as sheer numbers of bugs detected. I will revisit this idea later in the chapter (see "Managing Validation" on page 65).

Second, *look closely at the microcode.* Although microcode seems to have disproportionately more bugs than anything else in the chip, if you understand the x86 and the design process, that outcome is understandable. The x86 is an extremely complex instruction-set architecture, and most of that complexity is embedded in the microcode. You might think that a company that has successfully implemented x86 chips for close to 30 years would have "solved" the microcode problem long ago, but they haven't, because no such solution exists. Every time the microarchitecture must be changed, so must the microcode, and all fundamental changes to either will expose new areas in the microcode, for which the past is a poor guide to correctness.

Microcode also tends to be buggy because, unlike hardware, it tends to remain changeable right up to a few weeks before tapeout. Late in project development, if a significant bug is found in a functional unit, the unit's owner will often ask to make a small change to the microcode that would ameliorate the conditions under which this particular bug would manifest. And very often, such a change is indeed possible and does what the functional unit's owner wanted. The unit owner is now happy, but as he walks away smiling, another unit's owner comes in looking worried and contrite, and the process repeats. A project's last few months can see a lot of such changes, and taken together they can make a hash out of previously respectable-looking microcode source. These microcode fixes are also uniquely susceptible to the late-change syndrome, common to all engineering endeavors: If you make a change to an engineering design late in

> *If you make a change to an engineering design late in the project, that change is at much higher risk of bugginess.*

the project, that change is at much higher risk of bugginess than other design aspects. The team is tired, the pressure is high, and there is not enough time left to redo the past two or three years of testing and to incorporate the effects of this new change on the design. Although unrelated to its microcode, the infamous Pentium FDIV flaw was due to exactly such a late change to an existing design.

TRACKING BUGS. At first glance, it seems pretty clear what validation needs to do: Create a comprehensive list of tests such that a model that passes them all is considered to be of production quality. Then test the RTL models, identify the tests that do not pass, find out why, get the designers to fix the errors, and repeat until finished.

In the real world, however, the validator's life is often messy. The tools have bugs, the tests can be faulty, and because the RTL model under test is not a stationary target, tests that passed last week might fail this week. One design bug might prevent several tests from passing, and one of those tests might have found a quite different bug. Or a validation test might have assumed correct functioning was of one form, but the design engineer might have assumed something different. Is that a design bug? You cannot tell because you need more information.

Also, a validator chasing one specific test commonly stumbles across something else quite by accident. Said validator would be within her rights to ignore New Phenomenon B, on the grounds that she should not allow herself to get distracted while trying to nail Presumed Bug A. But experienced designers and validators have learned that if something serendipitously pops up during testing with "I'm probably a bug" written on its forehead, you have two choices. You could let it go back into hiding or deal with it now. If you let it go, the odds are extremely high that it will come back and bite you later. Given that you will almost certainly have to deal with it sometime, it is best to capture what you can about it now so that you can reproduce it later when you can focus on it. *Then* go back to chasing Presumed Bug A.

We dubbed any incident found during testing that could have a bug as its root a "sighting," and we learned to be very dogmatic about these incidents from our experience in other design projects. The rule was that anyone had to report a sighting to a general database, along with the specific RTL model, the test that generated the sighting, the general error syndrome, and any information a validation engineer might need to try to reproduce the sighting. See Figures 3.1 and 3.2.

A validation engineer, typically but not always the one who filed the sighting, would then attempt to reproduce it and find its root cause. Were other bugs recently found that might explain this sighting? Have any tools or test deficiencies been found that might be

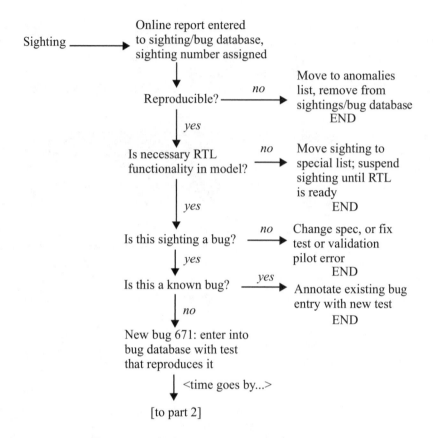

Figure 3.1. Sightings-to-bugs flowchart, part 1.

relevant? After checking the easiest answers first, the validator would then begin zeroing in on exactly what wasn't going according to plan and what might be causing the problem. In many cases, he could collect evidence in a few hours that a real bug in the design was the culprit, and would then officially change the issue's status from "sighting" to "bug."

Once an issue attained the status of bug, it was assigned to the most appropriate design engineer—whenever possible, the person who had put it into the design in the first place. This was not a punishment. Rather, the idea was to let the person who owned that part of the design be the person who fixed it and, thus, minimize the odds of the fix-one-break-two problem occurring (an all-too-common occurrence, in which the fixer introduces two new bugs while attempting to fix the first one).

A few hours or days later, depending on the bug's severity and the designer's workload, the design engineer would come up with a fix and was expected to build and check a model that embodied it. This sanity checking had a three-pronged goal: (1) determine that bug was really gone, (2) establish that nothing had broken as a result of the fix, and (3) ensure that the previous hole in designer's unit tests was now filled so that this bug could never come back. Once the design engineer's model passed this sanity check, he or she could mark the official issue status as "fix pending."

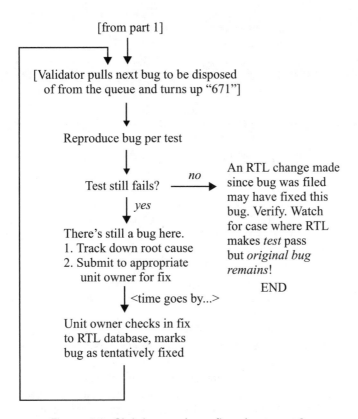

[from part 1]

[Validator pulls next bug to be disposed of from the queue and turns up "671"]

Reproduce bug per test

Test still fails? —— *no* ——▶ An RTL change made since bug was filed may have fixed this bug. Verify. Watch for case where RTL makes *test* pass but *original bug remains*!

↓ *yes*

There's still a bug here.
1. Track down root cause
2. Submit to appropriate
   unit owner for fix

↓ <time goes by...>

Unit owner checks in fix to RTL database, marks bug as tentatively fixed

END

Figure 3.2. Sightings-to-bugs flowchart, part 2.

We deliberately withheld the authority to mark the issue as resolved, saving that role for the validation engineer who filed the issue in the first place. That validation engineer had to then demonstrate that the previously failing test now passed, and that the new fixed model also passed some minimal regression tests so as to catch any obvious system-wide cases where the new fix broke something that used to work.

We found this process extremely valuable because it guaranteed that at least two project engineers had deep knowledge of both the bug and its cure. It also removed the temptation for the design engineer to continually short-circuit the process by simply unilaterally deciding it really was not a bug or he "thought he had fixed it" or any of the thousand other delusions a creative person can rationalize his way into.

MANAGING VALIDATION. Inherent in both the mismanagement of design errors and our process for successfully handling them is a critical requirement: Successfully manage the validation effort. This takes sublime judgment, which I have been able to distill into four don'ts (since the first step in doing something right is knowing what *not* to do).

First, *don't use the validation plan as a performance measure.* A validation manager finds herself embedded in a design project that values objectivity and measurement. She is asked to provide indicators and metrics by which her superiors can gauge her team's overall progress. Because the validation plan most closely resembles a list of tests to be run, an obvious metric is to measure how much of the plan the team has accomplished at any given time. The flaw in this thinking is that the validation crew has conceived the plan while carefully considering all the technical corners of the design it must cover. You cannot reasonably expect them to anticipate how the sequence of those tests will jibe with what the design is capable of at any given week, nor with what the design team may actually need that week.

More important, validation teams learn as they go. And the main thing they learn is where their own plan had holes and weaknesses. If a validation team is being managed strictly to the fraction of the plan they have completed, they may become fatally discouraged about adding any more tasks to it.

Second, *don't use the number of bugs found as a performance measure.* Late in the project, after most of the RTL has been written and built into a chip model, validation applies their accumulated mass of tests, along with randomly generated code and other methods, to try to find any design errata. The rate at which they find bugs depends on a mix of the design's innate bugginess, how close to the surface the bugs are, how many computing resources are available to the validation team, and how quickly the team can resolve the list of currently open sightings. Measuring validation's output strictly in terms of bugs found per week can quickly distort the entire validation process. Coverage matters, too. If validation finds that all their testing has turned up very few bugs in functional unit X, but revealed a veritable bug killing field in functional unit Y, they must be allowed to increase their pressure on Y without completely giving up on X.

Third, *don't use the number of tests passed as measure of project health.* Design projects running at full speed can be intimidating to upper management. They see the schedule deadline looming large, design errata being found at a steady or increasing rate, and a steady stream of bad news (higher power needed, performance deviations, larger die size), with no guarantees that the stream will not turn into a flood. They are tempted to ask the crucial question, "Is this project lurching toward a tapeout convergence, or is it exploding right before my eyes?" How can they tell?

One indicator they look at is the rate at which new bugs are manifesting in the design. Managers want the design errata rate to decrease steadily toward the tapeout window and then essentially hit zero per week for several weeks before taping out. That is what they would *like,* but that is not what happens. What happens is that by the time the RTL has matured enough to run the really tough tests and the validation crew has disposed of the easier bugs, not much time is left before formal tapeout. In fact, as the validation team gets more expert at wielding their tests and debugging the failures, the overall errata rate may well go *up* in the project's last few weeks.

To avoid upper management's wrath, the validation team might choose to accentuate the positive. It is easy to rationalize. After all, the validation plan called for every combination of opcode and addressing mode to be checked, so it is not necessarily duplicitous to report that all those seem to work, instead of concentrating your overall validation firepower on the areas yielding the most bugs.

Resist the urge to even think in that direction. Instead, let the project's indicators tell you the truth and guide whatever actions are appropriate. If some particular part of the design is generating more than its share of bugs, increase the design and validation resources assigned to it. Pay attention to the type as well as the number of bugs. The bug pattern may reveal an important lesson for either of these dimensions. And once having formed as accurate a picture as possible of the project's health, relay that picture to your management, the bad with the good. (Then take your licking with aplomb. That is why they pay you the big bucks.)

Fourth, *don't forget the embarrassment factor.* Imagine a design error such that the RTL model is yielding this result: $2 + 2 = 5$. (Ignore for the moment that a bug that simple would never make it into the wild, since the operating system would never successfully boot on a machine broken this badly. In fact, for a bug this egregious, the rest of the design team would probably invent some unique punishment that is too terrible to put in print.) There is a class of bugs that would prove beyond reasonable doubt that the design team simply hadn't ever tested whatever function they are found in. Worse, the implication to the buyer is "If they didn't test *that,* what else didn't they test?" For this reason, every opcode and every addressing mode really should be tested at some point in chip development, and anything else with a high embarrassment factor, whether or not this "coverage" testing is detecting design errata at a high rate.[4]

Plan to Survive Bugs that Make It to Production. Those who are not engineers know two certainties: death and taxes. Engineers know a third: there are no perfect designs. Every single product ever made has had shortcomings, weaknesses, and outright design errata [6].

The goal of the first two parts of my avoid/find/survive product-quality algorithm is to *prevent* design errata in the final product. The focus of the third part is to minimize the severity and impact of the errata that make it into the product. Some bugs are hardy or well disguised enough to complete that journey. The FDIV flaw was a subtle, complex bug that survived both design and validation.

I once worked on a microprocessor design team (not at Intel) whose motto was "From the Beginning: Perfection." We even had that slogan emblazoned on our T-shirts.[5] But the chip, far from being perfect, underwent an aggravating 13 steppings (design revisions) before it was really production ready. I believe a significant contributor to this was that the project team took this slogan *too* seriously. Once the project team convinces itself that a perfect product is an achievable goal, that mindset absolves the team from considering what they will face when the silicon comes back from the fabrication plant. Then, when it comes back from the fab in an obviously imperfect state, the design team will not have provided themselves any resources with which to debug the chip.

NASA has a well-tested methodology for dealing with unforeseen eventualities. For mission-critical facilities on a spacecraft, for example, NASA provides backups and sometimes backups for the backups. But merely providing the additional hardware is not enough. You must also try to anticipate all possible failure modes to make sure that the backup is usable, no matter what has happened.

Malfunctioning microprocessors are infuriating devices to debug in the lab. Computers in the 1980s were of medium-scale integration, and you could usually directly measure whatever signals or buses turned out to be of interest. With microprocessors, especially those with caches and branch-prediction tables, an awful lot of activity can occur on the chip with no outwardly visible sign. By the time it is externally visible that things have gone awry, many millions or even billions of clock cycles may have transpired. You could be chasing a software bug in the test, an operating system bug, a transient electrical issue on the chip or on the bus connected to it, a manufacturing defect stuck-at fault inside the microprocessor, or a design error. At this instant, as you stand there helpless and be-

[4]Sometimes, the corporate embarrassment factor has nothing to do with design or validation. The FDIV flaw is an example. See "Was the P6 Project affected by the Pentium's floating point divider bus."
[5]Here is a depressing thought: I got that T-shirt in 1980 and I can still wear it today. The microprocessor it was associated with has been obsolete, useless junk for well over 20 years.

> *During design you should have provided an entire array of debug and monitoring facilities, with enough flexibility to cover all the internal facilities.*

fuddled in the debug lab, the scales fall from your eyes, and you see clearly and ruefully that during design you should have provided an entire array of debug and monitoring facilities, with enough flexibility to cover all the internal facilities you wish you could observe right now.

Having learned this lesson on previous machines, we architects imbued the P6 and Pentium 4 microprocessors with a panoply of debug hooks and system monitoring features. If a human debugger has access to the code being executed and wants to see the exact path the processor is taking through that code, all she needs from the microprocessor is an indication of every branch taken. When that sequence of branches diverges from what was expected, she has a pretty good idea of the bug's general vicinity and can begin to zero in on it.

There are two subtleties in providing debug hooks. The first is not to use their existence as a crutch to do a poorer job at presilicon validation (a fear upper management often expresses). The second is to take validation of these debug hooks as seriously as you do the chip's basic functionality. After all, "If you didn't test it, it doesn't work" applies to all aspects of the chip, not just the mainstream instruction-set architecture stuff.

A Six-Step Plan for High Product Quality

There are no sure-fire recipes for getting a product right. But there are effective tactics and attitudes. Here are six good ones.

1. Incorporate only the minimum necessary complexity in the project in the first place. Do not oversubscribe the team.
2. Make sure the design team and corporate management agree on the right level of product quality. Empty aphorisms like "achieve highest possible quality," "no product flaws," or "20% better than competitor X" are worse than useless because they lead to insidious cases in which the design team is invisibly and actively working at cross-purposes to project management, executive management, or itself.
3. Do not let the design team think of themselves as the creative artists and the validation team as the janitorial staff that cleans up after them. There is one team and one product, and we all succeed or fail together.
4. Foster a design culture that encourages an emotional attachment by the designers to the product they are designing (not just their part of that product). But engineers must also be able to emotionally distance themselves from their work when it is in the project's best interests.
5. Make sure the validation effort is comprehensive, well planned, and adequately staffed and funded, with the goal of "continuously measuring the distance from the target," thus ensuring product quality is converging toward success.
6. Design and religiously adhere to a bug-tracking method that will not let sightings or confirmed bugs fall into the cracks.

The idea that the design culture should encourage emotional attachments, yet the engineers must be able to sometimes turn that emotion off, may seem inconsistent or even mystical, but it is actually quite simple. The emotional attachment just means the engineer cares about what she is designing. She wants to get it right, and she wants the product to succeed. To do a proper design review, however, the designer must check her ego at the door, and realize that it is in the best interests of the overall goal—a successful product—that her design undergo some rigorous scrutiny [28]. The commitment to the overarching goal is what will guide the engineer in knowing when to override the emotional attachment.

The Design Review

Designers make mistakes, but good designers strive to avoid making the same mistake twice, and they usually succeed, particularly if another equally talented designer is diligently checking what they have created. Software engineers have learned this as well [29]. Practitioners of extreme programming also practice extreme reviewing, calling for the checker to sit at the elbow of

> *Designers make mistakes, but good designers strive to avoid making the same mistake twice.*

the coder to check the code in real time as the coder first enters it [23]. Hardware design practices a less extreme form of cross-checking, called the design review (although "extreme designing" might be worth trying some day).

In most cases, a design review is a formal process whereby the engineer of the unit being reviewed presents her design to a panel of peers who then try to find any holes or errors in that unit. Design reviews have many styles, but they all include some kind of panel of peers. For the P6 and Willamette projects, our panel consisted of formal reviewers who were expected to do preparatory reading and study before the event, and 10 to 20 other interested designers and observers. The observers were not necessarily expected to actively contribute, although they sometimes did. Their role was to learn about their neighbor's unit design and to reinforce in everyone's mind that this project took its design reviews seriously.

The reviewers must have enough information to be able to follow the review and contribute to it. The unit designer has to furnish this information, particularly that which establishes the design's context: its place in the overall system; the function it is expected to fulfill; its constraints in terms of power, performance, die size, and schedule; and early alternatives to the approach that was eventually selected. Depending on the design itself, the designer might also need to provide block diagrams, pipeline and timing diagrams, and protocols, as well as describe finite-state-machine controllers and possibly furnish the actual source code or schematic diagrams.

When design reviews are done properly, the outcome is a list of ideas, objections, concerns, and issues identified by the collective intellect of the review panel. The reviewee then e-mails that list around to all attendees and project management, along with plans for addressing the issues and tentative schedules for resolving all open items. The overall project managers incorporate these issues and schedules into the overall project schedule and begin tracking the new open items until they are resolved.

At the review's outset, the team should designate a scribe to capture the ideas, suggestions, proposals, and any questions the review team asks. These will range from observations to pointed queries to suggestions for improvements or further study. These ideas and the interchanges between the presenter and the reviewers are the very essence of the review. The job of distilling this important but sometimes unruly stream of information is critical. The project should already have a central Web site accessible to all project engineers. After the meeting, the scribe should not only distribute minutes to the review participants, but also archive them onto the project Web site. Engineers who could not attend the review can then check its conclusions and spot surprises or inconsistencies.

The scribe should strive to be a neutral observer as much as possible. He or she will probably have to fight the urge to put a personal spin on what was said (and especially *why* it might have been said). Some value judgments are inevitable, of course, and many such judgments will turn out to be extremely useful. But one of the reasons the scribe should circulate the meeting minutes is precisely so that other attendees can check them for objectivity and completeness. These other attendees will want to check them, because they may well find their own name on the list of follow-on work to be done.

The scribe cannot be the presenter. Try that, and you will not get either job right. The presenter is utterly engaged in making sure the reviewers are getting the technical information they need to do an adequate job of covering the design. Presenting the design itself to people who are trying to poke holes in it is an intellectual exercise not for the faint of heart; it causes the presenter to make constant mental leaps from "This is how it works" to "This is why it doesn't work some other way" to "My intuition says your wild idea won't work, but I can't fully articulate why at the moment," and so on. The presenter is the one person at a design review who is 100% occupied and cannot take on any other roles.

Many design review meeting notes are appropriate for wider distribution than just to the attendees. It is not uncommon, for example, for the reviewers to suddenly realize that an issue is of far wider scope than just the unit under review. The reviewee must ensure that such issues reach the proper forum for global resolution.

How* Not *to Do a Review. A design review can also be counterproductive, whether because of the reviewee's defensive attitude or management's lack of monitoring. Since I have already established that people often learn by mistakes, here are a few ways to get a first-class education:

> *Have everyone deliberate on the world's greatest solution to a minor issue.* Reviews are not a great place for group thinking. Engineers like living in the solution space; give them a problem, and they will smile as they do an irreversible swan dive into that space. Multiply that by 30 people in a design review setting and you have an enjoyable but useless afternoon. It is more important that the entire unit be reviewed to at least an acceptable level of thoroughness than to hammer one item flat and miss several others entirely.

> *It is more important that the entire unit be reviewed to at least an acceptable level of thoroughness than to hammer one item flat and miss several others entirely.*

> *Measure the design's success inversely to the number of issues identified.* In this scenario, the reviewee exits the review gloating, "They didn't lay a glove on me," and actually believes the review's success is inversely proportional to the length of the issues list identified in the review. That person should immediately be fired for incompetence and eminent stupidity for having wasted a lot of very busy people's time and gotten nothing for it. My experience is that the people whose designs are so outstanding that they have little need for design reviews are the same ones who

least mind having their work checked by their peers. I do not think that is a coincidence.

Do nothing while the meeting degenerates into an emotional minefield. The "mines" can be either a reviewee who believes the design is his baby and glowers at anyone who dares criticize it, or reviewers who see the review as an opportunity to inflict a little professional payback or humiliation. Either attitude can permanently damage relationships and will prevent any forward progress on improving the design. To defuse the mines, project management must make it clear that design reviews are important, and, if necessary, personally attend the review to keep emotions in check.

Do not worry if people become sensitive or zealous about the review process. There is a fine line between reviewing work and sticking your nose into other people's business. A mature, professional team dedicated to designing the world's best products will find this line and observe it scrupulously. Project managers must monitor the process and make sure no designers are being driven quietly crazy by anyone else, under the auspices of the design review culture. Oddly enough, in my experience both designers who won't let anyone see their work and reviewers who are overly assiduous about checking others' work are likely to be doing substandard work. Either behavior should be a warning flag to project leaders.

As a reviewee, feel free to ignore certain issues the review raises. Reviewees cannot be allowed to judge the validity of an issue. If it was important enough for a reviewer to bring up, it is important enough to be properly disposed of. Simply ignoring it is not an option. Neither is proof by assertion or simply glowering at the reviewer.

When to Do a Review. Some companies or design groups have a long list of reasons to avoid design reviews. "There's not enough time in the schedule" tops the list and indicates a far deeper problem with project management. If a project does not have enough time to check that they are getting the product right, it will not have enough time to fix the product later (when they discover that they got the product wrong). Design reviews, properly done, facilitate vital communication among designers and between the design team and project leadership. If the project cannot make time for a review, it does not have enough time to do the product properly. And a project leader who does not see that is probably not doing his job properly either.

Design reviews do not have to be done every day, or every time the design changes. A good rule of thumb is to review every important subsystem in the design at least once when the design has matured enough to have worked out the essential elements but is still flexible enough to allow changes. And at least one joint design review should be held between the product team and any external interfaces required for that product's success. For microprocessors, this means at least one joint design review between the CPU and the chip-set designers.

ANOTHER ONE RIDES THE BUS

Sometimes we CPU architects tend to take for granted any system elements outside the chip's pins. We need to know bandwidths, latencies, and the capacities of the main memory and the chip's frontside bus, but beyond those we are content. For P6, we were able to leave that external world in the extremely competent hands of our chief bus designer, Gurbir Singh, and his talented first lieutenant Nitin Sarangdhar. Gurbir had previously designed the bus for Intel's i960 CPU, and the proposal he and the team came up with for P6's bus seemed eminently reasonable, implementable, and competitive.

Some voices in the company wanted us to reuse the Pentium's bus. They argued that changing the bus design had many unfortunate side effects, such as forcing the industry to change its tooling, routing, and motherboard placement rules for the chips. Chips that were compatible with the last generation's sockets could be sold as system upgrades and had a previously established and tested set of chip-set components.

This was all true, but the trouble was that the Pentium (P5) bus simply was not up to the system performance levels we needed with the P6 design. The Pentium processor and all its predecessors had been in-order designs. Because instructions could not be reordered, if a load instruction missed in the cache and had to retrieve the missing information from memory across the bus, that load and all other instructions in the CPU had to wait until that access was satisfied. In the Pentium's day, main memory was not very far away; it took only a few clock cycles to retrieve the needed cache line. That was a noticeable but not crippling loss of performance.

P6's clock rate was much higher, and if the product road map were to unfold over the next several years the way we had envisioned,[6] it would go much higher still. Main memory comprised dynamic RAMs (DRAMs), which were improving with time, but mostly in capacity, not in speed. This meant that the disparity between fast CPUs and relatively slow main memory was bad and about to get much worse. Making all instructions wait just because a particular load instruction missed the cache was likely to become onerous, especially for an intrinsically out-of-order engine that otherwise had all the capabilities required to avoid that cost.

To address this issue, Gurbir designed the P6 frontside bus to be transaction-oriented. Chips that connected to the bus were known as bus agents, and any bus communication would occur, by definition, between a bus agent pair, according to strict protocols and using the bus wires as little as possible. A CPU performing a cache line refill (as per the example I gave earlier) would arbitrate for bus ownership and send a message of the form "I request that whoever has data corresponding to system physical address A please send that data to me as soon as possible." All bus agents would hear that request, and normally the Northbridge chip, responsible for controlling main memory, would respond. The request for the cache line was one bus transaction; at some later time, after memory had had enough time to look up the information, another transaction would be initiated (this time by the Northbridge) and the information would be presented on the bus for the initial requestor's edification.

This transaction orientation is a standard feature of most modern microprocessor buses, despite its complexity and the implication that all bus agents must continuously monitor the bus and track the overall state, even for transactions that do not have direct relevance to them. But it is a good trade-off between the expensive (wires, motherboard routing, and CPU package pins) and inexpensive (transistors on the CPUs).

As a newly designated project manager on P6, my first mistake was in thinking that technical reasoning would be a satisfactory way to resolve any issues associated with the bus. After all, that is how we would attack any open issues inside the CPU's design. But as it turned out, the rules were (and still are) different for buses because just as multiple

---

[6]The road map did unfold exactly that way. More magic from Moore's Law.

bus agents share buses in a computer system, so multiple corporate entities share the bus design, and each has a vital interest in it.

Worse, the corporate group most responsible for the design of the Pentium bus, and the i486 bus before it, had not completely bought into the idea that P6 needed its own bus. They were just beginning to realize that a group of CPU designers in Oregon had had the audacity to go off and design an x86 CPU bus without their blessing, and were demonstrably unwilling to accept that fait accompli.

All I knew at the time was that contradictory, vociferous e-mails were raising the average temperature of my inbox to dangerous levels. To resolve the problem, I started by personally interviewing all the principals. Gurbir and the P6 bus implementers told me that they had already implemented a complete bus design in RTL and done substantial testing on it. Any changes to the basic design would seriously impact the project's schedule and they did not think the proposed changes were worth making given that cost.

On the other side was Pete MacWilliams, an Intel Fellow who had been instrumental in all prior x86 buses, but who had found himself immersed in Pentium issues until only very recently. One of Pete's cohorts, Steve Pawlowski, was also helping us by reviewing the bus specification from the chip-set point of view and offering ideas and criticisms. Pete asked us to consider some ideas on how to improve the P6 bus, and after looking at them, I agreed that most were in fact improvements. Had it been even a year earlier in the project, we would have adopted them without further ado. But schedule pressure was so high at this point in the project that this decision was no longer an easy one.

I decided to bring all the combatants into one room for a day to see if reasoned argument could let one side persuade the other. (Yes, I was that naive.)

The meeting opened with my standing at one end of a long table. On one side sat six P6 bus engineers and on the other sat Pete and a few of his coworkers. As I looked at the faces of those present, it suddenly dawned on me—there was not going to be reasoned persuasion here. Instead, the day would end with my having to break the tie, and when I did, the "winning" half of the room would think I had simply acquiesced to the obvious, whereas the other half would think I was a complete idiot. After listening carefully to the arguments, I concluded that the improvements were not worth the cost to

> *Half of the room would think I had simply acquiesced to the obvious, whereas the other half would think I was a complete idiot.*

the schedule on the first product, but could be added to some later proliferation design. I thanked everyone for their help in resolving this and asked Pete to stay involved with the P6 system design because of his extensive experience.

That was not the end of it. I don't think Pete was terribly unhappy that his suggestions had not been accepted, but apparently his boss was. A few weeks later, I found myself in a room of general managers and VPs. Pete's boss started the meeting by stomping around the room, shouting about how his group had always had the charter for designing computer CPU buses, that such things had to be done with an eye toward the future, not just because it was convenient for one particular chip, and how on earth could we believe a group of microprocessor designers knew anything about buses?

At first I was bewildered. Who was this guy, and why did he seem so emotionally invested in my project? Was he faking his anger just to make a point? But the other attendees seemed to be taking him seriously. Then I got annoyed at how far from reality his viewpoint seemed to be. And then I got mad. Really mad. I fired back, "We *had* to design a new bus for P6 *precisely because* the buses you and your team had produced were so thoroughly outmoded and unusable for modern designs. We have laid a solid foundation for the next 10 years of microprocessors at this company, a trick your team has not succeeded at, and we did it with no help from you. Then, after we no longer need your help, you show up and propose to damage our schedule just to assuage your egos. Why don't you just go away and let us design world-class products?"

This particular VP seemed to enjoy being addressed in this manner about as much as I had when he was yelling.

Looking back with 12 years of perfect hindsight, the man did have a point—it was, in fact, his group's charter to guide the CPU buses for the corporation. I now appreciate much better than I did then that such a role is absolutely necessary. The root cause of the conflict was partly our naiveté as a new x86 design group (not many people cared what bus was on the i960, but many people care about all aspects of x86 designs) and partly my own lack of understanding about how Intel was organized. On the other hand, I had valid points too; we really did put a solid bus into existence, a bus that is still being employed in various forms throughout the product line, 14 years after its conception. This is a testament to the strength of Gurbir Singh's original vision and the cleverness of many designers and architects along the way. And there was probably a nontrivial component of the legendary architect's ego involved. Anyone who wants to tell me that we botched some aspect of a design I am proud of had better start by acknowledging that context first. Otherwise, I will assume they are trying out for the Monday Morning Quarterbacking League and my interest level will drop precipitously.

Ultimately, the decision, which was made several levels higher than mine, was to compromise: Adopt the ideas that Pete felt would be the most necessary for good performance and early bus testing and refuse the ones that would have the worst impact on schedule. It's a good thing that Pete is such a nice guy and great technologist, because the whole episode left a very sour taste in a lot of P6 designers' mouths, including my own.

4

THE REALIZATION PHASE

It's always questionable to try to do something too cleverly.
—Albert Einstein

The concept phase produced about three feasible avenues down which the design project could travel successfully. The refinement phase investigated those avenues and identified the most promising. Now, the realization phase had to translate this winning idea into a product.

This phase can seem sudden and more than a little scary. Yesterday, the project was an abstraction—a collection of ideas, concepts, and new terms that a few people kicked around. Today, dozens of bright, experienced design engineers are taking these ideas at face value, studying them intently and internalizing them. Hundreds of people are being organized into small groups to work on respective subunits that seemed to be a lot less defined yesterday. People are creating T-shirts with drawings and caricatures based on technical terms you conjured out of thin air only a few weeks ago. Dozens of people are using terms that you invented and you wonder if they are using them in the way you intended.

> *People are creating T-shirts with drawings and caricatures based on technical terms you conjured out of thin air only a few weeks ago.*

At this time in the P6 project, I remember being overwhelmed by the many people who were taking our architecture ideas seriously. It is one thing to put a brave face on your uncertainty when convincing upper management that they should invest hundreds of mil-

The Pentium Chronicles. By Robert P. Colwell
© 2006 IEEE Computer Society

lions of dollars in your concepts. It is quite another when you see your peers staking their careers on the idea that you and the rest of the concept team have come up with something that has enough integrity to be implementable, is aggressive enough to beat the competition, and is flexible enough to survive the surprises ahead. Either they have bought into your vision, or they have put their trust in you; both prospects induce humility.

Those who are key players in a start-up know what it means to be fully and irretrievably committed to a technical vision and how grateful you are when others make similar sacrifices. Shortly after I joined Multiflow Computer, a VLIW start-up, I was copying some documents related to building a house when the VP of engineering walked in. When he realized that I was that deeply committed to making the company a success, the look on his face communicated volumes. What *he* knew then was exactly how precarious the corporate finances were and how badly things could go for us if the worst happened. All *I* knew was that no start-up had a hope of succeeding unless we first burned the lifeboats. My attitude was full speed ahead and do not look back. Samuel Johnson said, "Nothing will ever be attempted, if all possible objections must be first overcome." This kind of mindset will serve you well in the realization phase, in which a multitude of objections will arise daily.

> *Nothing will ever be attempted, if all possible objections must be first overcome.*

By its nature, the realization phase has many concurrent activities, most of which center on further development of the register-transfer logic (RTL) model, an executable description of exactly how the final microprocessor chip will behave under all circumstances. The project's refinement phase began with the behavioral RTL coding and the realization phase will convert that to the final structural RTL form from which the circuit and layout efforts will work. The finished P6 RTL model had approximately 750,000 lines of source code, clearly a nontrivial software development.

OF IMMEDIATE CONCERN

To get a feeling for what the realization phase is like, consider what would be involved in building a new high-rise [24]. The concept phase of that project has only a few participants: the buyer, the financier, the builder, and the architect. The refinement phase has more, as choices are considered and made, various possibilities weighed, and ground is broken.

But the building project really gets into high gear in the realization phase, when the blueprints have been drawn, the steel skeleton is up and the building site is crawling with hard hats. The building crew can now work at full speed, because the plans and the infrastructure are in place. There are huge cranes to lift the pieces of the upper floors into position. There are temporary service elevators to bring workers to any floor. The army of supply trucks has been organized into an intricate choreography. And while some teams work at completing the building's core structures, other teams put the building infrastructure in place, such as plumbing, electrical wiring, elevator service, and fire suppression equipment. Yet more teams work on finishing the interior according to the blueprints.

When you stand across the street from a project in the realization phase, you get a visceral sense of the concurrency in this phase. Small wonder that during this part of the project, more work gets done per unit time than at any other phase.

In a chip development, the concept phase comes up with some overall project alternatives, and the refinement phase narrows those down to two and then selects one. It in essence sets up the project scaffolding needed to support the concurrency in the realization phase. Because of this relationship, it is crucial that the realization phase not be undertaken until the preparation work is complete. If you wait a week longer than necessary to crank up your project into the full-out execution mode of the realization phase, you will at worst have delayed your project by a week. You can often make up that week by inspired management later. But if the project is allowed to begin the realization phase before the project direction has been firmly and confidently set and before all team members have internalized it, you will pay a much higher price than a one week slip. Subtle errors will creep into interfaces, designers will make choices that may not be obviously wrong but still are seriously suboptimal, and everyone on the team will get the wrong subliminal impression that, overall, the project is further along than it really is. This impression can itself cause errors in judgment that validation or management has to notice later on. It is a much better idea to guide the project purposely and judiciously from refinement to realization.

SUCCESS FACTORS

When the realization phase begins, the team has settled on one direction and has made some progress toward the RTL model that describes the actual product. The classical output of the realization phase is a prototype, a single instance of the product being developed. For silicon chips, the production engineers actually make several wafers' worth of chips on that first run, but the principle is the same—build a few, test them, fix what's broken, and when the time is right, move the project to the production phase (see next chapter).

The realization phase puts the pedal to the floor and designs a real product that conforms to the ideas from the earlier project phases. Whereas errors in the earlier phases could impact schedule, an error in the realization phase may directly affect hundreds of design engineers who are working concurrently. Assiduous project management and communication are key to the realization phase.

Balanced Decision Making

As a design proceeds, design engineers make dozens of decisions every day about their unit's implementation. They strive to balance their decisions in such a way that they meet or exceed every major project goal (performance, power dissipation, feature set, die size) within the schedule allotted. The very essence of engineering is the art of compromise, of trading off one thing for another. In that sense, any decision by any design engineer might impact performance.

> *The very essence of engineering is the art of compromise, of trading off one thing for another.*

At the beginning of the P6 project, we thought the relevant architect should bless all performance-related engineering decisions, but this requirement, though ideal in theory, quickly became impractical. There were simply too many such decisions and not enough architects to implement them and stay on schedule. We eventually established a rule, proposed by Sunil Shenoy: If you (the design engineer) believe that the performance impact of the choice you are considering is less than 1% on the designated benchmark regression suite, you are free to make the choice on your own. Higher than a 1% performance hit and you must include the architects in the decision.

This 1% rule generally worked well and certainly salvaged the overall project schedule. On the downside, the model ended up absorbing quite a few < 1% performance hits. Dave Papworth likened this to mice nibbling at a block of cheese: Mice do not eat much per bite, but over time the cheese keeps getting smaller.

> *Mice do not eat much per bite, but over time the cheese keeps getting smaller.*

The performance hits were usually independent of one another, and their combination at the system performance level was typically benign. But occasionally, the combination would be malignant, noticeably dragging down overall performance and drawing the ire of architects and performance analysts. Over time, the cumulative effect of these minor performance losses would cause aggregate system performance to sag imperceptibly lower almost daily until performance engineers would become alarmed enough to notify project management that performance projections were outside the targeted range. We would then essentially stop the project for a week, intensively study the sources of the performance loss, repair those areas, and reanalyze. We repeated the process until performance was back where we expected it to be.

Why then was the 1% rule important or even desirable? The simple answer is time. There weren't enough architect-hours to try to oversee every design decision that might affect performance. Picture a team of 200 designers, each making 10 decisions a day that might affect performance. We used the 1% rule, not because it was perfect, but because the alternative (utter chaos) was unworkable.

Documentation and Communication

We architects were creatively relentless in our attempts to transfer information. The first document written as a general introduction to the P6 was "The Kinder Gentler Introduction to the P6," an internal white paper intended to convey the general philosophy of the P6 microarchitecture. Next was "The P6 Microarchitecture Specification," or MAS, the first of what became a large set of documents detailing the operation of every unit on the chip, including new features, basic operation and pipelining, and x86 corner cases that our proposed design might affect.

Capturing Unit Decisions. Once the realization phase is underway, each unit group must begin to record their plans and decisions. For the P6 project, these records were the microarchitecture specifications. Each MAS described how the unit would execute the behaviors outlined in the unit's behavioral specification. Each unit group maintained their own MAS, which grew with the design, and distributed it to all other units. All MASs were written to a common template, so designers from one unit could easily review the MAS from another unit.

Each MAS included

- Pipeline and block diagrams
- Textual description of the theory of operation
- Unit inputs and outputs and protocols governing data transfers
- Corner cases of the design that were especially tricky

- New circuits required for implementation
- Notes on testing and validation, which we required so that design engineers could think about such things during the design, when it is easiest to address them

MASs were begun early in the realization phase, well before all the major design decisions had been collectively rendered. This timing was purposeful—the act of writing this documentation helped identify conceptual holes in the project. We began each MAS as early as we could, but only when we knew enough about the design that it was not likely we would have to tear the MAS document up and start over.

Integrating Architects and Design Engineers. Perhaps P6's strongest communication mechanism was not a videotape or document at all, but the architects' participation in the RTL model's debugging. Some engineering teams have the philosophy that the architect's job is finished when the concept phase documentation is complete. That is, once the project's basic direction is set, the architects are free to leave and start another project. This idea is reminiscent of the pipelining concept that underlies all modern CPU designs. It works brilliantly there, so why not apply it to people too?

I am sorry, but pipelining people, especially architects, is a monumentally bad idea. The architects conceived the machine's organization and feature sets and invented or borrowed the names for the various units and functions. They know

> *Pipelining people, especially architects, is a monumentally bad idea.*

how the machine is supposed to work at the deepest possible level of understanding, and in a way that other engineers cannot duplicate later, no matter how smart or experienced they are. The software industry is famous for inadvertently introducing one bug while fixing another one. Exactly the same malady will strike a chip development. It is all too easy to forget some subtle ramification of a basic microarchitecture canon and design yourself into a corner that will remain shrouded in mystery until chip validation, when the only feasible cures are painful to implement.

The architects are the major corporate repository of a critical knowledge category. Every design decision reflected in chip implementation is the result of considering and rejecting several alternative paths, some of which might have been nearly as good as the one chosen and some of which might have been obviously unworkable. The point is that the alternatives probably looked very appealing until the architect realized some subtle, insidious reason that the particular choice would have been disastrous later on.

If no one retains that crucial information, future proliferation efforts will suffer. Downstream design teams will have to change the design in some way, and if they stumble across one of these Venus flytrap alternatives, their product may be delayed or worse. The original architects are the best ones to tend those exotic plants and instruct others in their care and feeding.

Another reason not to pipeline architects is that architects, like all engineers, must use what they have created to solidly inform their own intuitions about which of their design ideas worked and how well, and about which ideas turned out not to be worth the trouble. Pipelining the architects is equivalent to sending them driving down a highway with their eyes closed. They may steer straight for a short time, but without corrective feedback, they will soon exit the highway in some fashion that will not do anyone any good.

PERFORMANCE AND FEATURE TRADE-OFFS

P6 was an x86 design from the heyday of x86 designs. High performance was the goal, and the reason our chip would command high selling prices. But performance was not the only goal; trade-offs were necessary. Making sure that the design team had the information needed to make these trade-offs consistently and in an organized fashion was both a technical and a communication problem.

(Over-) Optimizing Performance

In the preface to this book, I used the analogy of a sailing ship to describe some aspects of chip design. The project's realization phase also fits with the ship metaphor, except that this ship is attempting to navigate its cargo through tricky waters. While most of the vessel's crew go about their daily tasks of keeping the engines running and the ship clean, maintaining supplies, and doing most of the navigation, the captain must keep an eye on the overall voyage. Each crew member's individual task is difficult and pressure-filled, and the human tendency is for each to become accustomed to thinking of their task as something of an end in itself. It is up to the people on the bridge to constantly remind themselves and everyone else that they did not set out on this journey just to cruise around. Success will ultimately be measured by whether the cargo gets to the right port at the right time.

I will not presume to tell you how to run your particular ship, but I will point out some of the hazards along the shipping channel.

Perfect A; Mediocre B, C, and D. In this type of overoptimizing, the architect perfects one design aspect to the near exclusion of the others. This shortchanges product quality because architects working on idea A are, therefore, not working on ideas B, C, and D, and as the project lengthens, the odds of including B, C, and D go down. And idea A often has an Amdahl's Law ceiling that is easily overlooked in the heat of battle: Idea A may have been conceived as a solution to a pressing, specific performance problem, but any single idea may help that problem only so far, and to improve it further would require much more sweeping changes to the design, thus incurring further development costs and project risks. One must not become so myopically fixated on one project goal that other goals are neglected. B, C, and D will not be achieved as a by-product of achieving A.

The Technical Purity Trap. A common tendency, especially among inexperienced engineers, is to approach a development project as a sequence of isolated technical challenges. Rookies sometimes think the goal is to solve each challenge in succession, and that once the last problem has been surmounted, the project will have ended successfully. Experienced engineers know better. Subtleties abound, circumstances change, buyers' needs change, technical surprises arise that require design compromises, and schedule pressure only gets worse. Truly great designs are not simply those that post the highest performance scores, regardless of the costs. Great designs are those for which the engineers had a clear vision of their priorities and could make intelligent, informed compromises along the way.

> *Truly great designs are not simply those that post the highest performance scores, regardless of the costs.*

Why do engineers tend to focus on performance to the exclusion of other factors? To answer this, consider the responses of two engineers, one new and one experienced, to the question, "Which is a better car, a Mercedes S-class sedan or a Ford Taurus?" The new engineer will eagerly compare the technical details of each and easily reach the conclusion that Mercedes is by far the superior vehicle. The experienced engineer would then ask, "If the S-class sedan is so superior, why does Ford sell 15 Taurus models for every S-class car that Mercedes sells?" because she knows the comparison involves more than simply sorting horsepower ratings. Cost, in particular, is key. If these cars cost the same, the sales ratio would likely be considerably different.

The lesson is to follow the money. If Ford engineers forget why people are buying the Taurus, they may err in designing new cars, pricing their vehicles so high that the buyer either can't afford the car or realizes that at that price, he can shop at quite a few more car manufacturers. Likewise, if Mercedes designers lose track of why people buy S-class luxury cars they will alienate their customer base. Suffice it to say, rich people do not like to waste money any more than the less fortunate.

This lesson translates well to computers. Designing the "fastest computer in the world" is a great deal of fun for the designers, but it is an engineering joyride reserved for very few. The rest of us must design machines that accomplish their tasks within first-order economic constraints.

In an insidious way, microprocessor vendors who succumb to the allure of trying to be the fastest computer will win in the near term, but they will lose in the long run, a decade or more down the road. The reason is simple: Only a small market—at most a couple of million units a year—will pay large premiums to keep a niche vendor afloat. A user base that small cannot support the design costs of world-class microprocessors, not to mention the cost of state-of-the-art IC processing plants (fabrication plants, or fabs). When that vendor is inexorably driven out of business by these extraordinarily high costs, the mainstream, cost-constrained vendor is still there. And with one or two more turns of the Moore's Law wheel, that mainstream vendor inherits the mantle of "world's fastest" without having even tried for it.

Voltaire is often credited with the saying, "The Best is the enemy of Good," which means that myopic striving toward an unreachable perfection may, in fact, yield a worse final result than accepting compromises on the way to a successful product. Everyone wants their product to be the best; achieving that is great for both your career and your bank account. The trap is that taking what appears to be the shortest path to that goal—technical excellence to the exclusion of all else—can easily prevent you from reaching it. In plainer terms, if you do not make money at this game, you do not get to keep playing.

The Unbreakable Computer

Several of us P6 architects were interested in designing a computer that would never crash. Anyone who has experienced the utter frustration of a particularly inopportune system crash will empathize. As computer systems visions go, this one is killer. No matter what happens, no matter what breaks in the hardware or the software, the machine can slow down, but it can't stop working. That would be nice, wouldn't it?

That hardware designers have no control over the operating system or the applications should have shown us an upper bound on system stability that fell far short of our "unbreakable" vision. But even things we *could* control stubbornly refused to configure into anything approaching unbreakability. Permit me a Bill Nye moment (you know, the science guy with the great jingle): Electrically speaking, we live in a noisy, hostile universe.

Electromagnetic waves of all frequencies and amplitudes are constantly bombarding people and computing equipment. Very energetic charged particles from the Big Bang or cosmic events collide with atoms in the atmosphere to generate streams of high-energy neutrons, some of which end up smashing into the silicon of microprocessors and generating unexpected electrical currents. Temperatures and power supplies fluctuate. Internal electrical currents generate capacitive and inductive sympathetic currents in adjacent wires. The universe really does conspire against us.

The universe really does conspire against us.

On the basis of the statistics we observe from these and other events, we design recovery mechanisms into our microprocessors. If one of these unfortunate events occurs, the machine can detect the anomaly and correct the resulting error before it can propagate and cause erroneous data to enter the computation stream.

Error detection and correction schemes have their dark side, however. They impose an overhead in performance and complexity and a real cost in die size. Worse, although they help make the machine more reliable, they are not foolproof. For example, if an error correcting code is applied across a section of memory, then, typically, a single-bit error will be correctable, but if two bits are defective, our scheme will note that fact but be unable to correct it. And if more than two bits are erroneous, our scheme may not even notice that any of them are wrong.

The most stringent constraint on the ability to design an unbreakable engine, though, is that while the "state space" of a correctly functioning microprocessor is enormous, the possibility space of a malfunctioning machine is many orders of magnitude larger. Basically, unless you are designing an extremely simple machine, you cannot practically anticipate every way in which the machine might fail, which is what you need for a detection and recovery scheme. Moreover, even if you could somehow catalog and sandbag every single-event failure, it still would not be good enough. Failures can and do occur in pairs, or triples, or n-tuples.

Perhaps the day will come when a very different approach to this problem will present some affordable solutions, but today the best we can do is buttress the machine against its clearest threats and test it extensively and as exhaustively as human resources will permit.

Machine reliability raises some interesting philosophical issues, though. If an error is detected, should the machine attempt to roll back to a previous saved (presumably correct) state and restart from there, hoping that this time the error will not manifest? Many databases have this capability. Indeed, the Pentium 4 has an equivalent, in that forward progress of the engine is self-monitored, and if too much time has elapsed since forward progress was last detected, a watchdog timer will flush the machine and restart it from a known-good spot.

So although a rollback approach will work in some scenarios, in many others its success will be questionable. A four-CPU system, for example, has up to 12 caches among the CPUs, all controlled via the MESI (Modified-Exclusive-Shared-Invalid) protocol, a coherence scheme in which caches trade information as necessary to ensure overall consistency. But if just one of these caches were to fail in such a way that that cache's local error-correction mechanism could not fix, all four CPUs (the entire machine) would be potentially compromised, because the broken cache could have contained data that simply was not anywhere else in the system.

After considering some fairly aggressive schemes to improve system reliability, we finally decided to do conservative improvements to Intel's previous "machine check architectures," checking and reporting on errors, but making no heroic attempts to roll back to presumably safe checkpoints, and making no promises to users along those lines. Maybe some day we will.

Performance-Monitoring Facilities

As recently as the 1980s, computers were still being implemented with ICs of such limited complexity that it took many hundreds of them to comprise a system. Interconnecting so many separate chips meant that the printed circuit boards (PCBs) had to carry thousands of wires. And while these chips and interconnects meant higher manufacturing cost and possibly an impact on system reliability, having easy access to them during debug and test was an unalloyed blessing. Test equipment vendors such as Hewlett-Packard and Tektronix sold logic analyzers that could collect digital information from anywhere in the machine. If the system was malfunctioning, a technician could track down the problem by following the symptoms wherever they led. Likewise, if a performance analyst wanted to know how often a given functional unit was being used, she could attach her test equipment directly to that functional unit and simply monitor it.

Then, along came microprocessors. Early microprocessors were not so bad. Lacking substantial internal state such as caches and branch prediction tables, these CPUs had to signal all their activities on their buses. If they needed the next instruction, you could see the request on the bus and the memory's response to that request. True, you could no longer just attach your logic analyzer and watch the program counters sequencing merrily by, but the machine could not go too far awry before giving unmistakable clues on the bus.

To enhance performance, microprocessors began including internal caches in the late 1980s and branch prediction tables shortly thereafter. Modern microprocessors can have several megabytes of cache, more than enough for the processor to execute thousands or even millions of instructions before any external evidence of what the processor is actually doing appears on the frontside bus. If something went wrong at instruction N, and the engineer trying to debug it does not learn of the malfunction until instruction N plus one million, that engineer is about to have a bad day.

At Multiflow Computer, we had included a set of performance-monitoring facilities directly in the computer itself. With no recourse to logic analyzers, you could get the machine's diagnostic processor to "scan out" the performance-monitoring information and present it in a variety of useful ways. After having used and loved that facility for several years, Dave Papworth and I resolved to provide something similar in any future designs, especially microprocessors, in which overall visibility is the most restricted.

Counters and Triggers. For the P6, we therefore proposed and implemented a set of hardware counters and trigger mechanisms. Our intention was to provide enough flexibility so that the performance analyst could set up the performance counter conditions in many ways to help zero in on whatever microarchitectural corner case was turning out to be the bottleneck in his code. But we could not spend a lot of die area on the facility, and we absolutely wanted to avoid introducing any functionality bugs associated with the performance counter apparatus.

Intel eventually commissioned a software group to create a good user interface to these performance counter facilities. Their program is called VTUNE, and is of tremendous value to programmers tuning their code for maximum performance.

We designed the performance counter facility originally for ourselves, with an eye toward minimizing die size and designer time. (Yes, we had to sneak these features in, and you can only do that if overall impact is very small.) We asked the designers of various chip units to provide for measurements of certain features, which they dutifully did. Unfortunately, sometimes they had to use signals that had already been qualified with other signals; some measurements would include certain global stalling conditions, whereas others might not, for example. This sometimes led to user confusion.

Some of the items we architects wanted to measure were so detailed and deep in the machine that, for users to actually understand them, we would have had to publish much more than prudent intellectual property guardianship would allow. We chose not to publicize these because they were simply not going to be of much use to anyone outside Intel.

Protecting the Family Jewels. Another problem we had was one of the major performance-related things any programmer would want to do: correlate the micro-op stream to the assembly language stream that spawned it. That correlation is fundamental to the way P6 works, and the performance-monitoring facility could provide the micro-op information required. The only problem was that this was tantamount to publishing our microcode. The programmer merely had to generate a program with every x86 instruction in it and VTUNE would report the microcode streams corresponding to each. But Intel's microcode was considered part of the family jewels, so exposing it at this level was out of the question.

I proposed a compromise. For any x86 instruction that mapped into a single micro-op, VTUNE would accurately report the mapping. After all, for these simple operations, what the micro-op must do was no mystery. But for complex instructions, VTUNE would report only the first four micro-ops and how many others were required to realize a given complex x86 instruction. Performance-sensitive code would not normally use these complex x86 instructions anyway, and if it did, programmers would be unable to change anything about the micro-op stream even if they wanted to. This is still how VTUNE operates today.

Testability Hooks

In the late 1990s, the Focused Ion Beam (FIB) tool debuted, and for the first time silicon debuggers could make limited changes to the chip. This capability was and still is supremely important because design bugs are extremely good at hiding other bugs. Suppose, for example, that a bug is in the floating-point load-converter unit (FPLCU). Until that unit performs its job properly, you cannot test the floating-point adder, multiplier, divider, and so on. Without an FIB tool, a failing diagnostic would have led the technician to the FPLCU, but he would have had to stop there and place all floating-point tests offline until the FPLCU was fixed on a new silicon stepping. Getting that new stepping could easily take three to six weeks, depending on how busy the fab plant was with current production.

Now suppose the floating-point multiplier also had a bug. The time to get silicon with a working floating-point multiply would probably be closer to 17 weeks—two weeks to identify the FPLCU bug, a week to conceive and implement the fix for it in RTL, six weeks to get the new stepping back from the fab plant, a week for further testing, a week to find and resolve the new floating-point multiply bug, and six more weeks to get *that* stepping back. An FIB machine lets you reach in and fix or work around the FPLCU bug, so the floating-point multiply bug hiding behind it becomes apparent.

We were not sure we would have an FIB tool in the P6 generation, so to help expose bugs hiding behind other bugs and generally give engineers more tools during debugging, we gave the P6 an extensive set of debug/testability hooks. Our intention was that for any feature that was not crucial to the chip's basic functioning, there should be a way to turn it off and run without it.

An example is the "fast string move" capability in the P6 microcode, which had an extremely complex implementation. We worried that, despite all our presilicon testing, some piece of real code might cause it to fail, so we wanted a way to turn it off and revert to the existing known-correct string-handling microcode if necessary.

We tried to minimize power dissipation in the P6 by not clocking any units that did not absolutely need it, but we worried that the designers could easily have missed something in the logic that handles the power-down circumstances. To make us feel better, we provided a separate power-down-disable control bit for every unit.

A truly insidious psychological artifact rears its ugly head in designing perfomance-monitoring facilities. Designers and validators are very, very busy people. They routinely miss important family events and give up holidays, weekends, and evenings attempting to keep their part of the overall design on schedule. They, therefore, value their time and energy highly, and ruthlessly triage their to-do lists. When items appear on those lists that are not clearly and directly tied to any of the major project goals, those items inevitably become bottom feeders. Consequently, they get less time during design, which implies that they are probably less well thought out than the mainstream functionality. By then there is less time to validate them, and the validators are always way behind schedule at this point, so these items also get less testing than they deserve.

Moreover, during debugging, performance-monitoring facilities that are not working quite right will not hold up the activities of very many people. That's not to say that debuggers do not depend on their tools. If the testability hooks intended to speed debugging are themselves buggy, the confusion they generate can easily outweigh the value they bring.

The only way I have ever found to ensure that performance monitoring and testability hooks get properly implemented and tested is to anoint a special czar, whose job is to accomplish that. Without that czar, the shoemaker's children will still go barefoot.

GRATUITOUS INNOVATION CONSIDERED HARMFUL

Engineers fresh from college are uniformly bright, inquisitive, enthusiastic, and clue-challenged, in the sense that they are somewhat preconditioned to the wrong things. Perhaps at some point in the college education of every engineer (myself included), someone put us in a deep hypnotic trance while a voice chanted, "You are a creative individual. No matter what someone else has designed, you can do it better, and you will be wildly rewarded for it." Or maybe new engineers just lack the experience to know what has been done before and can be successfully reused, versus what is no longer appropriate and must be redesigned. Whatever the reason, almost all new engineers tend to err on the side of designing everything themselves, from scratch, unless schedule or an attentive boss stops them from doing so.

This disease, which I call "gratuitous innovation," stems from confusion in a designer's mind as to why he is being paid. New engineers think they are paid to bring new ideas and infuse stodgy design teams with fresh thinking, and they do contribute a great deal. But many of them lose sight of an important bottom line: They are paid to help create

> *"Gratuitous innovation" stems from confusion in a designer's mind as to why he is being paid.*

profitable products, period.[1] From a corporate perspective, creating a wildly profitable product with little new innovation is a wonderful idea because it minimizes both risk and investment.

Engineers who understand that the goal is a profitable product, not self-serving new-patent lists or gratuitous innovation, will spend much more time dwelling on the real problems the company and product face. To be sure, in some cases, new ideas will bring about a much better final product than simply tweaking what has already been done, but my experience is that unless you restrain the engineers somehow, they will migrate en masse to the innovation buffet.

An example is the design of microprocessor circuits. Integral to any such design are catalogs of cell libraries, existing designs that accomplish some list of desired functions. The library may contain more than one entry for accomplishing a given function, with one entry optimized for speed and another for die size. Engineers who are optimizing their design for reuse can often find existing cell-library components. Engineers who are optimizing their design for their career (whether real or only perceived because their managers know this game) will tend to insist on creating custom cell libraries, thinking that only in that way will they end up with their names on patents.

It can be fun to get wooden plaques bearing the seal of the U.S. Patent Office and your name, but it's much more fun, and ultimately much more lucrative for all concerned, to concentrate on the product and its needs. Real innovation is what attracts many of us to engineering in the first place. Never confuse it with the gratuitous version, which only adds risk to the overall endeavor.

VALIDATION AND MODEL HEALTH

So far, I have devoted this chapter to the architects and design engineers with a few validation mentions here and there. I am about to correct any misunderstanding about that: The real work of validation is concentrated in the realization phase, and the primary task is to drive the RTL model to good health and then keep it there.

A Thankless Job

Corporate management has a difficult job overseeing microprocessor development. Projects like P6 and Willamette take 4+ years of efforts by hundreds of people, cost hundreds of millions of dollars, and potentially affect company revenues by many tens of billions of dollars. If things are not going well in a development effort, managers want to know as early as possible so that corrective actions can be taken.

As the RTL model develops, upper management can collect statistics such as number of new RTL lines written per week and track that running total against the original esti-

---

[1] I once learned this same lesson in an entirely different guise. I was playing guitar in a band, and we liked playing tunes from the band Chicago. One night, several horn players from a local college sat in with us and man, we thought we were hot. The crowd overflowed the bar; standing room only, all night. At the end of the night, the bar owner said he wanted to talk to us. We thought he was going to lavish praise on us, but instead he said "You guys need to understand something. I don't pay you to provide great music. I pay you because the folks who buy the expensive drinks like to have music. Those people are 40-year-olds, not the 20-somethings you packed in here tonight, who nurse one ginger ale for three hours. Don't ever do that again."

mates of how many lines are needed to fully implement the committed functionality. The original estimates are usually too low and managers continuously revise them upward as the project matures. These revisions tend to be predictable, and you can make reasonably accurate extrapolations for final RTL size surprisingly early in the project.

But when the same upper management focus turns to presilicon validation, difficulties abound. The validation plan shows all the tests that must be run successfully before taping out, and there is a running total of all tests that have run successfully, but neither is terribly helpful. You cannot simply measure the difference between them, nor can you simply extrapolate from the improvement trend.

When the validation plan is conceived at the project's beginning, its designers try to account for all that is known at that time by asking questions, such as

- Which units will be new, and which will be inherited unchanged from a previous design?
- What is each new unit's intrinsic degree of difficulty?
- What is the most effective ratio of handwritten torture tests versus the number of less-efficient but much more voluminous random-test cycles on each unit, and on the chip as a whole?
- What surprises are likely to arise during RTL development, and what fraction of overall validation effort should be held in reserve against such an eventuality?
- How long will each bug sighting take, and how long will it take to resolve them?
- What role will new validation techniques play in the new chip (formal verification, for example)?

During RTL development, upper management was clearly unhappy about how their quick-and-dirty, validation-progress metric was behaving. Perhaps more to the point, they were unhappy that the fraction of the original validation plan that was being accomplished week by week was not shrinking on any acceptable trendline; in fact, it appeared that the fraction of overall weekly validation effort was shrinking, not growing, because the validation team was alertly adding new testing to the plan as they learned more about the design, and the plan was growing faster than the list of now-running tests. In effect, for a while it looked as though the validation effort was falling behind by 1.1 days for every day that went by.

After a week of unproductive meetings on the topic, management asked us to conceive a metric that we would be willing to work toward, one that would show constant (if not linear) progress toward the quality metric required for the chip to tape out.

Choosing a Metric

We proposed a "health-of-the-model" (HOTM) metric that took into account what seemed to me, Bob Bentley, and his team, to be the five most important indicators of model development, and we weighted them as seemed appropriate:

1. **Regression results.** How successful were the most recent regression runs?
2. **Time to debug.** How many different failure modes were present, and how long did it take to analyze them?
3. **Forward progress.** To what extent was previously untried functionality tested in the latest model?

4. **High-priority bugs.** Number of open bugs of high or fatal severity.

5. **Age of open bugs.** Are bugs languishing?

We then began tracking and reporting this HOTM metric for the rest of the project.

The fair amount of subjectivity in these indicators was intentional. We recognized that the strong tendency is to "get what you measure," and we did not want the HOTM metric to distort the validation team's priorities until we had accumulated enough experience with it to know if it was leading us in the right direction. Because we were the ones who had conceived the validation plan, we knew it was a very valuable, yet necessarily limited, document. Despite our best efforts to be comprehensive and farsighted, if history was any guide, we would discover that some parts of the validation plan would place too much emphasis on some part of the design that turned out not to need it, while other parts would turn out to be the most problematic and require much more validation effort than we had expected. We did not want to find ourselves unable to respond appropriately to such exigencies on the sole basis of some document we ourselves had written, knowing only what we knew two or three years ago.

Another reason for the metric's substantial subjectivity had to do with managing your manager. I believe there is a generally well-placed but occasionally extremely dangerous penchant within Intel to insist on quantifiable data only. It is simply corporate culture that if someone asks, "Is this chip's performance projection on track?" the preferred answer has the form, "A best-fit linear extrapolation of the last 6 weeks of data indicates a probability of 0.74 with a standard deviation of 0.61," not, "The indicators say we're marginally on track, but my instincts and experience say there's a problem here."

Management wanted to know when the chip would be ready to tape out, and they did not want to hear that the chip would tape out when the design team, the project leaders, and the validation team all agreed it was ready. They wanted a mechanical way of checking that all pieces were trending toward success. Then they could confidently reserve the right to "shoot the engineers" (see the section "Of Immediate Concern" in Chapter 5) and unilaterally declare tapeout.

Health and the Tapeout Target

The problem is that judging the health of a chip design database is not so easy. You can pick a metric at the project's beginning and then measure against it every week, but the metric itself is subject to revision as the weeks roll on, and it is not easy to go back, add something to the metric, and extract the necessary data from the old records. Basically, whatever metric you pick at the beginning is what you are stuck with throughout. You can revise the weightings, but even that is problematical.

The RTL model achieves its full functionality only toward the end of the development cycle, and the validation team can no-holds-barred test only that mature model. When a bug is found and fixed, you should assume that the fix may break something that used to work, but you cannot repeat every test ever run on the project. Again, judgment is required to know how much additional testing is appropriate, given particular design errata.

We picked a score of 95 as our tapeout target, knowing that upper management could eventually hold this score against us. As big, expensive chip development projects near completion, a kind of tapeout frenzy tends to break out in the design team as well as across the management chain. On the plus side, it inspires all concerned to do whatever it takes to finish the job. On the minus side it encourages management to sometimes discount the opinions of technical people, especially opinions that they do not want to hear, such as, "This chip is still too buggy. It needs at least three more weeks of testing." It is a management truism that a "shoot the engineers" phase of any design project is necessary, because without it engineers will continue polishing and tweaking well past the point of diminishing returns. By picking a fairly lofty target, we hoped we were placing it sufficiently out of reach so that we would never face the problem of having management wave our indicator at us and say, "You said this score was good enough to tape out, so you have no right to make it any higher now. Tape this thing out."

Metric Doldrums

Our HOTM metric did not behave as intended. We had hoped that if we weighted the five indicators properly, the overall score would start low and climb linearly week by week toward the final score that would suggest our new RTL was tapeout ready. What actually happened was that the overall score did start low and climb for awhile, but then it stubbornly parked for many weeks at an intermediate value that seemed much too low for anyone to accept as being of tapeout quality.

After several weeks of watching the HOTM score languish, I began upping the pressure on my validation manager, Bob Bentley. Bob patiently but firmly reminded me of all the pieces built into the metric and showed me how the RTL status and new changes were affecting each one. That made sense in isolation, but we had created this metric so that we could feel comforted as the model's quality visibly climbed toward acceptability, and now that it *wasn't* climbing, my comfort level was dropping precipitously.

Finally, at one of these meetings Bob said (not so patiently), "Okay. You are pushing on the wrong thing here by pressuring validation. We don't put the bugs in. We just find them and report them." He was absolutely right. I turned my attention to the design

Validation does not put the bugs in. They just find them and report them.

team, its coding methods, individual testing, and code-release criteria, and we made many changes that immediately began paying off in terms of overall design quality.

The HOTM metric never did linearly climb to 95, but it started moving after that, so, in retrospect, I think it was a good exercise. Intel has since revised the HOTM many times to make it more useful as a project-guidance mechanism.

COORDINATING WITH OTHER PROJECTS

Another characteristic of the realization phase is that the project is no longer in a corporate vacuum. Its visibility has increased to the point that other projects are not just reading about it; they are comparing their own design projects to its official goals and methods. This exercise is vital, for several reasons.

The first and most important is that customers like to think that a big company like Intel has put a lot of corporate thought into creating and coordinating their various product offerings. They expect that the overall road map will be coherent and will allow them to design systems that will form their customer's road map later on. If Intel puts multiple products into the same product space, it confuses the customers, and if those customers are foolish enough to design competing systems around them, the customers of the customers will also get confused.

Coordinating multiple design projects is also important because it can mean the difference between a potentially helpful interteam synergy or a destructive internecine turf war over influence with support groups, feature developments in common tool sets, and marketing campaign money. Big companies would like to believe that by fielding multiple teams, they are casting a bigger net over the design space; coordinating these teams is just collecting the best known methods from all of them and making those available to everyone.

In large companies like Intel, multiple design teams concurrently operate in various locations worldwide. Few are ever commissioned to directly compete with one another in the same product space; more often, each team's output is expected to fill some important hole in the product road map a few years hence. But the performance and feature sets of the various chips under development must be compared somehow, precisely so that the management and marketing teams can ensure that the overall corporate road map will make sense to the customers. This is a much more difficult task than it may appear.

Comparing two chip developments gives rise to several first-order issues. One is performance estimation, which I look at in the next section. Another is methodology: the simulators used, how they work, and their sources of possible inaccuracies. Design teams will have different beliefs about what is "best," and it's a virtual certainty that what one team considers an absolute requirement in a tool or design methodology will be rejected as anathema by another. And never underestimate the unpredictability of human psychology, which can easily subdue any rational technical decision.

Performance Estimation

Early in the project, when all you have are grand plans and a little data, performance estimation is an uncertain art form. Nonetheless, it is an art form you must engage in. Early estimations are crucial, even if they do show enough variability to warrant the scale dismal to stellar.

This uncertainty stems from many sources. When a design project is young, many of its major functional blocks are still in rough form. No one knows each block's ultimate contribution to overall performance; in fact, no one yet knows if a given block is buildable at all. Interactions between the various blocks are not yet fully understood. At higher levels of abstraction, there may be compiler, software library, and operating system developments that ultimately will affect delivered performance, but for now all you can do is guess at them.

The Overshooting Scheme. Dave Sager is a brilliant computer designer who was one of the principal architects of the Pentium 4. With many years of computer design experience, Dave has come to believe that the task of conceiving, refining, and realizing a computer microarchitecture is a process of judiciously overshooting in selective areas of the design, in the resigned but practical expectation that various unwelcome realities will later intrude. These surprises will take many forms, but the one common element is that they will almost never be in your favor. That clever new branch-prediction scheme you are so proud of will turn out to be a very poor fit to some newly emerged benchmarks. Your register-renaming mechanism, which looked so promising in isolated testing, will turn out to require much more die area than you had hoped, and the circuit folks will be engaged in hand-to-hand combat to make it meet the required clock speed.

Given that surprises will occur and will not be in your favor, your overall plan had better be able to accommodate any required change. Dave's overdesign approach assumes that you will eventually be forced to back off on implementation aggressiveness, or you will realize that the designs just do not work as well as you had hoped, either in isolation or in combination with other parts. He proposes that you not approach such thinking as if it were a contingency plan—that such eventualities are almost a certainty, given the complexity and schedule pressures of contemporary designs.

In essence, Dave's theory is that if the absolute drop-dead project performance goal is 1.3× some existing target, then your early product concept microarchitecture ought to be capable of some much higher number like 1.8×, to give you the necessary cushion to keep your project on track.

With both P6 and Willamette, we did, in fact, go through a process much like Dave's anticipated sequence:

- Early performance estimates are optimistic, and as performance projections gradually get more accurate, they yield a net loss in expected product performance.
- As the design team continues implementation, they constantly face implementation decisions that trade off performance, die size, schedule, and power. Over time, the cumulative effect of all these small trade-offs is a noticeable net loss in performance.
- Projected die size tends to grow continuously from the same root causes so, eventually, the project faces a double threat with no degrees of freedom left from which to seek relief.

When we reached this state in P6, we basically suspended the project for two weeks, purposely placing the performance analysis team's concerns on project center stage. Anyone not directly engaged in the performance war was tasked with finding ways to reduce die size. These "all hands on deck" exercises actually work quite well, and tend to give everyone a chance to step back from their daily grind and revisit the bigger picture. With that new vantage point, they can often spot things that would otherwise have gone unnoticed.

Not every team can follow Dave's suggestion. Sometimes, it is all a team can do to even get close to the requested performance target, let alone try to overshoot it. The schedule may not let you innovate in the microarchitecture area, or the team may be comprised solely of circuits experts unqualified to tackle architecture. Of course, the corollary to Dave's thesis is that if you do not purposely try to overshoot, and the customary bad news does arrive at your project's doorstep, you may end up with a nonviable product. Dave's suggestion is to face that issue at the beginning of the project, before a lot of time and money have been invested in it.

But even if every one of these design teams could successfully follow Dave's mandate, the teams would still disagree on important issues, and these differences of opinion directly influence their respective performance projections. Different slots in the road map can and do emphasize different applications; the large transactional database applications that rule the server domain are anathema to the mobile laptop space, for example. So if two teams wanted to compare their designs so as to inform corporate management, neither would let the other dictate the benchmarks to be used in the competition.

Server, desktop, and mobile product spaces do overlap, however, and it makes good sense to at least do sanity checks among them. If a part being designed for a different market segment happens to outshine the mainline part on some important application, that is as clear an early warning signal as any development project is ever going to get.

Psychological Stuff. Although it seems to surprise the public every time it happens, well-intentioned and well-educated experts can start with the same basic set of facts and reach opposite conclusions. In the same sense, performance simulations, especially the early ones, require a great deal of interpretation and are thus subject to the whims and personalities of their wielders. Some design teams are conservative and will not commit to any target that they are not sure they can hit. (Our Pentium Pro team was one of these, at least partly because Randy Steck, Fred Pollack, and I believed in this approach so strongly.) Other Intel teams had internalized company politics and reflected that understanding in their performance goals—promise them what they ask for now; if you later fall short, they will have forgotten about it, and even if they haven't, you can apologize later. Besides, tomorrow may never come.[2] Still other teams would aggressively choose the highest numbers from any uncertainty ranges and if necessary stack these rose-colored-glasses numbers end to end, on the grounds that (a) they are very smart people, (b) there is plenty of time left before project's end, and (c) nobody can *prove* the numbers cannot turn out this way.

We sometimes faced hostile management questioning along the lines of "Team Z has officially accepted a goal of delivering performance not much different from yours in less time, with less money. Why should I keep funding your project?" We tended to reply with "You don't have a problem with *our* project. You have a problem with *theirs*." A long moment would then ensue with said manager looking doleful and dubious. After all, he liked their story better than ours. Management would then direct us to go reconcile our differences with Project Z and report back as to which team had had to change their official plan-of-record (POR). Almost always, after a perfunctory attempt at reconciling the two points of view, neither team changed anything, and we would all forget about the episode until it repeated about six months later.

> *You don't have a problem with* **our** *project. You have a problem with* **theirs.**

I wish I could offer bulletproof, hard-won advice on this topic that anyone could follow and avoid the unpleasantness implied above, but I can't. When I was a boy, my mother warned me that I could not change anyone else's behavior, just my own. In the same way, I believe strongly that engineers must think straight and talk straight: tell themselves and their management the truth as best as they can.

If some other project cheats on this process, your project leaders will get an opportunity to point out these discrepancies, and then upper management must act, or at least actively interpret each project's predictions as needed.

Simulator Wars

Our P6 development demonstrated the value of simulators for performance projections to Intel management and technical ranks. The original Pentium chip was a relatively simple

---

[2]That sentiment was expressed by a leader of one of the company's other design teams. It was said over the second beer of a three-beer discussion, which is often the moment of truth.

extrapolation from the earlier 486 chip, and its presilicon performance tool consisted of a spreadsheet combining some rules of thumb about the machine's microarchitecture with other rules of thumb about the benchmarks.

As I described earlier (see the section "A Data-Driven Culture" in Chapter 2), we began the P6 project by writing our own performance modeling tool, a simulator of sorts, called the dataflow analyzer (DFA). This program started out as a very general out-of-order-execution analyzer, but that in itself made it useful only to the P6 project. Those of us who wrote this tool and used it to make performance projections eventually achieved some level of confidence in it, but engineers outside the project had no real basis on which to understand it or use it for comparative performance studies in their own designs.

By the mid-1990s, we had real P6 silicon and could directly calibrate DFA's predictions. But by then we were beginning the Willamette (Pentium 4) design and were finding that the basic differences between the Willamette and P6 engines were such that we had to invest a lot of software design effort to make DFA useful to Willamette and, in fact, ended up calling it NDFA, for "new" DFA. In hindsight, although DFA was a brilliant success for P6, for Willamette we should have dumped DFA and used a custom simulator; it would have been more efficient and accurate overall.

Most of us were uncomfortable with how difficult Willamette's NDFA was turning out to be, but few of us had the software skills to actually do something about the problem. One of us did: Mike Haertel complained long and loud about the problem, and when it became clear to him that we were going to try to stay with NDFA rather than formally commissioning what we believed would be an even riskier start-from-scratch simulator, he asked if he could write one himself. It is not uncommon for bright, creative engineers to become frustrated with their tools, to convince themselves that they could do much better, and to importune management to let them try. Sometimes, this is simply a case of hardware designers thinking software is easy. Most of the time, it seemed to me that they probably *could* do better, but it would take much more time than they were assuming, so it would be better for the project for them to continue tolerating the tool's shortcomings than to drop their project responsibilities while they fixed it.

But Mike Haertel was not the usual dissatisfied engineer. Given his outstanding skills in both hardware and software design, if he said he could write the simulator in a certain amount of time, then he probably could.

I decided to let him proceed, but with the proviso that his new simulator had to work quickly or we would abandon it quickly. I reasoned that if his simulator ideas turned out to be unworkable, we would not have made a large investment, and his new simulator had to be accurate with respect to the Willamette microarchitecture for it to be worth doing at all.

Mike pulled it off in eye-popping fashion. He called his new simulator "Willy" and convincingly showed its intrinsic advantages over NDFA. He even had a better user interface. The Willamette architects loved it.

But we should have known that nothing is ever easy. At exactly the same time we were getting used to Willy, we were informed that a central research group in the company had just created the New Standard Simulator Which We All Must Use (NSSWWAMU), and were politely given the proverbial offer we could not refuse. Willy was obviously redundant and a symptom of old-fashioned thinking. The new simulator was already standard everywhere in the company except our little Oregon outpost, and our upper management was squarely behind this standardization initiative. So get with the program, please.

Now, corporate "everyone do things the same way, please" initiatives are not new.

They appear with regularity every six months or so, and some actually yield real results. Others are an annoying distraction from the real work of designing competitive microprocessors. The way I routinely handled the second category of initiatives was to ignore them for awhile. If the ideas turned out to be not particularly well thought out and had appeared only because someone was running them up the flagpole to see if anyone would salute, they would go away on their own if left to age properly. By sitting on them for a while, I prevented the company from siphoning off people or focus from my project.

With both NDFA and Willy online, I felt no need for yet another simulator, so at first I tried giving this initiative my standard second-category treatment. After several months, however, it became clear that real people with real energy were behind this new simulator, and they had spent those months enlisting allies, including my upper management. The politeness went away, but the insistence did not. These folks were not easily discouraged.

I next tried my Backup Gambit B: Show that the new initiative, brilliant though it may be, did not apply to my particular project, so please come back in a few years when we start something new. Because we were the only design team in the company pursuing new out-of-order microarchitectures, we had so far escaped any corporate initiative for any new simulators well suited to out-of-order designs, which this new simulator was not. Unfortunately for Gambit B, it did not take much work by the NSSWWAMU folks to remove this objection.

So I resorted to Gambit C: Like the second-category treatment, C was a delaying tactic that gave at least the appearance, if not the reality, of taking the NSSWWAMU simulator out for a test spin. I asked Michael Fetterman, who like Mike Haertel is one of those rare people equally gifted at software development and microarchitecture design, to go investigate this new corporate simulator and make a recommendation as to how we could not reasonably be expected to use it. Unfortunately, Michael concluded that though Willy was a direct match for our project (which was no surprise, considering its origins) the corporate simulator could be made to do what our project needed, given enough time and effort to make the switch. Fortunately, by this time, the Willamette project was far enough along that this effort was no longer a direct threat to our project schedule, which was a good thing, too, because I was out of gambits.

PROJECT MANAGEMENT

Having just delved into the psychological realm and exposed the occasional irrationality and unpredictability of microarchitecture design and development, it seems fitting to segue into project management. I will revisit people issues in more depth later (in "The People Factor," Chapter 6), but the realization phase of a project is the quintessentially management-driven part of a project, and it seems more appropriate to talk about some of the project management foibles here.

Awards, Rewards, and Recognition

I once took an Intel management course in which the instructor, Bill Daniels, told the class that he was a behavioral psychologist who knew what people would do, even though he did not know why. He gave the example of praise. People, according to Bill, respond in a predictable way to praise: They like it. Through his studies, he had identified the most efficacious times and methods for bestowing praise on coworkers or subordinates (or bosses). It surprised him that even telling people ahead of time they would be set up for praise did not seriously diminish its effectiveness once they got it. He then gave our class some minimal task at which we all

> *People respond in a predictable way to praise: They like it.*

succeeded and told us how well we had done and that he was pleased with us. Presto, the room was instantly full of beaming people, just as he had predicted.

Engineers are perhaps even more susceptible to this kind of benign manipulation because of their innate parsimony. When an advertiser wants to know how well their latest ads are succeeding, they commission a survey of the intended audience. We engineers get so many of these surveys that even if we wanted to, we could not participate in all of them, so some advertisers have taken to inserting a crisp new dollar bill in the survey envelope. This additional financial incentive does not create more hours in our day, nor is it even close to the amount it would take to fairly compensate us for the 15 minutes we will have to invest in the survey. Yet that dollar bill works—no engineer is going to throw it away (an unforgivable waste), and having accepted it, will feel duty bound to complete the survey.

Finding the right incentives to get a large design team to its maximum output and then keep it there for years is crucial to a project's success. Obviously, getting paid for work done is a key motivator, and design teams are full of professionals who will always try to give a day's work for day's pay. But if that is all management is getting from their team, real trouble is afoot.

The difference between getting maximum output from a team and getting only a day's work for a day's pay cannot be overstated. An absolute requirement for achieving a world-class product is a design team that is fully committed at every level and at all hours. Sound technical ideas I have had or have witnessed others contributing have come during showers or while walking around aim-

> *The difference between getting maximum output from a team and getting only a day's work for a day's pay cannot be overstated.*

lessly or driving—any activity other than sitting at a desk actively pondering the problem. Something about being outside the pressurized corporate environment while engaged in a task that can be performed without your entire consciousness tends to free up the creative muse and let the really good ideas bubble up into view. (Yes, driving *ought* to be done with your entire consciousness, but empirical evidence and the preponderance of cell phones on the ears of one-handed drivers suggest that such focus is seldom achieved.) When your design team is routinely reporting creative solutions to their troubles, and a large fraction of those are coming from pondering in off-hours moments, you know that your team is fully engaged and giving the design everything they have.

So what motivates a team to go above and beyond the call of duty, to think it worth pondering a problem during mundane activities? Career advancement is one reason. A team's top producers are, in effect, investing their time and energy speculatively, trusting in the team's management to notice their standout performance and take the appropriate action when the time comes, be that promotion, pay raises, or stock options.

But for most people, an even stronger incentive than "What's in it for me?" is "What will my peers think?" The act of engineering a product is pitting your training, talent, intellect, and ability against both competitors and nature itself. This is the draw and the scary part of an engineering career, since no matter how many times you have succeeded at similar projects, the current project could always turn out to be the one that crashes and burns because the design team came up one good idea short. And the only people on earth who really understand just how truly great your efforts have been are your peers on the same design team. Coming from a peer, a little encouragement that your design is on the right track can boost your morale and confidence more than any other incentive.

As with military organizations, large companies learn that for very little expense, a lot of good will and bottom-line output can result from organized efforts to show recognition, especially the kind you get in front of your peers. Pay raises and stock options are important, but they are private transactions. Bill Daniels had it right—there is nothing like hearing your name called in an auditorium full of your peers to make you work like a madman so that it can happen again.

The Dark Side of Awards

The flip side of recognition is that for every person for whom performance recognition generates X units of good will, you might have four or five who would like to string you up. Among those watching the jubilant engineer make her way down the auditorium aisle to receive her award are those who are bubbling with righteous indignation. Hell hath no fury like an engineer who feels his contribution was overlooked, or worse, misattributed. The rage and betrayal he evinces are awesome to behold and terrifying if directed at you.

Anger at having your work misattributed to others is common in all fields. Thomas Edison had many helpers in his lab, even if it was generally just his name on the patents [9]. Eckert and Mauchly are not household names, but the von Neumann computer architecture that we all routinely use in today's microprocessors came from them, not von Neumann. Watson and Crick discovered the double helix topography of DNA molecules and deservedly won a Nobel Prize for it, except that Rosalind Franklin should also have been named. Indeed, the one thing you can reliably predict about each new set of Nobel Prizes is that they will compel someone, somewhere to step forward and claim they were unfairly excluded.

For all the team motivation reasons just described, Intel tries hard to recognize team members who rose to the challenge during chip development projects. They follow six steps, roughly summarized below.

1. Form a group to identify candidate achievements worthy of the awards in question while not overlooking any.
2. Ask that group to prioritize these achievements, which may be as varied as an extremely clever and intricate electronic circuit or an unusually effective marketing initiative or an innovative legal maneuver.
3. Decide whose names will go on the achievements that made the cut.
4. Weigh the results in a larger context. Overrewarding one group can result in a corporate net negative overall motivation, even if that group's output appears to warrant such action.
5. Look for "firefighting by arsonists." You must not reward extraordinary efforts that only became necessary because of earlier errors by the nominees. (Yes, this does happen.)

6. Achieve all of the above without talking to the engineers themselves, because these awards work well only
when they come as a surprise.

> *Do not reward firefighting by
> arsonists.*

Number 1 is relatively easy. All managers propose their own group's list of award-
quality activities. Number 2 could be tricky. The group might decide that a clever intricate circuit is just the result of the engineers doing their job, but readily agree that what
the marketing group accomplished was truly outstanding. That would be hard to sell to
engineers who face mainly technical challenges.

Numbers 4 through 6 should be doable if the group (and the staff) has learned to communicate honestly, directly, and diplomatically. By the way, one of the reasons for the
surprise element in Number 6 is that if an engineer believes he is being considered for an
award and then doesn't get it, he now has a good idea of what was prized over his own
work. And if he doesn't agree with that prioritization, his morale asymptotically approaches zero.

Number 3 is often ridiculously hard. Achievements large enough to deserve awards are
almost always built of stepping stones. Some are so substantial that nobody would overlook them, but some are right at the border of the twin cities It-Was-Their-Job-Anyway
and Without-Them-There-Would-Be-No-Great-Achievement-Here. If you step over to
the second city, you end up with three dozen names and glaring disparities between their
relative contributions. If you step over to the first city and painstakingly identify the five
major contributors, the next 15 on the list (not having as complete a picture in front of
them) will camp on your doorstep the next day, demanding that you right this great wrong
that was visited upon them by your ineptitude or malevolence (they don't always care
which).

I had my own battle with Numbers 3 and 4 in 1995, when we decided to nominate the
P6 project for two Intel Achievement Awards, one for the microarchitecture and one for
the Pentium Pro chip itself. The IAA is Intel's top individual award. Once a year, the IAA
awards committee solicits nominations, and they go through a company-wide exercise of
Numbers 1 through 5.

A short time after the nomination, communication through back channels revealed
that the IAA awards committee was not inclined to bestow two of their awards on the
same project (see Number 4). All our project management staff except me took this as
a positive sign—convert our two nominations into one joint one, and we would be a
shoe in.

Far from agreeing, I thought this was a horrifyingly bad idea. Intel awards IAAs every
year, but large design teams come up with a new chip only every four or five years. I
found it grossly unfair to penalize such design teams by making them self-select at most
one IAA prospect every five years. Moreover, we were just finishing a mountain of architecture work that led to the P6 microarchitecture, work that we were intentionally investing on Intel's behalf so that future derivative chips could benefit from our foresight. Giving this group of architects an award that, in effect, said "Thanks. Nice Chip" would
accomplish the opposite of motivating them. It was tacit proof that upper management did
not, in fact, understand what the architects had just accomplished and, therefore, could
not possibly appreciate it properly.

So I stood my ground and refused this compromise, and even threatened to stage a
public plaque-burning ceremony if they went ahead with it anyway. In the end, we did ap-

ply for both IAAs and got both of them (deservedly, in my view: it was a darned good implementation of a darned good microarchitecture).

Back to Number 3. I was in the group that decided who got various accolades for the P6 design, and assembled the list from design, architecture, and presilicon validation names. Intel even put a nice exhibit into the microprocessor museum in their Santa Clara Robert Noyce building with a picture of the design team's leadership and the entire list of names we had supplied.

But as soon as that exhibit opened, I got a polite but pointed e-mail from a system validation manager who wanted to know why the list had not included any postsilicon validation names. I had thought that exclusion appropriate because at the time they wanted the list, the included people had already invested five years of their careers in the design, whereas the postsilicon validation effort was still getting underway. Including the postsilicon validation list would have added hundreds of names to a list that was already hundreds long. And finally, the list that had been solicited was specifically the names of the people who had created this new chip, and it would have seemed an injustice to find the name of some postsilicon validation engineer who had not, to that date, had anything to do with the chip, whereas some of the design and architecture names had not taken vacations or holidays in several years.

The validation manager had a point, though. Postsilicon validation is just as necessary as design itself, and the people who perform that vital task are very often taken for granted by all concerned. Indeed, the only time they are very clearly visible to upper management is when an important design error has eluded them and manifested itself in volume production. It is very hard to keep a team motivated when they accurately note that the only time their supervisor even notices them is when they goof (especially when they were not the ones who caused the bug to take up residence in the first place).

I felt terrible about appearing to have joined the camp of people who undervalue validation, especially at the exact moment when I most needed them to grab the baton and run with it. But, in the end, you have to draw the line somewhere. Giving out awards is an exercise in compromise no less difficult than the design itself. So I reluctantly agreed to put the line between the design team and the postsilicon validation team and hoped any damage to the relationship between those groups could be repaired later.

Difficult judgment calls like this seem impossible at the time, but after enough time has elapsed, sometimes the right call appears much clearer. This did not happen with "Do we include postsilicon validation in the design award?" Years later, I still think of it as a toss-up, with strong negatives either way.

A similar issue arose concerning the names that should go on an IAA for the conception and realization of a certain chip feature. As the nominating manager for this issue, I had to construct the list of names to go on the award. I was in deep trouble. The list was long, with no clear breakpoints, and my own name was on it.

I prioritized the list as best I could and sanity-checked it with a few other managers. On a list of 20 names, my own was twelfth. Clearly, if I were to draw the line just under my own name, there would be a strong appearance of impropriety. But it was quite clear that the twentieth name had about 1% of the overall impact as the first few names, so including all 20 was not right either.

I ultimately decided to draw the line just above my own name. Everyone higher on the list than I would be named on the award, and everyone below me (including me) would not. That way, I figured people who believed their contributions should have placed them on the award list could at least not accuse me of malfeasance.

How naive I was! One of the people at the very bottom of the list and one person who was not even on it decided that a grave injustice had been visited upon them, and they embarked on an epic quest to rectify it. For the next couple of years, one manager after another, some quite high in the management hierarchy, called me. They explained they had been approached by one or the other of these aggrieved individuals and wanted to make sure justice was being pursued. I stoically defended my position and eventually the calls stopped.

Having lost all these appeals, one person simply gave up, but the other took to simply ignoring me or throwing visual daggers, depending on his whim. I was sorry that this episode permanently soured a working relationship, but I was very glad I had the foresight to anticipate a claim of impropriety and avoid the appearance of such by leaving myself off. People can get really worked up about perceived injustices, especially those to themselves. (I know the feeling. See "How would you respond to the claim that the P6 is built on ideas stolen from Digital Equipment Corp.?" in Chapter 7.)

Project Management by Grass Cutting

Intel used to have its new managers take a series of courses intended to help them develop the skill set necessary to lead a team to a successful outcome. One exercise I vividly remember began by randomly assigning the participants to three groups: executives, middle managers, and workers. The workers were asked to remove their shoes and sit in the meeting room in just their socks. The "executives" conceived a "corporate strategy" and tried to bring it to fruition by communicating it to the middle managers. The managers converted the strategy into tactics that the workers could actually do. But the entire exercise had been contrived mainly to get these points across:

1. It is extremely difficult for executives to enunciate a clear strategy and get it across to the middle managers and their underlings without serious distortion.
2. It is very hard for the workers to understand why the executives want what they seem to be asking for, and it is not always possible for the middle managers to do a reasonable job of making the necessary translations between the executive and worker levels.
3. Knowing what motivates the workers and middle managers is crucial for the executives to have any chance of success.

What was the point of taking people's shoes? In U.S. industrial culture, you might kick your shoes off when you are alone in your cubicle, but not in a meeting. As the designers of this training session understood, not having your shoes on in an office setting makes most people very uncomfortable, and until they get them back, the issue will continue to prey on their minds. You will not get their full attention until they are prepared to give it.

Executives must provide the necessary motivation on the workers' own terms.

And the executives must provide the necessary motivation *on the workers' own terms;* those terms cannot be imposed. In other words, though the company might be organized to bestow certain financial rewards on its employees, and employees will seldom turn those down if offered, the reality is that many other forms of compensation or recognition are also effective, and you have to talk to the employees to find out what they are.

We remembered some of the lessons of these sessions when running the P6 project. Engineers who are spending every waking hour at work do not have time to go home and cut the grass, for example, so we instituted a program by which the company would pay for a grass-cutting service for qualified people. We had to justify this program repeatedly to other organizations within the company, who thought it sounded suspiciously like a boondoggle, but when we explained the motivation, they were generally mollified.

Another perquisite we tried was to provide dinners and breakfasts for engineers working late or early. The rationale was that the cost of the catering was more than offset by the increased productivity of a hundred engineers not having to leave the campus and go searching for food. The catered food was generally a healthier choice than the fast food they might have found otherwise, but the catering was also a way to continually remind the engineers that their employer noticed the sacrifices they were making for the project and that we were trying to support them in any way we could. The effect on morale was immediate.

Later in the project, we began to notice that the project was exacting a toll, not only on the engineers directly, but also on their spouses and children. It occurred to us that these people were also part of the team, and that reaching out to our extended team might have a salutary effect on our engineers. One highly successful tactic was our Thursday Family Night dinners—we invited whole families to join us at the engineers' dinner. The design team loved it because they got a rare opportunity to enjoy their family, the engineers' spouses loved it because they did not have to prepare dinner, and the kids loved it because nobody yelled at them when they returned to the dessert table for seconds.

Again, peer recognition is important to an engineer's well being. As many soldiers have written, in the final analysis, it isn't love of country or even a sense of duty that keeps them going when all else has failed; it's a commitment to the person fighting alongside them. Design engineers operating in a team feel that same commitment. Nobody wants to be the one whose effort fell short and delayed or damaged the project. Conversely, praise from one's peers is an adrenalin rush for anyone.

To encourage this productive interaction between design engineers, Randy Steck instituted the Goody Drawer. Every few weeks, a volunteer would spend a few hours shopping for geek-friendly goods such as CDs, bicycle computers, soccer balls, and coffee warmers, and stock up the Goody Drawer. When an engineer noticed something noteworthy about a peer's performance, that engineer would grab the awardee and walk them over to the Goody Drawer, where they would get to pick one of the treasures.

Engineers may complain about their compensation relative to other professionals such as physicians or lawyers, but compared with the general population, engineers are reasonably well paid. So you might not think a $20 gift would particularly excite them. But it wasn't the price of the gift that mattered. It was that a peer noticed their work and found it exemplary enough to want to draw corporate attention to it. Peer recognition is powerful indeed.

Recognition by your direct supervisor is still important, of course. You do not get a pay grade promotion by peer vote, after all. The usual meritocracy mechanisms were too long term to play a strong role during a tapeout crunch, so we relied on smaller, quicker, more direct recognitions. Any manager could, for example, decide that any employee had earned a weekend for two at a local resort. This form of recognition was particularly valuable because it rewarded both the engineer and the spouse holding things together at home, an otherwise thankless job. It garnered the employee some brownie points at home when they were most needed. We used similar mechanisms to allow someone to bestow small cash awards on an employee or a group.

It might seem as though these little rewards are too mundane to deserve much attention by project leadership, but I don't think so. When a team is really cranking at full output, every person on that team has committed their livelihood, their career, and their sacred honor to succeeding no matter what it takes. They have every right to expect their management to exude this same take-no-prisoners attitude and to look out for their welfare during the sprint to the project's end. It is an article of faith, a covenant between engineers and their managers, that is fundamental to the success of the whole enterprise. Management should welcome every opportunity to reinforce the idea that they are holding up their end of this bargain.

Marginal Return from Incremental Heads

No matter how well you plan, and no matter how hard you work, your project will inevitably run into schedule pressure. At some point in the project, you will find that your team has considerably more work to do than time left in which to do it. This phenomenon is so common that other design groups in the company are counting on you to face what your progress indicators are telling you and officially announce a schedule slip.

> *No matter how well you plan, and no matter how hard you work, your project will inevitably run into schedule pressure.*

If you don't, they probably will, and they would rather you slip first so that they can slip their schedule for free.

If one design group is large, say, hundreds of people, and the other is more on the order of tens, the larger one will have to make the announcement first. Upper management would not stand for the smaller group to hold up the bigger one and would "parachute in" enough borrowed designers to redress the imbalance.

When the groups are roughly the same size, however, the interproject dynamic looks exactly like a huge game of "chicken," the demented teenager pastime seen in various movies, in which two drivers aim directly at each other, and the first to flinch and veer off "loses."

On some unfortunate day, you will have to announce the news of the necessary schedule slip to your upper management. This is exactly the kind of problem executives know how to handle. They can castigate the project managers severely for not having kept their project on track despite said executive's constant reminders of its overriding importance. They can use the opportunity to announce that they have lost faith in these leaders and will now investigate every nook and cranny of the project instead of continuing to take their word on anything. They can also lighten the load on the project by removing features or adding heads.

By the way, it is not necessarily a given that removing features actually reduces overall schedule pressure. It depends on the actual features, how much time remains to tape out, and how deeply the feature is embedded in the design. But these subtleties are not part of the executive's schedule slip calculus, and he is not much in the mood to hear you argue it just now.

When we reached the point of announcing a schedule slip in the P6 design, our executive VP said, "Okay. How many additional heads is it going to take to get this thing back on schedule?" For Randy's design team, there probably was such a number, but for an architecture team in the middle to late stages of a design, adding heads would only drain more time and energy off the chip and into training. When I respectfully declined, the VP gave me a shocked look and spluttered, "But you *can't decline* additional heads! As soon as you take on a management role, you can no longer say 'I cannot use additional heads.' It would be a sign of managerial incompetence."

We had the converse of that discussion a few months later. As I described earlier in the chapter (see "Health and the Tapeout Target"), at one time in the project our validation indicators (HOTM metric) seemed to be pointing to the dreaded "constant time to completion," meaning the project appeared to be slipping day for day. When our VP was informed of this situation, I proposed that the indicator itself might be a substantial part of the problem, and extra help on the validation team might relieve the other part.

His first reaction to this assessment was that if we could improve the present indicator, we should do so. His second reaction was to revisit the additional heads topic. He told me that he was asked for more heads all the time by managers who probably did have a legitimate use for them, but who also understood that the bigger their personal empire at next year's performance review, the more likely they would do well in that review. Unless it is mismanaged, a larger team can usually get more work done than a smaller one.

He then seemed to rethink his earlier statement, offering that we probably had enough validation personnel and that adding some might actually increase the project time. I agreed that the effect he was describing was, in principle, a possibility, but was not the case for our project. I probably should have left it at that, but I elaborated anyway. Given the amount of time remaining in the project, and the length of the learning ramp until the average validation engineer reached nominal efficiency, adding 10 heads to the 30 already on task was not likely to yield 10 heads' worth of incremental results. My estimate was that, all things considered, we would probably get five heads' worth of results from these 10 heads but that this would still pull the schedule in and reduce the eventual project risk of recall. Even so, I did get the additional engineers, and I think they were an asset both directly, by helping to write and debug tests, and indirectly, by demonstrating management's commitment to product quality.

Sometimes, you just can't estimate things any closer than this until you are staring directly at the work in the middle of the project. Some people sandbag their estimates accordingly—an expensive option that can lead to marginal returns on the extra heads, even early in the project—and these estimates will be sanity-checked against those of equivalent projects. If the executive becomes aware that a particular project leader routinely overestimates his real requirements, his future requests for additional money or people will be denied with no hope of appeal. I believe it is better to try to get it right during planning and hope for a boss who understands the uncertainties involved in doing something really difficult. Bosses *are* trainable; sometimes you just have to work at it.

Project Tracking

A new flagship microprocessor development effort involves several hundred design engineers, a new process technology from the fabrication plants, new design tools, a supervisory staff that has often just been promoted into their current jobs, and a great deal of uncertainty about product features, targets, microarchitecture, and circuits. With such a huge number of unknowns, it is virtually impossible to predict a project schedule a priori, no matter how fervently upper management demands it.

Instead, we took our best informed guesses and inflated them per hard-earned experiences of the past. Then we modulated those guesses to account for several important relat-

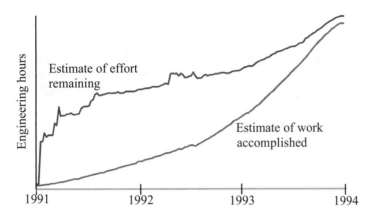

Figure 4.1. Project tracking rollup data.

ed factors, including our VP's management style,[3] what recent other projects had projected and how those projections had fared, and what our own design team was telling us about tools, personnel, and project difficulty.

These early estimates are useful only for very high-level planning, such as corporate road map and project costing efforts, project staffing, and management of related projects such as chip sets and tools. To really determine where a project is relative to its plan, you must track the project directly.

Randy understood this before anyone else and put a mechanism in place by which every project engineer would, on a weekly basis, report what he or she had accomplished that week and how much they estimated they had left to do before tapeout. Then Randy's Unix tools would roll all those individual estimates up to the project level. The difference between the combined joint estimate of remaining work and the combined joint estimate of what had been accomplished so far was, we hoped, proportional to how much work the project had left to do.

Things are never so simple, of course. In Figure 4.1, the lower curve is the aggregate estimate of how much had been accomplished to date, and the upper curve is the aggregate estimate of how much work remained to be done.

These curves hold some interesting lessons. First consider 1991–1992, the "start-up transient" year. Over several weeks, the designers thought hard about how the overall project was being partitioned, their own share of it, how they would have to go about accomplishing their part and how long that would take. As these weeks rolled by, the cumulative estimate fluctuated, but if you average it across the entire year it is clearly showing a general rise.

The message is one we didn't fully appreciate until a few years later: Where there is any uncertainty in scheduling, that uncertainty does not mean the final schedule could be longer or shorter with equal probability. I'll return to this thought shortly.

By 1992, the general estimate of total project effort remaining seemed to have mostly stabilized. For all we project leaders knew at that time, we would have a tapeout approximately on schedule, as the second tracking figure shows in Figure 4.2.

---

[3]Some VPs want a "best unbiased estimate," others want the "most aggressive schedule you can conceive of," and still others want two dates—a "50% confidence" aggressive date and a "90% confidence" date. We chose to provide a commit target and a stretch goal that was aggressive but not impossible.

How Not to Sell Management Visions

Andy Grove had a tradition of identifying the general direction in which he wanted the company to move every year. One year, "The PC Is It" was the message. A couple of years later it had morphed into "The Internet Is It." Such a directive may seem over-simplified, but Grove understood that it is almost impossible to convey any complex messages accurately to all corners of the company, and he also understood that simpler is better, as rallying cries go.

Intel's ubiquitous desire to constantly improve manifested itself as one VP tried emulating Grove's vision proselytization. Every year, this VP would try to enunciate his own desire for improvement in the engineering operations, but usually in terms either so apocalyptic as to be absurd, or so aggressive as to be humorous. The engineering rank and file just were not listening to him.

I am an engineer. I fix things. So I suggested that if this VP really wanted to get some mindshare from the engineers, he should work through the technical ranks and not use managerial mechanisms to get his message across. In effect, if you have sold the technical leadership, the engineers will follow.

He said, "Okay. You're on. Convene a meeting of the top 50 technologists in our microprocessor divisions so they can help me craft my message to the troops. Having been part of the message creation, these 50 will then help me get the word across." So I organized the meeting.

Things went well at first. The VP showed his draft foil set and we diplomatically suggested (well, okay, as diplomatically as engineers ever get, which admittedly is sometimes not much) that we could help refine them for maximum effectiveness to the troops. (Translation: Your foils are on the verge of being ludicrous and we will help push them closer to reality.) But after a few hours of discussion, this VP had had enough of our help. He began shouting at one of the best technologists he had, dressing him down in front of all his peers. Then he stormed out.

I think that in the process of injecting reality into his vision, we were frustrating him enormously. He seemed to feel that we were bending his vision and doing more damage than good. But this in no way justified his destruction of the nascent technical communication chain in such a personal way. In a sense, he was lucky because this particular technologist turned out to be surprisingly thick-skinned, and took the beating with aplomb, somehow understanding he was being berated on behalf of all the recalcitrant techies in the room.

The VP's behavior was the polar opposite of what had been promised and had exactly the effect you might imagine—he not only got no support from the technical intelligentsia in selling this message to the troops, but they exhibited much more than the normal amount of eye rolling when the presentation was eventually made.

When a message comes down through the management ranks, engineers will automatically view it with a certain amount of skepticism because they know the management chain is required to pass along such communications regardless of how any manager in that chain might feel about it. Not so with the technical ranks. The engineers have no reason to believe the Intel Fellows and the principal engineers are swayed by anything other than an argument's technical merits. Convince them, and they will carry the battle the rest of the way. The only trouble is, one does have to convince them, and it may be uncomfortable to find that the normal positional authority actually works against you.

<u>Figure 4.2.</u> Project tracking extrapolation as of 1991.

The Experiment. Still, Randy was concerned. Why did a constant inflation factor seem to be built into the estimate of effort remaining? Unless we understood where that inflation was coming from, we could not be sure it would remain linear. It just seemed somehow counterintuitive that so many people were discovering new work at a substantial fraction of the rate at which they were finishing existing work. Surely we could do a better estimation job if we put our minds to it.

Randy decided to experiment. He spent a week or two working with all the design supervisors, showing them the overall rollups and the inflation factor, soliciting their inputs on its source and asking them to rethink the methods they were using when creating their estimates of work remaining. One hypothesis was that the engineers were only looking ahead one task at a time, consistently underestimating each task by the same amount. Perhaps all they needed was to extend their planning horizons. If we could get all of them to cast their nets more widely and to apply the fudge factors that the data had implied so far, perhaps we could remove the inflation once and for all.

After Randy's exhortations, the team did indeed look harder and increment their fudge factors. The result was an immediate, noticeable, but not overwhelming increase in the estimated amount of project work remaining. Over the next few months, the new aggregate estimate of work remaining stayed relatively constant. The inflation seemed to have been vanquished.

But as you can see from Figure 4.3, relative to Figure 4.1 and Figure 4.2, the inflation was not really gone. It was just hidden by the artificially increased work estimates the experiment induced. In 1993, the inflation was back, and had picked up exactly where The Experiment had temporarily obscured it.

The Mystery of the Unchanging Curve. I have always thought it a little spooky that the accomplishment curve, which combines so much data estimated from so many people, would revert to its original shape after a perturbation like The Experiment. It suggests the presence of an intrinsic "blindness" factor with respect to estimating work remaining, and that this factor is reasonably common across people. If so, it probably stems from the same source that influences so many project management books, which almost always recommend that project planners strive mightily to create an accurate estimate and then double or triple it.

The accomplishment curve's nonlinear upward trend is likely the result of two large-project realities: fluctuating team size and the accumulation of expertise. Project teams

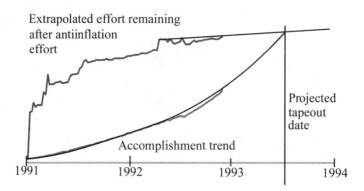

Extrapolated effort remaining
after antiinflation
effort

Projected
tapeout
date

Accomplishment trend

1991   1992   1993   1994

Figure 4.3.   Project tracking extrapolation as of 1993.

begin with perhaps a dozen people, and they ramp up to a peak that can number (as in P6's case) in the hundreds, a peak hit several weeks before tapeout. Because the team is growing over the project's lifetime, the amount it can accomplish per week grows as well. The peak-to-tapeout phase of a chip design, by the way, is exactly like standing on shore as a major hurricane hits land. The tapeout itself is the hurricane's eye. As it passes, everything is temporarily calm while the fabrication team does its work for a few weeks, and there is comparatively little you can do until the silicon comes back.

Expertise influences the curve because, after working on a design for a year or two, the design team becomes expert on the tools' use, weaknesses, and workarounds. Errors and failures that would have cost an engineer three days early in the project will cost her very little later because she will have learned how to stay out of trouble in the first place.

The work-remaining curve never actually did intersect with the accomplishment curve, mostly because it is no longer worth tracking when the project gets to within a few weeks of tapeout. We had always expected that when the difference between those curves reached zero we would have tapeout day. But that does not happen. Instead, as the engineers accumulate experience, they find more and more things they wish they had time to do. Validation learns a lot of very useful information as the project proceeds: which tests are finding lots of bugs and which are not, and which functional units are clean and which seem to be bug-infested. Validators will also pay attention to design errata being found in other chips in the company to make absolutely sure the company is never subjected to the agony of finding essentially the same embarrassing bug in two different chips. In general, validators will always be able to think up many more testing scenarios than any practical project will have the time and resources to carry out. And since their careers and reputations are on the line, they want to perform those tests. Project managers often have to modulate such work inflation, or the chip will tape out too late.

Flexibility Is Required of All

At the end of every engineering project is a crunch phase, during which the team is working at or beyond its maximum sustainable output and the mindset is very much that of a fight to the death. At that point, the engineers have been working on the project for years. All the fun and limitless horizons "This is going to be the greatest chip ever made" thinking has now given way to the cold realities of compromise. Or worse, by now all the project engineers have become painfully aware of whatever shortcomings the project now includes. Years have elapsed since the early days of boundless optimism, and the competition has long since leaked details of what they are working on. Their designs are not as close to fruition as the press believes (and maybe as the competition believes) but the engineers on *this* project cannot help but compare that paper tiger to their almost finished creation and wince.

Everyone is tired by this point—tired of working on this chip, tired of working next to these people, tired of doing nothing but working. Their spouses are tired of carrying the entire burden of running the home and family, and they may not be as inspired with the engineer's spirit of enterprise. Design engineers are always a cantankerous bunch, but with all this in the background, they are now positively cranky.

It is wise, nay essential, to manage projects so as to minimize this crunch phase. Six months in such a pressure cooker is about the most you can expect; longer than that and the project was not planned properly. Under no circumstances should an understaffed team be expected to make up for that management error by simply having a longer crunch phase. Design engineers who are dumb enough to fall for that ploy are not smart enough to design world-class products. You cannot have this one both ways.

Having said that, the P6 project's crunch phase lasted about seven months. Fortunately, the team came through it in fine form. I know that with several hundred people under this much pressure, some divorces and separations are statistically likely, but I still wonder if we could have done anything to improve that part of the equation.

One of the key design managers on the P6 had observed the overall schedule closely and noticed that the team began with a very few people and ballooned to hundreds. If the initial small group were to settle on a microarchitecture earlier, he reasoned, he could trade the wall-clock time saved for the same amount of time later and still hit the overall project schedule. If the architects would just get their acts together, he reasoned, the project would save a lot of money (since time saved multiplied by the number of heads affected is so different in the two cases). He believed the absence of late changes to the design would obviate the crunch phase. He unilaterally announced this plan at the beginning of the Pentium 4 development.

That was the start of two years of unpleasantness for the architects. Obviously, if we knew how to conceive a bulletproof, guaranteed-to-work microarchitecture on day 1, we would not have to spend days 2 through 730 continuing working on it. We do not know how to do miraculous conceptions like that. What we know how to do is this: conceive promising approaches to problems, refine them until our confidence is high, combine them with other good ideas, and stop when we believe the final product will hit the project's targets.

The manager in question did not like that answer. He proposed that if the project's architecture phase really had to proceed along those lines, then at least we could be honest about how expensive that part was. He was suggesting that we all spend more effort alone until such time as we could come up with a microarchitecture for which we could reasonably guarantee no more changes. If that made a 1.5-to-2-year architecture phase into a 2.5-year phase, so be it. At least the large design team would not be whipsawed by late changes. And he still believed he could avoid any crunch phase that way.

I think he also believed that if upper management saw the "true cost" of designing the microarchitecture, much more pressure would be applied to the architects (earlier) instead of to the design team (later). In that sense, he was probably correct. By the time upper management got serious about applying schedule pressure, the project was in its final one to two years and the architects were no longer the critical path.

I don't know how to prove this, but I believe that doing microarchitecture development the way we did on the P6 (and to an extent on the Pentium 4) is the optimum method. The architects get some time to think, and they tell management and the design team when their ideas have matured to the point of usability. Like everyone else, architects learn as they go. They build models, they test their theories, and they try out their ideas any way they can. If they are taking the proper types and number of risks, then some of these ideas will not work. Most ideas will work well in isolation, or the architect's competence is in question, but many ideas that look good in isolation or on a single benchmark do not play well with others. It's not uncommon to find two ideas that each generate a few percent performance increase by themselves, but when implemented together jointly degrade performance by a percent or two.

Designing at the limits of human intellect is a messy affair and I believe it has to be.

> *Designing at the limits of human intellect is a messy affair.*

The danger and schedule pain of design changes are real, but so are competition and learning. Projects must trust their senior technical leadership and project managers to make good judgments about when a change is worth making. Attempting to shut this process off by applying more up-front pressure to the architects does nothing useful, and I can testify from personal experience that it damages working relationships all around.

The Simplification Effort

The dictionary says one of the meanings of the word "complex" is complicated or intricate. But those characterizations do not do justice to modern microprocessors. Trying to

> *Complexity is a living, growing monster lurking in the corridors of your project.*

get your driver's license renewed can be complicated; complexity, in the context of microprocessor design, is a living, growing monster lurking in the corridors of your project, intent on simultaneously degrading your product's key goals while also hiding the fact that it has done so.

That is how it feels to a project manager, anyway. For large projects like P6, hundreds of design engineers and architects make dozens of decisions each day, trying to properly balance their part of the design so that it meets all of its goals: silicon die area, performance, schedule, and power. Every decision they make affects multiple design goals. On any given day, simulations may be telling a designer that her circuit is too slow; she redesigns it for higher speed, but now the power is too high. She fixes the power but it now requires more area than her unit was allotted.

Almost always, a designer's desire to fix something about a design results in a more complicated design. Part of the reason is that the designer would like to fix, say, circuit speed *without* affecting any other goals. So rather than rethink the design from scratch, the designer considers ways to alter the existing design, generally by adding something else to it.

On any given unit, this incremental accumulation of complexity is noticeable but not particularly alarming. It is only when you notice that hundreds of people are doing this in parallel, and you roll up the aggregate result, that the true size of the complexity monster lumbering around the project's corridors becomes apparent.

This complexity has many costs, but among the worst is the impact on final product quality in terms of the number and severity of bugs (errata). The more complicated a design, the more difficult is the task of the design team to get that design right, and the larger the challenge facing the validation team. While it is hard to quantify, it feels as though the validation team's job grows as some exponential function of the design complexity.

I used to go to bed at night thinking about what aspects of the P6 project I might be overlooking. One such night in 1992, I realized that this daydreaming had developed a pattern: It kept returning to the topic of overall project complexity. I knew that we were accumulating complexity on a daily basis and I knew that this complexity would cost us in design time, validation effort, and possibly in the number of design errata that might appear in the final product. What could be done about it? I briefly pondered going on a one-man crusade to ferret out places in the design where the injected complexity was not worth the cost, but there was too much work to do and not enough time.

The last time in the project that I had found myself facing a task too big to handle alone, I had successfully enlisted dozens of other people on the project and together we got it done. Was there a way to do that again? Back in the BRTL days, the design engineers did not have more pressing concerns and were relatively easy to conscript, but the project had since found its groove and everyone was incredibly busy all of the time. So asking them to put down their design tasks and help me with a possible simplification mission would not be a low-cost effort.

On the other hand, enlisting the design engineers themselves might have some tangible benefits besides additional sheer "horsepower" devoted to the task. They were the source of some of the added complexity, so they knew where to look. That could save considerable time and effort. And once they saw that their project leadership felt so strongly about this topic that we were willing to suspend the project for a couple of weeks in order to tackle it, perhaps the engineers would find ways to avoid adding unnecessary complexity thereafter.

We launched the P6 Simplification Effort, explaining to all why some complexity is necessary but anything beyond the necessary is an outright loss, and got very good cooperation from the engineering ranks. Within two weeks we had constructed a list of design changes that looked as though they would be either neutral or positive in terms of project goals and would also make noticeable improvements to our overall product complexity. This experiment was widely considered to be a success.

Just as I always do with die diets (mid-project, forced marches to make the silicon die smaller, mostly by throwing features off the chip), I wondered if some better up-front project management might have avoided the need for the Simplification Effort. I don't think so. I think it is useful at a certain stage of a design project to remind everyone that there are goals that are not stated and are not easy to measure but are still worth pursuing. Perhaps stopping the project periodically has the same effect that "off-site" events have on corporate groups—it gives people time to take a fresh look at what they are doing and the direction in which they are going, and this is very often a surprisingly high-leverage activity.

5

THE PRODUCTION PHASE

Two male engineering students were crossing the campus when one said, "Where did you get such a great bike?" The second engineer replied, "Well, I was walking along yesterday minding my own business when a beautiful woman rode up on this bike. She threw the bike to the ground, took off all her clothes and said, 'Take what you want.'" The first engineer nodded approvingly and said, "Good choice; the clothes probably wouldn't have fit."

I like this account of the overly focused engineering students for several reasons. First, it's funny because it twists the reader's expectations, playing to a stereotype of engineers as humorless optimization engines, while simultaneously rebutting that stereotype with the wry smiles of the engineers who read it.

But I also like it because it graphically demonstrates the single-mindedness required of the engineering profession. Early in the design program, ideas flowed like water—the more the better. Architects, managers, and marketing people were encouraged to roam the product space, the technology possibilities, and user models to find compelling product features and breakthroughs. As the project evolved through its refinement phase, the vast sweep of possibilities was winnowed to only a few of the most promising. The realization phase settled on one of those semifinalists and developed it to a prototype stage. This is nice, logical sequence that makes sense to most technical folks, who are often not prepared for what happens next, even though they think they are: production.

The Pentium Chronicles. By Robert P. Colwell
© 2006 IEEE Computer Society

After having spent 4+ years on the project, many engineers feel that their responsibilities have pretty much ended when they finish the structured register-transfer logic (SRTL) model. Their mindset is that they have designed the product they set out to create and now it is someone else's job to make tens of millions of them. How hard can that be, compared to the intellectually Herculean task that has now been accomplished? The answer is, very hard, and it requires a whole new set of skills.

To the eternal consternation of executives throughout Intel, it takes approximately one year to drive a new flagship design into production. A huge amount of work follows the initial tape out, much of which cannot be done earlier, even in the unlikely event that engineers were available. The production engineering team (the corporate production engineers plus a substantial fraction of the original design team) must prove silicon functionality and show that circuits and new features work as intended with the compilers and other tools. The chip power dissipation must be within the expected range, the clock rate must hit the product goal, the chip must operate correctly over the entire target temperature and voltage ranges, the system must demonstrate the expected performance, and testers must create the test vectors to help drive production yield to its intended range. Any of these requirements could become problematic, so a great deal of highly creative engineering must literally be on call.

Meanwhile, the marketing team is preparing the customers so that they will be ready when early production units arrive. These customers are preparing their own systems around this new chip, so they often have questions, suggestions, and concerns that require technical expertise to resolve. Technical documents must be updated and distributed. Collateral such as tools, performance models, and reference designs must be tuned to represent the chip's final production version.

Although not new to the production phase, the job of properly managing the sightings, bugs, and engineering change orders (ECOs) takes on a new urgency and importance. If the technologists who were judging bug dispositions during earlier project phases made an error, the project might suffer a schedule hit as the bug was later rediscovered and re-disposed of. But in the production phase, bugs that are not properly handled have a high likelihood of escaping into the wild, meaning into a customer's system, raising the ever-present specter of an FDIV-style mass recall. (See the section, "Was the P6 project affected by the Pentium's floating point divider bug?" in Chapter 7.)

The production team's responsibility then is to finish the job the design team has begun. In much too short a time, they must polish a raw, brand-new design into a form suitable for the safe shipment of tens of millions of copies. Tension is constant and comes from all sides: Management screams about schedules and product cost; validation constantly lectures on the dangers of another FDIV; marketing and field sales remind you that your project is late and that only an inspired performance by them will stave off the unbelievably strong competition that you have ineptly allowed to flourish; and the fab plant managers remind everyone of how many millions of dollars a day are lost if the chip isn't ready on time and their plants run out of things to make. The last source of tension is not a minor concern. Modern silicon fab plants cost almost as much to leave idle as they do to run at full production. Nothing out = No revenue = Very unhappy fab managers.

Validation is a good example of how much pressure is brought to bear in the production phase. Despite the millions spent on fast validation servers and the validation engineers who keep them busy, there is nothing like real silicon. In the first few seconds of running it, far more code is executed than in all the presilicon validation exercises combined. We are talking of ratios of 10 or 100 cycles per second for presilicon simulation to 3,000,000,000 cycles for real silicon. A lot of headaches can crop up in that many cycles.

OF IMMEDIATE CONCERN

The only job in the production phase is to bring the product to market. Unfortunately, that simple idea translates into knocking down every barrier that might otherwise prevent ramping up to large shippable volumes in a few months. In this phase, cleverness gets you only so far; brute force in the form of a lot of hard work by a lot of people must take you the rest of the way.

Functional Correctness

The first barrier to knock down is any remaining functional inaccuracy. It is a mistake to think that postsilicon validation is just an extension of presilicon testing. The two have unique advantages and disadvantages. Suppose you have a cache with 4 Mbytes of storage, arranged in 128 K lines of 32 bytes each. The RTL that instantiates that cache in the chip model will

> *It is a mistake to think that postsilicon validation is just an extension of presilicon testing.*

have a loop, essentially telling the RTL compiler each line's structure, causing that compiler to mechanically replicate that structure. Thus, in the RTL simulation universe, every line will behave identically. Knowing that this is how the cache was implemented in RTL, a presilicon validator can reasonably expect that if she proves line N correct, then line $N + 1$ is very likely functionally correct as well. Of course, good validators will always check the end conditions, such as the first last lines, and possibly other internal boundaries, but at the functional testing level, validators can and do exploit regularities to guide their testing to the areas of highest payoff. They can divide and conquer, testing each abstraction layer in isolation.

For a real silicon chip, however, all abstraction levels must *simultaneously* work correctly. If the RTL functionality contains an error, the microprocessor will not perform to satisfaction, even with perfect circuits and no manufacturing defects. If the cache line drivers have a circuit marginality, for example, access to lines close to the cache unit's edge might work at full speed, but those buried deep inside the unit or at its opposite edge might need more time than the clock rate allows. In this scenario, the presilicon tester's assumption about the mutual correctness of cache lines N and $N + 1$ would be dead wrong.

Manufacturing and physical characteristics cannot be ruled out in postsilicon either. When a postsilicon validator approaches a new chip, she knows very little about it, especially for the earliest chips. Fatal design errors could be preventing the chip from running any code out of main memory, for all she knows. Whole sections of this chip, or all chips at this revision level, could be completely unusable. Power-to-ground shorts might be preventing the chip from even powering up.

Fortunately, the errors are typically not on that scale. As validation and design engineers test more and more of the design over the first few weeks of new silicon, they sometimes find outright design errors, but more commonly they find areas that just need improvement. Meanwhile, the presilicon validation team is completing its validation plan and probably finding more design errata.

Speed Paths

Another important obstacle is any design artifact that might be keeping the chip from reaching its clock target. The maximum clock rate of a microprocessor has been its principal marketing feature and a first-order determinant of its eventual performance.

Even in time-tested designs, silicon manufacturing has a speed curve. Multiple fab plants worldwide built to the same standards and using identical equipment and processes will not produce the same chips. Some will function at faster clock rates than expected; others will be slower. If everything goes well, the median will be close to what the earlier circuit simulations predicted.

With a cutting-edge, flagship design, however, odds are that the chips will not be as fast as the design team intended. This is hardly surprising, since it takes only one circuit-path detour or some overlooked design corner to limit the entire chip's speed. Typically, tens to hundreds of these speed paths are in a chip's initial build, and the production engineering team must identify and fix them before mass production can begin.

Speed-path debugging can be extremely tricky. The presilicon RTL simulation involved tremendous complexity, but at least the engineer could monitor any set of internal nodes of interest as the simulator was running. With postsilicon debugging, you simply cannot reach every set of internal electrical connections. Instead, you end up making some inspired guess, inferring what the problem might be, and then making even more inspired proposals about how to prove your conjecture.

In the past, engineers addressed speed-path debugging by increasing the supply voltage, which tended to make all circuits faster. This strategy quickly lost its appeal when the chip's power dissipation became untenable, since it increased as the square of the voltage difference. In effect, when the voltage goes up a little, the clock goes up proportionately, but thermal power goes through the roof. Even without the thermal power concern, you can raise the supply voltage only so high without running afoul of physical constraints such as oxide thickness and long-term chip reliability.

The production team uses a host of techniques, nearly all proprietary, to drive aggregate chip speed up to its target. I can generalize and say that the process is human-intensive. The circuits effort proceeds around the clock with multiple tag teams of experts, and it is punctuated by new tapeouts followed by weeks of waiting for the "new improved" chip to come back from the fab plant, so that the process can start all over again. Eventually, the fab plant begins reporting high enough yield at the desired clock frequency to warrant higher volume production, and the speed-path team can wind down.

Chip Sets and Platforms

For the same reasons that thoroughly testing a CPU design's performance presilicon is impractical, it is even harder to test its performance with its accompanying chip set and platform (motherboard) design. Chip sets are designed on a very different timeline from CPUs; 9–12 months instead of 48, for instance. This means that even if you could hook the CPU and chip set simulations together presilicon, the chip set does not even exist until the final year of CPU development.

This increases the odds of more surprises when the actual chip set and CPU silicon first meet in the debug lab. The bus interfaces for both the CPU and chip set reflect certain policy decisions. In isolation, these decisions may seem innocuous, but when the two interfaces begin communicating, these decisions could easily turn out to have unfortunate consequences in certain corner cases.

There are some remedies for such interaction problems and we did use some of them. For the P6, we emulated the entire CPU, connected to a real chip set (although not the chip set being designed for it) in a large reconfigurable engine from Quickturn, Inc. (now owned by Cadence Design Systems). On the Pentium 4, we simulated the CPU and a mockup of its chip set as extensively as we could to help drive out mutual incompatibilities.

In the end, the one thing you can count on is that surprises are inevitable, and the production team will have to find them, identify them, decide which must be fixed (and how), and which can be lived with. This takes time, people, and a good working relationship with the early development partners.

> *The one thing you can count on is that surprises are inevitable.*

SUCCESS FACTORS

Because the production engineering team comprises design, validation, management, marketing, and product engineers, it must balance a variety of concerns on a very tight schedule. There is no time to explore nuances in someone's point of view. Communication must be direct, succinct, and frequent.

To satisfy this requirement, we created the "war room," a designated room for daily meetings, during which the team assimilated new data and decisions, planned out the next day's events, and coordinated with management. (Some politically overcorrect team members attempted to call it the peace room, but after a few months of tie-dyed shirts and responses of "Hey, chill, dude" instead of "I'll get right on it," we reverted to the original name.)

The war room was fundamental to the production engineering team's main job, which was to nurture the product to a marketable state, an effort that entails such unenviable tasks as writing test vectors and managing performance and feature surprises.

Prioritizing War Room Issues

The war room team must successfully juggle a steady stream of sightings, confirmed bugs, new features, marketing issues, upper management directives, and the constant crushing pressure of a tight schedule. On a daily basis, however, its most important function is to prioritize the list of open items to ensure that they can be disposed of within the required schedule.

Some issues on the war room list will be quite clear: "This function does not work correctly, and it must. Fix at earliest opportunity." A clear priority is when the team knows that the errant function is preventing a lot of important validation. In that case, they might decide that a new part stepping is appropriate. New steppings cost at least a million dollars each, and they require more coordination with external validation partners. Every project has a budget for some number of postsilicon steppings, so commissioning a stepping effectively fires one of the project's silver bullets. Because steppings also take a few weeks for the fab plant to turn around, it makes sense to combine multiple fixes into one stepping whenever possible.

Other war room issues are not as black or white. Sometimes, the team finds that new features with no correspondence to any previous chips have some corner case that does not quite work as intended. Such features have no x86 compatibility issues, and waiting for a stepping or two could possibly save money and time. The war room team faces some tough decisions in these gray areas, but they must make them or risk losing the schedule.

Perennial gray-zone cases are performance counters and test modes. Performance counters are a set of non-architecturally defined features that let programmers tune their code for high performance. There is more than one way to measure some complex system phenomenon, so if one way doesn't work or produces results that are slightly off, it is probably not worth a new stepping just to fix it. In fact, depending on the schedule status and many other factors, some issues are simply marked "future fix" or even "won't fix."[1]

Upper management can and does get directly involved, and not always for the reasons you would think. There is a silent period around any official corporate disclosure that might affect the company's stock price. During that time, all corporate officers must avoid any stock transactions because they know more than external investors and cannot trade on that knowledge. If an important bug comes to their attention during times when the trading window is open, the window shuts abruptly and remains closed until the bug has been resolved. Typically, most executives wait this out with relative patience, but those who were planning to pay for a boat or house through sale of stock become maniacally interested in resolving the errata. In these cases, the team might wish the war room had been encased in lead under some unspecified hunk of rock.

Managing the Microcode Patch Space

The microcode patch facility is an example of what the war room had to deal with. The facility is an important feature of Intel Pentium microprocessors starting with the P6, and to understand its importance to the production phase, some history is in order.

Minicomputers of the 1970s and 1980s had reloadable microcode, and when design errata were discovered, it was fixed by someone writing new microcode and distributing it to the field. Beginning with the P6, Intel mimicked this process with the patch facility—a new microcode facility that provided the ability to fetch an alternative microcode source. The patch facility can handle a fairly arbitrary subset of the microcode ROM because every time the microprocessor powers up, one of its tasks is to read from a predesignated area of system memory to see if what is there looks like a valid microcode patch. After some nontrivial checking (after all, we want the machine to accept only legitimate Intel-supplied patches, not some hacker's evil output, and we want to make sure the revision level of any patch found is appropriate to the CPU's stepping), the patch would be accepted, and whatever bug or bugs that patch was aimed at would manifest no more.

The catch is that the microcode patch space is limited, which means that only so many patches can be applied. If someone finds a design error after that, the choices are bleak: evict a previous patch, forget about patching the new error, or recall the silicon (the latter usually at huge expense and inconvenience for both the customer and Intel).

Obviously, then, someone must zealously guard the microcode patch space. If a bug is merely an irritation or lends itself to a workaround, it should not be allowed to take up permanent residence in that space.

---

[1]The choice "won't fix" might be valid in three scenarios: (1) if the fix could break something else of far greater significance, (2) if the feature in question has a conceptual error for which there is no fix, or (3) if the feature was solely for Intel's production engineers and they have decided they can get along without it.

This is not as easy as it sounds, because microcode is a versatile medium in a micro-processor such as Intel's, and almost anything beyond a certain complexity threshold will involve microcode. Translation: A suitably clever microcode patch can, in principle, fix a surprising number of bugs that have nothing directly to do with microcode.

You can also ameliorate certain chip set bugs that involve bus modes in this way. On the other hand, is that wise? If a small microcode patch can prevent the recall of a large number of motherboards, it is justified, but if the patch uses up half the CPU's patch space and accomplishes nothing more than shaving two weeks off the chip set's development schedule, it is probably not worth a permanent patch.

It takes exquisite technical judgment to be able to weigh what is known about a bug, its severity, how long it will take for a future stepping to arrive that fixes it, the volumes of all affected chips, how full the patch space already is, and how many future bugs are likely to appear that would use up more of it. No formula, algorithm, or algebraic equation, no matter how cleverly applied, can tell you how to wield the microcode patch space.

Your best resource for that is the most senior technical person, which in our case was Dave Papworth. Intel owes Dave an eternal debt of gratitude for the stellar job he did on this task for the first six years. Validation would inform the war room of the important sightings and bugs and Dave would essentially inform the war room of how the bugs were to be disposed of. It was like watching Michael Jordan play basketball or Tiger Woods play golf. Some people are so good at what they do, they make it look easy, no matter how hard it is, and it is only when you try it yourself that the amazement takes over.

PRODUCT CARE AND FEEDING

As every parent knows, or will find out when the time comes, you don't actively raise your children until they hit the magical age of 18 and then launch them into the world, reducing your parenthood to mere observation of their progress. Do launch them (a 30-year-old camping on the sofa is not a pretty sight), but the process of guiding, correcting, nudging, fixing, helping, and otherwise adding value must go on.

The same is true of a product. As with your children, you invest heavily in preparing them for the world and you hope that they are so ready that they will be a raving success with or without you. But they have strengths and weaknesses, and areas where some inspired collaboration can make a big difference. Your "product" continues to need you even after production has commenced.

Test Vectors

You were not sure you could run an entire marathon. Sure, you trained for it, hitting the pavement every night until your shoes wore out and your knees begged for mercy. But until you were actually part of the sweating, groaning, moving mass, you could not be sure if the training was enough. So you set a modest goal: Finish the race with some dignity, at least at a slow jog.

Finally, the big day arrives, and you run and run, and run some more. When you are sorely tempted to walk, some disembodied voice calls out, "Keep it up! Good job! You're halfway there." So you pick up the pace, persevere through the pain, keep your eyes on the backs of the people ahead of you, and try not to notice that your watch seems to have stopped. After agonizing hours, you hear shouts and see crowds leaning into the road, urging you on. Yards ahead is your goal and you are still on your feet.

You lurch across the finish line in a kind of dream state, certain that you have never been this tired in your life and convinced that no one with a shred of sanity does this more than once.

And then a man rushes up to you, all business. "That was great," he says, "but you're already late, so change into your biking gear, and remember your target speed is 179 km/hr! Oh, and make sure your swimsuit is handy. Come on, buck up! This is only the first leg of your triathlon!"

The sinking feeling of this spent marathoner only approximates what design engineers feel when they have made it to tapeout only to be told to hurry up and generate production test vectors, which everyone needed yesterday.

Test vectors are an artifact of the silicon manufacturing process. Through an incredibly elaborate series of chemical, mechanical, and photolithographic processes, silicon is transformed from being little more than sand (silicon dioxide) into microprocessors with hundreds of millions of transistors and billions of wires. Before they are even cut away from the wafer, each die is individually powered up and given rudimentary testing. Testing at this stage saves work and expense for packaging, since it makes no sense to package a die you know is nonfunctional.

The testing procedure is relatively straightforward. A robotic arm positions an array of metallic whiskers over each die. The whiskers are lowered onto the bond pads of the die under test, the die is powered up, and its inputs are driven in sequences of logic values that cause good chips to respond in certain predictable ways.

Less intuitive are conjuring up the required inputs and defining the expected outputs, tasks that make up the largely unrewarding job of writing test vectors. As you might guess, nobody is eager to volunteer for this. It is a deadly dull, error-prone, and open-ended process. You cannot test everything; there is not enough time and you are allocated only a certain number of input vectors. For most of the design project, design engineers spend each new day building on what came before. If they did a great job preparing for part of their design, that part will be commensurately easier to complete, so they are motivated to do a great job. With test vectors, there is always a sense that you are doing it for someone else, someone you do not even really know. It can be challenging to keep someone interested in a task that they view as forced charity.

On any mandatory march like test vectors, it is imperative to properly supervise the design team. Their leaders must make sure that everybody contributes equally. If whiners can get off the test vector writing hook, word will circulate that whining gets you what you want, and you can guess what happens after that. Project leadership must clearly show how much this task is valued and ensure that those contributing to it are being noticed and recognized. The engineers will still grumble, but the task will be completed within the weeks or months allocated.

Performance Surprises

Early silicon is scarce, so it must be allocated to customers that are best prepared to help nurse it through its infancy. Companies like IBM, Dell, and Compaq/HP have traditionally been extremely valuable partners in testing early silicon and reporting any observed anomalies in functionality or performance.

As I hope the earlier chapters of this book made clear, tremendous effort and cost is expended presilicon to ensure that basic functionality is correct. Most of this effort is in the form of RTL simulations, which are cycle-by-cycle accurate with respect to the final silicon.

Correctly executing code is only a prerequisite. The final customer *assumes* the code will execute properly, but that is not the only reason why they bought the chip. Customers buy new computers because

> *Correctly executing code is only a prerequisite.*

they believe that new computer will do things their previous one could not, such as run new applications, or old ones much faster or more reliably. The problem with performance is that it is much more difficult than functionality to simulate presilicon. The basic reason is "state," the amount of information that must be accumulated before the machine is ready to do some particular task. A modern processor has caches, branch predictors, and other internal databases that must be warmed up over many millions of clock cycles.

So even though presilicon testing has reasonably wrung out the initial silicon, the SRTL that defined that silicon has had relatively minimal performance verification. Therefore, performance surprises await early silicon, and such surprises are never in your favor.

Benchmarks are the only plausible way to tune a developing microarchitecture and find at least some of those surprises. The real code that will run on the designers' new system is intractable. It is too big, uses libraries that do not yet exist, and is aimed at an operating system that is not even accessible yet. It also makes no sense to run existing applications. You would have to run thousands of them, which is hardly practical, and even then, they cannot cover all the design corners.

Benchmarks are supposed to represent the real code in all the important performance-related ways, while being much more manageable in terms of slow simulations. But which benchmarks? And who chooses them?

In yet another feat of deft judgment, the design team (in particular the performance analysts) must consciously predict which software applications will be the ones that really matter in a few years, and then find or create benchmarks and a performance-prediction method on which they can predicate the entire project's success or failure. The trick is to fit all the benchmarks into the acceptable simulation overhead space, so one benchmark cannot take up so much space that it becomes the only one that gets analyzed presilicon.

All these uncertainties leave a lot of room for errors, changes, and misjudgments. A very common error is to fixate on the benchmarks that the team relied on for the previous chip generation. Another is to incorrectly anticipate how the buyer's usage model will change. We were somewhat guilty of this with P6, having conceived and designed a workstation engine in 1990 that ended up being used as a Web server in 1996. We got lucky, however, because our basic design turned out to be compatible with the performance rules of an I/O-intensive Web server workload. But it is always better to correctly anticipate the workloads that will be of interest and then find ways to model those workloads that are compatible with the methods to analyze presilicon performance.

When the chip goes into production, the pool of people able to run real code on these chips goes up enormously, as does the number of software applications. Consequently, chances increase that some of those applications will stray outside the expected performance envelope. The envelope's outsides tend to be asymmetric, however. The applications that run faster than expected will delight their users, but delighted users rarely call to tell you how happy they are with their applications. Disgruntled users, on the other hand, will forcibly bring slower-than-expected applications to your attention, along with their deepest convictions that you have wronged them. Analyzing the software in question and working with the application developer will resolve most, if not all, of these slowpoke applications. Often, the developer has used a suboptimal set of compiler switches, or the user's system was not configured for highest performance, or the software vendors did not follow the performance-tuning rules (or at least the rules were not clear in some area crucial to this particular application).

Many performance issues in early silicon can be dealt with via compiler changes, operating system changes, or software vendor education. An example is the original Pentium Pro's handling of partial register writes. Because of historical artifacts in the x86 register definitions, it is possible to directly address various subfields of a nominally 32-bit register like EAX. But the P6 microarchitecture renames registers by keeping track of register writes and register reads, and rather than triple the complexity of the register renamer, we chose instead to provide only enough functionality to correctly handle partial register writes. Used as we intended, this scheme was reasonably inexpensive and yielded very good performance. P6 marketing had a campaign to make this and several other performance tuning hints available to the software vendors well before P6 silicon arrived.

We received confirmation that this tuning scheme worked when shortly after we had sent P6 early production units out, a report came back from the field support engineers that the developers of the game Monster Truck Madness were unhappy with the performance they were seeing. A cursory inspection of their code showed it was riddled with partial register usage, which a compiler change quickly fixed.

Feature Surprises

Geologists can read the Earth's local history by interpreting the various rock strata. If there were such a thing as a computer geologist, Intel's x86 architectural origins would be somewhere around the Paleozoic Era, as Figure 5.1 shows.

> *If there were such a thing as a computer geologist, Intel's x86 architectural origins would be somewhere around the Paleozoic Era.*

One such era relied heavily on 16-bit code, a mode in which the CPU used only 16-bit data registers and coincides with when dinosaurs first roamed the Earth.

As I described in the section, "Legacy Code Performance" in Chapter 2, we P6 architects had to make an explicit choice as to what kind of code our new machine would optimize: older 16-bit or newer 32-bit. This was not a question of running one and jettisoning the other; P6 had to get correct answers no matter what kind of x86 code it encountered. The choice confronting us was how to strike the best performance balance between old and new.

After not much debate, we decided that 32-bit code was clearly the future and that if x86 were going to keep up with 32-bit-only competitors such as MIPS, Sun, HP, and IBM, we needed to go after that target directly. If we lost that war, we might sell one more generation of x86s but we would fall further and further behind everyone else. If we were going to catch up to our non-x86 competitors, it was now or never. For the long-term good of the x86 franchise, we adopted a formal target of 2× for 32-bit code and 1.1× for 16-bit code[2] and proceeded to optimize P6 for 32 bits.

We had many meetings with Microsoft, swapping notes and ideas about the future of

---

[2]We were not so much concerned with speeding up 16-bit code by 10% as we were trying to avoid being slower than Pentium on any particular code. The 10% was our margin against that prospect.

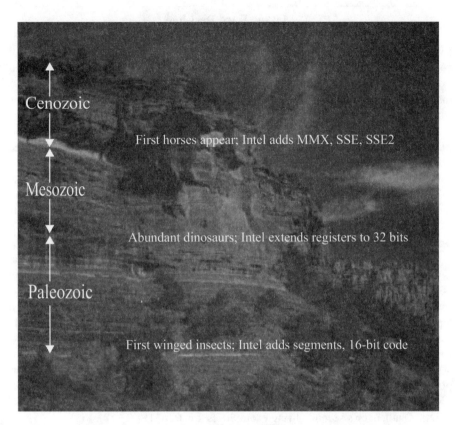

Cenozoic

First horses appear; Intel adds MMX, SSE, SSE2

Mesozoic

Abundant dinosaurs; Intel extends registers to 32 bits

Paleozoic

First winged insects; Intel adds segments, 16-bit code

Figure 5.1. Intel history of an ancient architecture. Photo by John Miranda (www. johnmirandaphoto.com).

DRAM sizes and speeds, hard-drive evolution trends, and our respective product road maps. From 1991 to 1993, Microsoft made it clear that Chicago, which eventually became Windows 95, would be their first 32-bit-only operating system. Then, in 1994, they announced that a key piece of Chicago would, regrettably, remain 16 bits: the graphics display interface.

This was unhappy news. It was far too late in Pentium Pro's development to change something as fundamental as our overall optimization scheme. But we were not too worried; after all, Windows 95 would be a desktop operating system, and the Pentium Pro was not intended as a desktop CPU. (Its two-die-in-package physical partitioning afforded much higher performance, but at a much greater manufacturing cost and, thus, with constrained production volumes.) Unix dominated servers and workstations, and Unix was strictly 32 bits. We knew that proliferations of the original P6 chip would be aimed at desktops, but we bet that the original Pentium could hold that market segment for the year it would take the Pentium II team to put in some 16-bit tweaks and retarget the P6 for desktops.

That is exactly what happened, although, in retrospect, it is clear that we made a riskier bet than we had intended. The Pentium chip did, in fact, hold its own on the desktop, but luck played a larger role than we foresaw—AMD's K5 chip turned out to be late and

---

Making Hard Decisions

Eventually, I would find myself excoriated for the decision not to emphasize 16-bit code performance, but looking back at the experience, I am unrepentant. You cannot explore every idea to equal depth, cover every base, hedge every bet, and refuse to make any decisions until all the data is available. All the data is *never* available. This is true not only in engineering, but in every important human endeavor, like marriage, family, and choosing a job or home. To choose one path among several is to fundamentally exclude other sets of possibilities; you cannot have it both ways. With perfect hindsight, our decision to optimize 32-bit performance was exactly the right one. A subsequent P6 derivative microprocessor added 16-bit performance tweaks, and since that particular part was aimed at desktops, where 16-bit code was still important (legacy and Windows 95), we were covered in that market. Meanwhile, our 32-bit optimized part was opening new markets for Intel in workstations and servers, where 16-bit code was irrelevant, and those markets became major new revenue streams.

LDS Elder Robert D. Hales says, "The wrong course of action, vigorously pursued, is preferable to the right course pursued in a weak or vacillating manner." Engineering is about taking calculated risks, pushing technology into new areas where knowledge is imperfect, and if you take enough risks, some of them will go against you. The trick in a project's concept phase is to know when and where you are taking risks and to make sure you can either live with a failure (by permanently disabling an optional but hoped-for new feature, for example) or have viable backup plans in place. And never forget Will Swope's dictum: Your backup plan must be taken as seriously as your primary plan; otherwise it is not really a backup plan. Thinking you have a backup plan when you really do not is much more dangerous than purposely having none. The Space Shuttle Challenger's second O-ring exemplifies this trap [19].

To choose A is not to choose B. People who try too hard to get both, as a way of avoiding the difficult choice between them, will end up with neither.

---

very slow. Lack of competition, combined with a vigorous marketing campaign centered around dancers wearing colorful bunny suits, made a success of Pentium long enough for the P6-based Pentium II to become ready, with its improvements to 16-bit code performance.

I consider our 16-bit choice on the original P6 to be among our best decisions. We recognized an important issue, considered all of its ramifications, placed an intelligent bet on the table, and won. To me, making such compromises openly and rationally is the essence of great engineering.

Not everyone saw it that way. In 1996, under the guise of conducting a routine interview, an industry analyst took me to task in no uncertain terms over our 16-bit choice. How could we have been so expressly incompetent in failing to recognize how much 16-bit code remained in the world? Did we not realize we were threatening not only Intel's immediate future, but also the future of the industry as a whole? What unmitigated hubris, what fatal ignorance! As far as this man was concerned, all the people involved should be chained to the same rock as Prometheus and undergo the same liver surgery.

Over the next few years, different internal groups within Intel would sporadically "discover" the Pentium Pro's perceived weakness. E-mail flew, presentations were given, and task forces were formed. If there ever is a Monday Morning Quarterback league, it will not lack for players.

What all these objectors fail to see is that design is the art of compromise. You canot have it all. In fact, you cannot have even most of it. The Iron Law of Design says that, at best, you can have a well-executed product that corresponds to a well-conceived vision of technological capability/feasibility and emerging user demand, and that if you strike a better compromise than your competitors, that is as good as it gets. If you forget this law, your design will achieve uniform mediocrity across most of its targets, fail utterly at some of them, and die a well-deserved and unlamented death.

Executive Pedagogy and Shopping Carts

An important part of product care and feeding is to expect the unexpected, and I had many opportunities to exercise that philosophy during the P6 project. Corporate management was beginning to show interest in our microarchitecture, and requested that I give them a tutorial on how it worked.

This was a frightening prospect. *I* knew how it worked, but I also knew how unprepared our executives were to grasp out-of-order, speculative, superpipelined microarchitectures. How could I give them some intuitions about our motivations and choices in the design of this complicated engine?

The night before I was to give this talk to our executive VP, I still had not solved this conundrum. I knew I could always be boring and pedantic, and give the listener a straight-up data dump. If they could not keep up, too bad.

But that is just not my style and, anyway, I was proud of our design and I really wanted our executives to understand, at least to some extent, how thoroughly cool it was. So I decided to pitch the talk at my mother—a smart person, but one with no technical background. If she could follow the discussion, then Intel execs might, too.

I did not think my mother would have the patience or interest to learn enough about microarchitectures to approach this topic on its own terms. So I started thinking about analogies, and I finally came up with one involving shopping carts and supermarkets, one with enough parallels to an actual microarchitecture to illuminate the concepts without too much distortion.

I also happen to like this analogy because it supports one of my pet conjectures: Computer design looks a lot more mysterious than it is because familiar ideas tend to be hidden by engineers who rely heavily on the passive voice and routinely forget to eschew obfuscation. Actually, computer science has very few original concepts. Once you get past the buzzwords and acronyms, you can fairly easily explain the ideas using a range of familiar contexts. I happened to pick grocery shopping, which nearly everyone has done at some time.

Picture your favorite supermarket. You go to the store with your shopping list in hand, a list similar to that in Figure 5.2. As you push your cart, you stop and grab items off the shelves that correspond to your list. When you have gotten everything on the list, you go to the front of the store, pay for the merchandise, and leave.

In this analogy, your shopping list corresponds to the software you want to run, and the speed at which you move through the store is your clock rate. The "program" terminates when you leave the store. The other correspondences depend on the type of microarchitecture.

Consider the venerable Intel 486 processor, an in-order, single-pipeline scalar microarchitecture with a cache but no branch prediction. The 486 shopper gets a cart, but no map

```
┌─────────────────────────────┐    ┌───────────────────────────────────┐
│        Shopping List         │    │         Computer Program          │
│                              │    │ main()                            │
│   1. milk                    │    │ {                                 │
│   2. cookies                 │    │    char i, a, err=();             │
│   3. diet peach ice tea      │    │    for (i=0; i<imax; i++){        │
│   4. potato chips            │    │    write_flash(i,i*2);            │
│   5. chicken                 │    │    a = read flash(i);             │
│   6. wine                    │    │    if (a !=i*2)                   │
│   7. frozen pizza            │    │       {                           │
│   8. toothpaste              │    │       err=1;                      │
│                              │    │       break;                      │
│                              │    │       }                           │
│                              │    │    }                              │
│                              │    │    ...                            │
│                              │    │ }                                 │
└─────────────────────────────┘    └───────────────────────────────────┘
```

<u>Figure 5.2.</u> The uncanny correspondence between shopping lists and computer programs.

of the store, and has to pick items off the shelf in the order they appear on the list (no looking ahead allowed). Lacking a branch predictor, the 486 shopper starts at the beginning of aisle 1 and linearly searches the entire store for item 1 on his list. When he finds item 1, he returns to the beginning of aisle 1 and repeats the process for item 2, and eventually for the remaining items on the list. Because the 486 had very slow clock rates, relative to the chips that came later, our 486 shopper not only traverses the aisles many times, but he does so quite slowly. He has no branch prediction table, so he learns nothing as he goes; he must start over in order to find each new item on the list. But he eventually does manage to find every item on his list and successfully exits the store.

The shopper who corresponds to the Pentium processor (also an in-order architecture) must search for items in 1, 2, 3, . . . , *n* order as well. However, because the Pentium is a two-pipe superscalar design, the Pentium shopper gets two shopping carts. Whenever the items on the shopping list happen to be near each other on the store shelves, the Pentium shopper can grab them both, one in each hand, and toss them into their respective carts. The Pentium also has a branch predictor, so after the shopper has traversed the store a time or two, he has constructed a kind of map and does not have to return to aisle 1 and linearly search the entire store for each new item. Finally, since the Pentium has a faster clock rate, he walks the aisles faster, and gets the job done much faster than the 486 shopper.

The shopper who corresponds to the P6 microarchitecture has a unique shopping experience. P6 is an out-of-order, three-way, superscalar, superpipelined machine with branch prediction and speculative execution. So the P6 shopper gets three independent shopping carts with three helpers to push them. Each helper gets a copy of the shopping list, but this time can grab items in any order that is convenient (because the architecture is out-of-order). The helpers know where everything is because of P6's advanced branch prediction, and they all wear special running shoes because the P6 clock rate is much higher than the Pentium's. But they can also grab items off the shelf and put them into their cart before they have even read the whole shopping list; that is the speculative execution. The shopper sends the helpers off to load their carts while she stands at the front of the store. When the helpers have finished their lists, she checks their carts before paying, in the likely case that they got creative and brought something she did not want.

When I first presented the "shopping cart analogy" to our executives, I was a bit worried that they might feel it was oversimplified or condescending. But they loved it. When they heard about this analogy, our marketing department also loved it, and one of them produced a graphical simulation of the whole thing. Eventually, P6 marketing put this simulation on Intel's Web site, where it stayed until a Pentium marketing person saw it and realized that, although it made P6 look great, it did so at the expense of Pentium, which was still being sold.

Our marketing folks also used this simulation to explain P6 to outside groups, including a TV station's camera crew, who got completely carried away and proceeded to go to a local supermarket where they staged the whole thing. I do not think their version really got the point across, though; you had to see the items being found and crossed off the shopping list, and remember the equivalent rates for the other two microarchitectures, to reach the right conclusions. The sheer spectacle of TV reporters running around throwing random store items into their carts was definitely entertaining, but even *I* had trouble seeing any relationship to what is in a microprocessor.

Interestingly, I also showed the computer-based shopping cart simulation to groups of grade school children, and they enjoyed it to the same extent and for much the same reasons as our executives had. I leave it to the reader to glean any significance from that.

MANAGING TO THE NEXT PROCESSOR

Part of the production phase necessarily involves looking beyond the current project. Engineers love novelty, so they will not normally do the same thing over and over unless they are compelled to do so. The exception is the basis for much marketing folklore: engineers who will not stop polishing long enough to get the product to market. Typically, however, most of us look forward to skipping the mundane issues of speed paths, performance divots, and functional errata, along with the daily management browbeating to meet impossible schedules. The temptation can be overwhelming to chuck it all and jump into the marvelous new project that is welcoming fresh ideas.

The draw is intensified by the knowledge that a new design project is often marked by a kind of land rush. In 1889, the U.S. government sponsored a race in what is now Oklahoma. To settle the land, the government promised that homesteaders would own up to 160 acres after they had settled on and cultivated the land for at least five years. A new design is parceled out in a similar way: The functional blocks are up for grabs and get locked down fairly quickly. The way in which various engineers "settle" a design's various parts has a profound effect on the eventual design and on job satisfaction over the next several years.

An experienced engineer—the kind you want working on the preproduction team—is likely to be anxiously watching the rest of the team driving their mules at a furious pace across Oklahoma's landscape, while trying without much enthusiasm to resolve the tricky issues of finishing the "old" chip. Ultimately, these faithful few must trust project leadership to reserve some homesteads for them. Those leaders would be wise to honor that trust.

THE WINDOWS NT SAGA

There was a time when you could design a computer without using a computer to do it, but that time was well before the P6 era. For the P6, the question was which computers to use. With only a few senior engineers on the project, it was relatively simple to try a few engineering workstations, and then ask management to standardize on the one we liked best. This turned out to be IBM's RS6000 line, running their AIX version of Unix.

All computing platforms have their unique set of quirks and vagaries. We dealt with the RS6K's by dedicating a set of very talented software engineers to serve as the design team's first line of defense. These folks were invaluable at figuring out when an unexpected problem was a designer's own pilot error, the fault of the tools being used, a design flaw in the workstation or its operating system, or some combination of these possibilities.

As we were entering the home stretch of P6 development and beginning to plan the follow-on Willamette project, the question of what engineering workstation to use became an issue.

I argued that engineers ought to use their own designs whenever possible because they can then devote themselves to their creations in a way that abstract professionalism does not quite reach. An engineer who worked on the controls for the jet engines on the Boeing 747 told me that he and a colleague went along on that engine's first flight. A military pilot once told me that a parachutist commonly packs his own chute, and when he can't, the person who did pack it has to jump, too, using a randomly chosen chute. Both these practices tend to focus the practitioner's full attention on the task and to expose that person to any flaws in its execution. Errors can still be made under such circumstances but, surely, the odds of careless mistakes being made will be minimized.

At the P6 project's outset, no Intel microprocessor-based workstation was suitable for use by an industrial design team. The P6 itself turned out to be a formidable performer for engineering design, however, and I wanted the Willamette design team to "eat their own dog food."

Unfortunately, Intel was a newcomer to the workstation market in the mid-1990s and although the traditional desktop PC vendors were offering very reasonable workstation designs, we saw no operating system as the obvious right choice. Our design team had lived in a Unix environment for so long and so successfully that they believed the only thing worth arguing about was the Unix vendor.

But Intel upper management had other concerns. We were told on several occasions that the entire design tool chain—both Intel-developed and Intel-licensed—would migrate to Microsoft's Windows NT as soon as possible. Moreover, management was worried that no credible Unix vendor would listen to Intel's complaints or entreaties when we needed special features or fast bug fixes. Intel managers also profoundly distrusted the emerging Internet model in which seconds after you posted a question about a bug, 20 responses would appear, 18 of which were blatantly wrong, but two of which were potentially quite useful.

So we Willamette project managers were given a choice. Either we could go with Unix, but from a standard vendor with its own self-supported Unix, or we could go with any reasonable x86/P6 hardware platform vendor, but run Windows NT. The only standard vendors with their own Unix at that time were IBM, Hewlett-Packard, Sun, and Silicon Graphics, and their machines were much more expensive than standard desktops.

With perfect hindsight, I wish we had chosen a Unix-based solution, *any* Unix-based solution. Instead, we chose to switch to Windows NT, the start of a struggle that grew worse with time.

It was not that Windows NT was substantially less stable than the competing Unix alternative. It may or may not have been, but the real problem was primarily that the entire design team had spent many years creating and maintaining software tools under Unix and no time at all doing the equivalent under Windows. In a misguided and ultimately counterproductive effort to make Unix folks feel at home in Windows, our tools group created a range of tools, shells, and alias lists so that we could migrate the hundreds of design tools from Unix to Windows. What we did not anticipate was that, for many reasons, it is better to rewrite tools from scratch when migrating them to Windows from Unix. Instead, we ended up wielding these seductive tools to get a quickie port on Windows, only to discover that they were of the same flaky consistency as grandmother's best dinner rolls.

This list conveys a flavor of what these quickie ports from hell collectively evinced:

1. A bug sighting is reported to the software tools team. A software wizard is dispatched to reproduce the problem, which we will call Problem A.

2. The software expert wrestles with the bug report and, after playing with the various reported facts, believes she has successfully reproduced Problem A. Remember that she has had access to the operating-system source code all her career, but with Windows NT she does not, so she can only guess at any bugs or limitations it might be causing.

3. With her understanding of the bug, she proposes a fix, usually a change to the quickie-port scripts and tools. She tests the fixed script for a few days and becomes convinced that she has solved Problem A. Her fix is released to the general tool-using population.

4. A new problem, which we will call Problem B, is reported. Because it is seemingly unrelated to Problem A, Problem B goes to a different tools expert, who begins the same process outlined in (2) and (3), but, unbeknownst to him, Problem B is indeed a direct result of Problem A's "fix." Worse, Problem A was not really fixed; lack of access to the operating system source code caused the first expert to guess slightly wrong. She was right enough to make the symptoms of Problem A go away temporarily, but wrong enough that only minor changes to tool use or the dataset make Problem A come back. Meanwhile, the change to fix Problem A has now broken something that used to work.

Figure 5.3 gives you the graphical equivalent of this destructive cycle.

After a few more of these "coincidentally" timed bugs, the software tools folks began to suspect that something more deliberate was causing them, and they laboriously puzzled out more of what the real operating-system/tools interactions must be on the basis of observed behavior. They began to propose more refined fixes, and the tools gradually got less flaky.

Many people believe that if you throw a frog into a pot of boiling water, it will jump right back out, but if you put it into room temperature water and gradually heat it to boiling, it will stay in it until it is too late.[3] That is how our forced migration away from Unix

---

[3]The moral of the story is valid, but the story itself is an urban legend. In reality, frogs have more sense. They try to get out of the increasingly hot water, with an urgency proportional to temperature [8]. Who makes these things up, anyway?

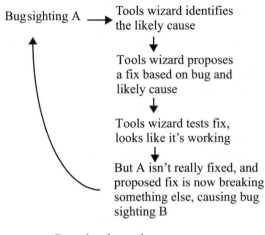

Round and round we go...
from one bug, we now have several

Figure 5.3. Lack of access to source code forces guessing and more bugs.

felt. Because the tools environment *seemed* to get gradually more reliable, we stuck to the plan, hoping that when the software-tools folks found and fixed the few really big bugs, our design tool chain would once again exhibit the overall level of reliability to which we had become accustomed. But it never did. Instead, the software tools folks just kept patching and guessing and trying to infer what was wrong. And as the development schedule marched on, they had less and less time to backtrack and replace major sections of the tool chain with code specifically written for the Windows NT environment.

Some of them also began exhibiting worrisome behavior. Whenever they saw me, they would point in their best Ghost of Christmas Future imitation, and in a hollow, eerie voice wail, "*You* did this to me! I *hate* you! I quit!" And I would gingerly talk them down from their Windows-induced psychosis. But upper management held firm—Windows NT was the future, and we simply had to adjust.

Later in the project, as the RTL matured, the validation team began using massive cycles for their validation exercises, and they found that the overall tools environment had matured to an asymptote that was an order of magnitude away from what they could live with. In classic Intel tradition, they did not ask permission, but simply brought up Linux on several hundred validation servers and re-ported whatever tools were needed. Within a few days, they were once again merrily running their tests and enjoying the kind of computing system stability we had not seen in several years.

And in the ultimate irony, the same management that made us walk the plank in this manner eventually bestowed the company's highest technical achievement award on the validation and computing support personnel who had reverse-migrated us back to Linux. Another quintessentially Dilbertian moment in the annals of technology.

PRODUCT ROLLOUT

Like most large companies, Intel carefully stage-manages product rollouts. Senior marketing executives collect information from the technical people who created the product and combine that information with their own imaginations to come up with the glitzy extravaganzas you see at rollout affairs. Rollouts also require a certain awareness of what you should and should not say during interviews, which takes more training than you might think. (Or maybe just more than I had.)

On Stage with Andy Grove

Marketing rollouts of new high-tech products usually include selected product users and early adopters, whose job it is to say, "Without Intel's latest and greatest processor, my life would be devoid of meaning," and "Now that the Pentium Pro exists, my applications leap tall buildings in a single bound." I am not criticizing them, of course; I went to Bill Daniels' lectures (the human behavior expert cited in the section, "Awards, Rewards, and Recognition" in Chapter 4), and I am no different from anyone else who likes praise, regardless of the circumstances.

As Randy Steck and I were soaking up the adulation, even the less-than-spontaneous variety, Andy Grove invited us onto the stage. The applause that followed seemed genuine, and after nodding our thanks, we moved out of the spotlight and waited for the final fireworks.

They came a little earlier than I expected. During the audience question-and-answer session immediately after our appearance, Andy fielded the first few questions, and then someone remarked, "Rumor has it that the Pentium Pro's 16-bit performance is hardly better than Pentium's. What caused a design gaffe like that?" Andy had no idea if the questioner's premise was correct, and if it was, what the best answer might be. So he looked back at us.

My feet moved almost of their own volition, and I found myself standing in front of a microphone, squinting into very bright lights, with Andy Grove looking at me expectantly. I took a deep breath and began what I hoped was a spirited defense of our design choices in the matter of 16-bit performance. I do not remember if I inflicted the entire history of this choice on the questioner, but I do remember that my aim was to drive a stake through this question's heart. When I got back to Oregon, many members of the team thanked me for my performance. I asked them if my answer made any sense, and they gallantly said, "It doesn't matter. It was the conviction with which you spoke that counted." It was a great experience, even if it made me feel at the time like a waterboy who had accidentally been sent up to bat against a major league pitcher.

What still irks me about that question is that it shows how little people understand design decisions. If events had transpired in a way that made the early P6's 16-bit performance seriously deficient, then someone could legitimately criticize our collective judgment on this issue. But to insinuate that this choice was an unconscious, default decision, a simple oversight, is to cast aspersions on our competence as designers. Judgments that turn out wrong are crucially different from judgments that no one ever made, and that difference is what distinguishes great design teams from mediocre ones—Great teams can make wrong calls, but they make all their calls based on the best information available at the time. It is this deliberate, informed decision making that stacks the odds in their favor.

How Not to Give Magazine Interviews

Intel faces a perennial problem: How much access should magazines, TV, radio, and Web site gurus be granted to techies and geeks? A supplementary problem is how to train the technical talent to understand that blurting out the entire truth to a question is not the only option.

Old jokes often contain old truths. A hoary engineering favorite is the one in which three convicts are in line to be executed, the third of which is an engineer. The first puts his head in the guillotine and the executioner pulls the lever, but the blade gets stuck halfway down. Because of some ostensible double jeopardy principle, the convict walks away a free man. The second convict puts his head in the guillotine, the same thing happens, and he also walks away. Then the engineer walks up, but before he puts his head on the block, he points to the track of the blade and says "Hey, I think I see how to fix where that blade is getting stuck."

Randy Steck and I spent a few days entertaining various magazine editors from all around the world, giving interviews on the design, the team organization, and other topics of interest. Many of these interviews ended up being published in languages neither of us could understand, so I never did get to read what they quoted me as having said. I hope it was intelligent. But I have had many occasions to read the raw transcript of a speech I had given or legal depositions I have made, and they always make me cringe. I often wonder how anybody gets any coherent information out of what looks to me like quasirandom walks through various idea spaces, separated by nonsequiturs and expostulations. Maybe they just like the panache with which I attempt them.

At one magazine interview, I decided to take a break while interviewers kept talking to my Intel compatriots. As I headed for the door, I heard the questioner ask about our PowerPC competitors (which were very new at the time): "How do you think P6 will fare against the forthcoming PowerPC chips?" As I walked past, I thought, "Who cares how fast any chip is if it cannot execute the right kind of code?" The next day, I saw that quote in the newspaper and realized I hadn't just thought it; I had said it aloud, and they had heard it. I wonder how my PR handlers at Intel would have felt if they had known that that quote was as big a surprise to me as it was to them.

Someone from the *Wall Street Journal* was interviewing us later that day, and asked what we had done as a result of corporate's learning about the FDIV flaw. Without thinking (enough, anyway) I said, "We learned many things about the public and its relationship to technology, and we realized that as bad as FDIV turned out to be, it would be far worse if Intel made the same mistake twice. So we pounded the crap out of the floating-point units in the P6." Naturally, that's the quote they ended up using, and it was sent over the wire services to a huge number of local newspapers, including ours. Some friends bought a new hammer, wrote "craphammer" on its handle, and left it on our front doorstep. My mother saw the papers and threatened to wash my mouth out with soap. I guess it just does not pay to get too technical with the noncognoscenti.

Speech Training

As the P6 project was winding down, our general managers had the great idea that we should prepare the project leaders to give coherent public presentations. They hired Jerry Weissman [11] to tutor four of us for a week on how to structure our foils and deliver them for optimal effect.

Jerry was a great coach. He had all of us do a quick presentation that was videotaped for later reference. Then he began working on us. He correctly noted that most technical presenters are deadly dull, believing their job is to inundate the listener with data and to pack as much as possible onto each Powerpoint foil. If the foil will not accommodate all the data, they use a smaller font size. Yet, as Jerry pointed out, none of us actually *like* to sit through such presentations.

We had all been to technical conferences and the universality of Jerry's truths was self-evident. Jerry suggested that even technical folks like a good story and that no one was going to remember all the data anyway. He advised us to pick the one or two major ideas we hoped we could get across and then structure the talk around them. He had numerous suggestions for structuring the Powerpoint foils. No more than four bullets per foil. No more than four words per bullet. Place words so that they enhance the graphic, not obliterate it. Build the foils so that the sequence makes sense.

He also had dozens of great ideas on how to present the story. Do not grip the podium; it makes you look like you are scared. And do not hide behind it. Let the audience see you. When they sense your mastery of the material, they will relax and accept the message better.

Jerry also stressed practice. He suggested that we practice our talks in the shower, while driving, while eating lunch, in front of friends, in front of coworkers, in front of strangers, in front of pet iguanas—in front of any entity that will sit still long enough.

It was decided that we would introduce the P6 at the IEEE's 1995 International Solid-State Circuits Conference (ISSCC '95), a kind of Superbowl for microprocessors, and that I would be the presenter. I had attended many conferences, but never that one, so I did not know quite what to expect. But I definitely said a silent thanks to Jerry and my own general managers for having put me through this training, because I soon found myself alone on an enormous raised platform in front of 2,000 conference attendees, wearing a wireless microphone headset. I felt like Madonna but with a lot more clothes.

My talk followed those of a few others, who had described competitors to Intel's products, and who had obviously not taken Jerry's class because they did that techie data-dump thing. The session chair introduced me and I walked behind the podium. Then I walked around it and stood next to it, per Jerry's instructions. Out of the corner of my eye, I could see that this action had startled the session chair, who got halfway out of his chair, presumably to address the problem he thought I had or to give this idiot speaker some additional instruction, since the dummy obviously did not know he was supposed to stand *behind* the podium. I launched into my talk, and he resignedly sat back down, the emergency averted.

At several points during my presentation, audible gasps circulated through the room; they were among the most gratifying sounds I have yet heard in my career. One of these occurred when I pointed out that we had made the P6 an intrinsically multiprocessor-capable engine; all you had to do was connect a second (or third or fourth) socket to the pins of the first one and install another P6 chip in it. Another occurred at the end, when I pointed out that I had prepared the talk on a P6 system. This told the technically astute in the audience that P6 was already healthy enough to run Microsoft's Powerpoint application, and the only way to run Powerpoint was to run Windows first. With that single remark I had given them a lot of information that led to one conclusion: The project was very far along. This out-of-order stuff was working.

I have been grateful for Jerry Weissman's training on other occasions as well, in particular, at the Microprocessor Forum. I have presented at that conference a few times and it was always a surreal experience. Instead of sitting in the audience and listening to previous speakers before taking my turn, I was kept backstage, like a rock star before a gig (or a convict as the engineer in the joke above was repairing the guillotine). If that were not bad enough, I had to speak immediately after AMD's Jerry Sanders on one occasion, which meant that we briefly occupied the same cramped space, much to my amusement.

After being introduced, I discovered that the monitor I was supposed to use to see what slide the audience was seeing was almost invisible from where I stood because of the in-

---

Trash-Talking Helps the Opposition

My antipathy to AMD's Jerry Sanders stemmed from interviews he had given in 1995, in which he had opined that "The reality is the (P6) is inferior to the Pentium. . . . The Pentium is a better part" [36]. I didn't much care what his technical opinion was of the P6, but what he said next, I did care about. "The guys who conceived of the Pentium were better than the guys who conceived of the P6." It doesn't matter which guys were truly "better," and Sanders' opinion on it mattered even less. What got my attention was that the CEO of a rival company had decided to not just trash the P6, but to personally attack its designers as well. Why he thought that was appropriate or useful to AMD, I could not guess, but I took it personally and decided to do with that quote what sports teams do with trash-talking by their rivals: they post the quotes in the locker room for additional inspiration. So maybe I should thank Mr. Sanders, because in the wee hours, when I was tired and wanted to quit for the night, I would see that quote on the wall and feel reinvigorated.

---

tense glare of multiple spotlights trained squarely in my eyes. I could not see even one person in the audience, much less discern the real-time feedback the audience normally provided. If that were not bad enough, I next found that if I turned my head even slightly, out of the corner of my eye I could see a 20-foot image of my own face, tracking my movements in real time. It was incredibly disconcerting, and if I had not practiced my talk so many times that I had memorized it, it would been very difficult to stay on task. I do not know how Mick Jagger does it.

6

THE PEOPLE FACTOR

Good people aren't good because they never cause harm to others. They're good because they treat others the best way they know how, with the understanding that they have. Too often in our public life we condemn people for well-meant errors, and then insist that everyone should forgive people whose errors were intentional and who attempted, not to make amends, but to avoid consequences. Good and bad have been stood on their head by people who should have known better. How do we live in such a world?

—Orson Scott Card, **Rebeka**

To say that the P6 project had its share of people issues would be an understatement. Any effort that combines extreme creativity, mindbending stress, and colorful personalities has to account for the "people factor," the simple idea that people will say and do just about anything given enough time. The people factor is probably the least understood aspect of hardware design, and nothing you learn in graduate school compares with what a day-to-day, long-term, high-visibility, pressure-cooker project can teach you about your coworkers, or yourself.

I considered filling this chapter with sage advice about managing and coping, but I ended up mostly relating stories of stuff that worked and did not work. I am confident the reader will draw the appropriate conclusions.

The Pentium Chronicles. By Robert P. Colwell
© 2006 IEEE Computer Society

HIRING AND FIRING

The 1990s were a period of very strong growth in Intel's workforce. Early in the decade, the company had around 22,000 full-time employees; by 2000, the number had quadrupled.

Our design teams were growing, too. The inexorable march of Moore's Law made ever more transistors available to chip designers, but schedules were not lengthened commensurately, and though design tools were improving, they did not make us twice as productive every 18 months. In other words, we were falling behind, and we compensated by hiring more help. Design teams as large as Intel's—hundreds of engineers, tools designers, and layout experts—require a highly organized, disciplined process for hiring, forming, and managing the team.

Rational Recruitment

Approximately half the P6 and Pentium 4 design teams were recent college graduates (RCGs) when they joined us. Hundreds of RCGs were walking around who not only had never designed anything, but also had never held a full-time professional job. On the surface, this probably seems a little crazy.

I would like to think our recruitment scheme was solely responsible for our stellar selection of RCGs, but I know better. Still in all, it worked well enough for us to staff both the P6 and Pentium 4 projects with hundreds of engineers, and we were justifiably proud when many of those RCGs went on to have very successful careers.

Part of our recruiting scheme's success is that it was impressively rational. We began by fishing in the steady stream of resumes made available by the company's usual campus representatives, and farmed out the most likely fits to the project leaders. Design engineers would phone screen the candidates for 30 to 60 minutes, essentially checking for a match between the candidate's knowledge and the resume's strong points. About half the phone screen candidates who passed were invited to Oregon for a site visit.

Those interviewing the visiting candidate had two goals: Sell the candidate on Intel, the team, and the merits of living here (not *at* Intel, but somewhere nearby; we did not want to scare them), and assess their ability to do the work and the candidate's fit with the team. We had cleverly isolated six major technical areas—architecture, microarchitecture, software, logic, circuits, and layout—and determined that successful candidates should be expert in at least one. A design team expert from one of the six areas then spent an hour with the candidate, gently probing his or her knowledge and training. The interviewer scored the candidate's knowledge of that area from 1 to 10, with 1 being clueless and 10 being world-class expert. When the expert in that area was finished, the candidate would move to the expert in the next area, and so on. By the end of the interviewing, we had six scores for each candidate.

Few candidates scored at either extreme; middle scores between 3 and 7 were by far the most common. For calibration, we routinely reminded interviewers that 5 was supposed to be the mean score expected of a candidate. Most candidates would score very well on one or two areas, relatively poorly on one or two, and middling on the rest. If the personality fit was good, such candidates could expect a job offer.

The interviewers would meet to discuss the candidate, and occasionally, one would say, "This candidate didn't know much about X, but seemed to be an expert at Y." The Y interviewer would then raise her eyebrows and say, "That's funny. I found that this candidate doesn't know anything about Y, but they sure talked a good game about X." To get to the root of this contradiction, we would ask the X and Y interviewers to explain the

---

The strcpy Programming Test

As part of our interview to determine skill in the software technical area, we asked the candidate to write the C code for the strcpy (string copy) utility. This is a presupplied function in the C/Unix runtime library, so most candidates would never have previously considered how it must be implemented, but it is a very simple task for any reasonably experienced programmer to sketch out a workable version of strcpy within a few minutes.

Most candidates who said they "knew C" passed this sanity check easily. But we were surprised at how many candidates who had claimed extensive C programming experience on their resume were unable to conjure up a plausible strcpy. Some would stumble around for a few minutes and then admit that they had heard of C, but never actually seen it. Others would write out code that looked suspiciously like Fortran, using array syntax instead of C's pointers. We did not necessarily fail candidates who performed poorly on this test, but if their resume did not match their interview, we looked much harder at their references.

---

questions they had asked. Listening to these interview questions, the other four interviewers would look around guiltily, as they realized that they themselves might not have fared all that well on this interview.

Hiring and the Promotion List

In 1999, Jim Aylor of the University of Virginia invited me to give a talk at the Microelectronic Systems Education Conference in Arlington, Virginia [25]. The invitation was in response to requests from professors who wanted to know how effective their students were when they entered industry and how well prepared we thought they were during recruitment. I viewed this talk as an opportunity to show off our well-crafted recruitment process, and solicited some help from Intel's human resources department so that we could show how actual data on promotions and career advancements correlated to our hiring process.

Initially, I didn't even think to question whether the data would support my belief that our hiring process was effective. But as I looked over several years of promotions data from the corporate database, I began to realize that my intuitions were way off. I had thought that the higher the interview score (the candidate's average expertise level across the six technical areas), the more likely they would be to "catch on" at Intel and move on to great things. But there really was no statistical correlation between our interview scores and the odds that a particular person would get a promotion within a few years after having been hired. (All "fast-track" performers get such promotions.)

This was somewhat distressing, at least initially. It just seemed so logical that people with higher evident technical ability would be better positioned than others with respect to promotions, but the data did not show it.

This made me suspicious. If my intuitions were wrong about this, where else might they be wrong? Well, surely a higher college grade point average ought to be correlated with career success. After all, the GPA is a result of native ability, hard work, and demonstrated mastery of difficult technical material, all of which seem essential to success in industry. But, again, the data did not bear this out. It was clear that Intel did not hire engineers with GPAs below approximately 3.2, but once someone was hired, a higher GPA did not in any way predispose its owner to faster promotions.

I was feeling a bit desperate at this point. If interview scores and GPAs did not predict future success, how about advanced degrees? Wouldn't MSEEs and PhDs be able to exhibit higher levels of mastery as well as the perseverance to tackle something and finish it no matter what? Again, the data stubbornly refused to support even this soundly logical assumption. If anything, PhDs appeared to be underrepresented in the ranks of the newly promoted.[1]

By this point, the pattern was clear, and I was pretty sure how the next attempted correlation would turn out, but I pressed on, comparing the alma maters of the fast-trackers to Intel's list of preferred "focus" schools. I found nothing. There were unmistakable differences in the educational background of students who came from, say, MIT, and those who came from second-tier universities, but focus schools were only slightly better represented in the promotions lists. And even that correlation was questionable, because Intel hires disproportionately more students from its focus schools so, naturally, there would be more of them in the fast-track category.

None of this was particularly alarming. After all, our recruitment process was accomplishing its basic mission of finding good technical talent. Asking it to also predict which candidates would excel at climbing the corporate ladder was beyond what we needed. But when we discussed the implications of my correlationless findings, it was still worth asking, "If a candidate's background and training doesn't lead to corporate success, what does?"

We concluded that no single quantifiable metric could reliably predict career success. However, we also felt that fast-trackers have identifiable qualities and show definite trends.

One quality is a whatever-it-takes attitude. All high-output engineers have a willingness to do whatever it takes to make a project succeed, especially their particular corner of it. If that means working weekends occasionally, doing extracurricular research, or rewriting tools, they do it.

Another quality is a solid, unflappable understanding of all the technologies they are using or developing. No one person can know everything, but fast-trackers have the drive to familiarize themselves with all aspects of their work, even those that are not required for their immediate task, and this gives them the necessary credibility to discuss their design with project experts, which in turn drives them up the learning curve that much faster. Finally, these high-output types seemed to innately grasp that they are members of a large team, which means that certain behaviors are very efficient while others are counterproductive. They know, for example, that the classic elbow-your-neighbor scramble up the corporate ladder does not work in a large design team that is competently managed, so they avoid that tactic. Instead, they are the ones always helping everyone else, sometimes directly and sometimes by sharing tools or tricks they have learned or developed.

When we can identify these high-output traits in an interview, maybe we will be able to confidently predict career trajectories. Until then, at least we know not to trust any of the obvious predictors, even education level.

---

[1] In retrospect, this should not be surprising because PhDs tend to get hired into higher pay grades, and the higher the pay grade, the longer the average period between promotions. Job effectiveness in the higher pay grades is a strong function of a person's ability to influence peers, and it takes time to build the necessary interpersonal relationships.

Firing

About the least fun you can have as a manager, unless you are Donald Trump, is to fire someone. And with a team as large as the P6, despite your best efforts at hiring only people you believe will be barn-burners, every manager will eventually have to deal with an employee who simply is not getting the job done in an acceptable way.

> *About the least fun you can have as a manager, unless you are Donald Trump, is to fire someone.*

Just as a stellar performer's glory tends to make his manager look good, a poor performer tends to drag down everyone around him. Large companies must have a process they can use to identify underachievers and help them get back to an acceptable output level. Failing that, there must be a way to remove from the design team and the company those who are not pulling their own weight. You might think that underperformers do not enjoy their reputation and are already making plans to leave. Unfortunately, that is not so; people with that much initiative tend not to get into performance trouble in the first place.

Except in television sitcoms, the trouble is not people who simply do not show up for work, or who take three hour lunches and then leave early. People who are that far off their required output are easy to deal with. The difficult cases are those in which a formerly competent engineer has been promoted beyond his comfort zone and has not adjusted to the new expectations associated with the higher pay grade.

> *The difficult cases are those in which a formerly competent engineer has been promoted beyond his comfort zone.*

Intel's pay grade scheme is intended to associate an employee's overall compensation with his or her contributions to the corporate bottom line. Intel calls this process a meritocracy and reminds every employee, including support staff, that all employees are expected to continually improve their performance and that they will be formally evaluated once a year to establish that they are keeping up with their peers [27].

As a manager, you often supervise people representing several pay grades. You have a reasonable working knowledge of what tasks are appropriate for which employees (otherwise you would not be an effective manager, which would not bode well for your own performance evaluation) but day to day, your group's pay grades are immaterial. The focus is on allocating the required work among the group in a way that gets it done in the required time.

The surprise comes when you attend the yearly ranking-and-rating (abbreviated as R&R) session on behalf of each of your team members. Suddenly, the members' pay grades are extremely relevant because that is the basis on which their output will be evaluated vis-à-vis their peers in other groups. Few things are as poignant as a manager's dismay when he realizes that the person he has been giving nothing but kudos to over the year is not doing at all well relative to those of the same pay grade in other groups. The manager often feels somewhat guilty, and more than a little duplicitous, because that employee contributed valuable output toward the group's bottom line and now will not receive the expected reward.

There is no arbitration for this. The manager must accept that he or she neglected to take the employee's pay grade into account in assigning tasks or simply did not notice or could not tell where the norm was for that pay grade. Now, instead of a raise, the employee will be getting feedback that those valuable outputs simply were not up to the quality or quantity of the employee's peers in that grade. The manager is probably thinking a root canal would be more enjoyable.[2]

The company's formal process for recalibrating the employee is a three-to-six-month "recovery" plan. A lot more direct supervision is involved—daily meetings in some cases—and careful record keeping. In many cases, this direct coaching is all the employee needs to get up to snuff and improve his rating at the next R&R. But occasionally, even the direct help, which can verge on micromanagement, does not fix the problem and the manager must resignedly conclude that the employee is simply not capable of operating at the current pay grade. A strategy that works in a surprisingly large fraction of cases is to demote the employee back to the pay grade at which they were successful.

Still, there are some cases in which a demotion is not appropriate, or the employee will not accept it. That leaves firing as the only option. It is not pleasant to have to walk someone to the door—not for them and not for you as their manager. Occasionally, an employee will thank you for having gone the extra mile in trying to get them back on track, and they will have realized that they simply were not a good fit for your group and should try something else. But if my experience is any guide, most will be upset, angry, fearful, and in the mood to tell you how you could have managed them better and how this is all your fault, not theirs. Those are the days when, try as you might, you cannot remember why you ever took a management job in the first place.

I once went through this course of events with an employee, a person who worked for someone who reported to me. After we both tried hard to modify his behavior and get usable output from him, we ended up walking him to the door. On the way, he regaled us with stories of how we had screwed up his life and how his only mistake was to have had the unbelievably bad luck of getting us as managers. It took a couple of weeks for the bad taste to go away, just long enough for another manager in Intel to (believe it or not) rehire him. Apparently, this manager had seen that his new employee was newly fired, but did not see fit to call me and ask what was behind the dismissal. Although this particular employee had not generated much legitimate technical output, he was more than capable of making a hash out of our chip design database had he been revenge-minded. Fortunately, he was not, but had it been up to me, the manager who blindly rehired him would have also been walked to the door on the grounds of self-evident incompetence and unjustifiable risk taking.

POLICY WARS

From time to time, project realities clash with corporate's idea of what the company should be doing at this particular time. During the P6, we encountered many such disruptions in the space–time continuum, and it is my fondest wish in sharing these stories that they inspire policy makers to walk around the hallways and observe operations before launching company-wide edicts.

---

[2]As employees go higher in the pay grades, this problem becomes less important, because it is an official tenet of Intel's meritocracy that employees "own their own careers." They are required to operate at their pay grade; it is not enough to just do what the boss tells them to do.

Corporate Disincentives

Chip development projects or, for that matter, any product development I have ever been part of, always feel like a log flume ride at an amusement park. These rides begin with a long uphill climb, where things happen rather slowly and the fun is minimal. Then the log-boat floats around several curves, with lots of gratuitous splashing and generally nice views, but it does not feel like you are going very fast or getting anywhere. Then you see the final drop off and time speeds up. The sense of inevitability mounts, and you have the distinct feeling that you are committed to getting to the end of the ride no matter what. (In Disneyland, animatronic bears and raccoons happily shout out that it is too late to do anything but hang on and wait for the finish, and why would you get on this ride, anyway? Chip developers everywhere will recognize *that* sentiment.)

In the "pre-drop-off" frenzy, key engineers are spending every waking moment working, whether at the plant or from home. Unless you can get a team to this tapeout crunch, death-march phase, you have no hope of meeting your schedule. Nature will conspire to throw obstacle after obstacle into your project's path, and the only way to prevail is to have every hand on deck, actively resolving issues as they arise. These crunch phases typically last six months, although I have seen them go on for as long as a year. Some would argue that you can do the entire project in crunch mode, but you surely risk burnout and then you would get the exact opposite of the efficiency you are seeking.

We were in the P6 crunch phase when word came down of a new corporate initiative, effective immediately. The initiative, "Back To Intel Basics," was an attempt to recapture Intel's history, in which every employee was required to be at work by 8 A.M. and those arriving *between* 8 and 9 A.M. had to sign a late list that their supervisors would see. I never understood why highly paid professionals competing on the world stage would require such babysitting or deserve that kind of official condescension from upper management. Luckily, I had managed to miss that era because they had gotten rid of that onerous absurdity before I started in 1990.

But I was getting a chance to relive that period four years later. Thanks to the new initiative, employees who could not be at work by 8 A.M. would need to provide a written explanation to their management. And we managers were to explain this new policy to the troops.

I objected vociferously. Half our engineering team had still been on the premises at midnight the night before, yet they were expected to be back by 8 A.M.? That was obviously ridiculous, and I could easily predict their reactions. "Sure, boss, from now on I'll be here at 8 A.M. And I'll leave at 5 P.M. I have no problem cutting back on my hours!" I respectfully declined to participate in this management error. But I was reminded that when I accepted a management position, I also implicitly agreed to pass legitimate directions from said management to my team. So I agreed to tell my team "I have been instructed to tell you that anyone who cannot be here at 8 AM is required to give me a written statement as to why." When I told the team that, in exactly those terms, they all looked puzzled. One finally said "If we write the memo in question, what would you do with it?" I said I would throw it away without reading it and that I trusted they were all adult and professional enough to know how to get their jobs done. I never heard another word about it.

Other corporate initiatives included a serious infatuation with Stephen Covey's *7 Habits of Highly Effective People* [33]. There were books, videos, and courses. I don't think we were ever formally measured on whether we had taken Covey training, but it was not far short of that. The idea of a win/win did permanently enter the corporate lexicon, and I think it was a great antidote to Intel's historical "constructive confrontation" procedure, which was sometimes wrongly interpreted as official corporate sanction to say whatever you wanted to a coworker.

A corporate initiative that I particularly disliked was, "Do chips in half the time with half the people." Talk about an unfunded mandate! The executives could just as easily, and with the same effectiveness, have promoted an initiative for each electron to carry twice the normal charge. As goals go, at least that one would generate interesting discussion, and in that context might even have useful outputs, but as a requirement from above, this kind of wishful thinking is very dangerous. Well-run design teams that mean what they say would be unable to commit to this target, but poorly managed teams might succumb to the ever-present temptation to tell management what they want to hear. For the next few years, that second-rate team would be the darling of the company, until the day they had to deliver the new design. At that point, everyone would realize that the team did indeed achieve a design with half the labor in half the time. They just forgot to create a viable product in the process.

An Intel initiative for several years now has been "Operational Excellence," or OpX. The basic idea is to execute well—make and meet commitments, do not accept mediocrity, and strive for continuous improvements across the board. So what's not to like about that? Plenty, but none of it is obvious, and therein lies the danger.

OpX emphasizes exactly the wrong thing. What makes companies like Intel successful is creating profitable products that compete well on the open market. The customer who plunks down hard-earned cash for an Intel machine does not ask, "How did you design this chip?" The product must stand on its own. In the final analysis, it does not matter how it was conceived and executed. You do not ask Johnson & Johnson how they made their cotton swabs, and you don't ask Pepsi how efficiently they formulated their soda. The only thing that matters at the point of sale is how good a product is and how much it costs, and that is where a design team must focus their attention.

Richard Feynman tells the story of the "cargo cult," a South Seas people who, in World War II, got used to having big airplanes land with lots of valuable things inside [18]. They wanted this to happen again, so they lit fires down the sides of the runway, built grass huts with bamboo sticks arranged like a radio antenna, and provided an islander to sit attentively with fake headphones on his head. But the planes did not come. The islanders had mistaken appearance for reality.

The insidious aspect of OpX is that when a team does create a world-class product, much of its development was indeed performed in ways congruent to OpX's goals, but in spite of OpX, or independently of it, not because of it. A good design team will naturally make and meet commitments, not accept mediocrity, and strive for continuous improvements across the board in their pursuit of a world-class product. They do not need OpX to spur that thinking.

Conversely, teams that have not conceived a world-class product, or who are simply not up to that challenge, will not benefit from the distractions of constantly analyzing their execution when they ought to be thinking about how their product will fare in the open warfare of the commercial marketplace.

If you win the Superbowl, nobody is going to say, "Well, maybe you won, but then again your methods weren't as good as the team that won last year." (And if they do say that, flash them your Superbowl ring and ignore them.) Likewise, it will be small consolation to the losing side if they are told, "Too bad you lost, but at least your uniforms are clean." And that is what is wrong with OpX. Teams that need it, need much more than it

provides, and teams that do not need it
will be hurt by its pointless distraction.

> *Teams that need OpX need much more
> than it provides, and teams that don't
> need it will be hurt by it.*

The Led Zeppelin Incident

Security guards are an essential feature of
today's workplace. The vast majority are
professional and compassionate and try to do the best job they know how. (The exception
is a woman guard I had to pass on my way out the door. Every night, she would look at
my badge, with a photo from circa 1990, then at me, and say the same thing: "Oh my,
how you've *aged*." And I would grit my teeth and think, "Lady, you're no spring chicken
yourself.")

But security guards are also agents of company policy, whose creation and motivation
was largely outside their scope of influence. Consequently, they can radically favor the
letter of the law over its spirit. In an engineering environment, that is a recipe for trouble.

This particular reality hit me hard one weekend when I was on a deadline to finish a
paper by Monday morning. Debug contingencies had prevented me from getting to it until that Saturday, so there I was on Sunday morning at 3 A.M., typing away, headphones
plugged into Led Zeppelin's first album with the volume cranked up as high as necessary
to keep me awake. The building was empty except for me and the security guard at the
front desk.

Someone tapped me on the shoulder. Startled, I turned in my chair, and found the security guard in my cubicle.

"Can I help you?" I asked somewhat warily.

"What are you listening to on those headphones?" he replied.

"Led Zeppelin's first album. Why?"

"Is that work-related?" he continued.

"Huh?"

"Corporate policy forbids listening to music on personal CD players."

"You're kidding, right?" I start turning back to my paper.

"No, not at all. First of all, listening to music could annoy the others around you."

I still thought, maybe this guy's joking, and turned fully around and look at him.
Hmmm, no smiles. Maybe he really *is* serious, I thought. "Uh, look around you. Do you
see any other people here? You were the nearest other humanoid. Are you saying you
could hear my headphones from 100 meters away?"

But the security guard did not give up easily. "Well, what if there were a fire, and the
alarm went off, and you couldn't hear it because you had the music up too high?"

At this point I was struggling with whether to feel annoyed that this guy was wasting
my time at 3 A.M. on a Sunday, or amused at how sincerely he was trying to obey his corporate directions and keep me and my phantom neighbors from burning up in an imagi-
nary fire.

I could feel annoyance getting the upper hand. "If I had the music up that high, it
would indicate that I have a very serious hearing loss. And with a hearing loss that profound, I might not hear the normal alarms anyway. What provision has the company
made for indicating a fire alarm to putatively hearing-impaired people such as myself,
anyway?"

The security guard looked around, saw the alarm horns, and realized no such provision
had been made for the hearing-impaired. He recovered nicely. "We're not discussing that.
We're talking about violating the company's rules about listening to music while at work."

Annoyance thoroughly trounced amusement, and even sarcasm beat a hasty retreat. "Well, tell you what. I'm going to sit back down, and you're going to leave my cubicle and go back to your desk at the front door. When you left my cube, the subject had been informed of his violation of a sacred precept of the company, so you can tell whomever needs to know that you did a good night's work. As for me, when you walk away, I'm going to start the Led Zeppelin song over again, because I hate to start in the middle, and then I'm going to finish the work I came here to do." (Appropriately enough, the Led Zeppelin song in question was "Communications Breakdown.")

A few days later, my general manager, Will Swope, asked me how things were going, and I related this story to him. He was aghast, promised to investigate, and said that in the future security guards would be permitted to approach the engineers only to ask, "Sir, can I bring you a cup of coffee?" I think he really did follow through with that, because the headphones issue never resurfaced. Of course, the fact that all new PCs and engineering workstations were equipped with CD-ROM drives complete with convenient headphone jacks might also have contributed. Intel security may have realized that this was a losing battle.

As a bonus, a few weeks later, the company added flashing strobe lights to the fire alarm system in that building.

Exiting the Exit Bag Check

From its earliest days, Intel had a formal company policy that all bags were to be checked upon exiting the premises. Like many high-tech firms, Intel knew that its family jewels were the intellectual property inside its best products. This IP existed in several forms, such as books, documents, and computer storage media, and the exit bag check was aimed at these targets. Intel also made large quantities of small computer chips that were quite valuable. Presumably, security guards would also be quite interested were they to spot an outgoing bag with a lot of chips inside.

Whatever its original motivation, by the 1990s, the exit bag check had long outlived its usefulness. Its main effect was to establish a constant line of from five to 15 irritated engineers, all just trying to get home after a very long day. But because their employer obviously did not trust them, they were expected to waste (by actual count) two to eight minutes per evening getting out the door.

The security guards tried hard to implement a consistent policy for bag checks for all U.S. sites. Unfortunately, it was pretty stringent, and the laptop bag I was using had nine zippered compartments. So every single night, the guard would exercise all nine zippers while I and everyone behind me did our best to enjoy the spectacle.

It got worse. In the mid-1990s, CD-ROMs became a popular way to distribute software, and writable CD-ROMs became common. In my laptop bag was a CD-ROM carrying case containing a mix of software, backup copies of presentations and other files, and music CDs. Every night, as the guard rummaged around in my bag, he or she would find this CD case, and feel obliged to open it and check the identity of each and every CD-ROM. Some guards also shared their opinions of my musical tastes, which I often found difficult to appreciate.

One night, I became exasperated with the CD-ROM part of the search and asked, "Exactly what is it that you're looking for in that CD case?"

The security guard said, "We have a report that a particular CD-ROM was stolen a few months ago and we're watching out for it."

"But the only way you're going to find it that way is if the thief is a certified moron.

Do you see that rectangular piece of plastic on the side of my laptop? That's a CD-ROM drive. Since the laptop is not powered up, you can't see what's in that drive. How do you know the CD-ROM you're looking for isn't in that drive?"

The guard looked wary, but interested. "Is it?"

"No!" I exploded, "And that's not the point. See all these people in line? They all have dial-up or cable access to Intel's computers from home. If they're not smart enough to get the information off the CD-ROM you're looking for and get that data to their homes without your knowledge, then *they're not smart enough to work here.*"

I realized I was yelling at the wrong person. The guards do not make the policies; they just implement what is handed down as best they can. I decided to change tactics and go after the policy makers.

I started sending e-mails to higher-ups, trying to figure out who was in charge of company policies about security and exit bag checks. I firmly believe that policies affecting the entire company on such a fundamental basis must be decided with the participation, or at least the full understanding, of the company's workers, never secretly or in a vacuum. Allowing small, secret groups to quietly determine general policies virtually guarantees irrational acts and inefficiencies.

For the next few years, I routinely traded e-mails with various company policy makers, urging them to rethink the exit bag checks and to clearly post the rationales for the various exit checks still being inflicted. I got a lot of encouragement from my coworkers. One very senior engineer told me that he had long ago decided to test the exit bag check policy by simply refusing to cooperate with it. When he first did that, he assumed it would bring the issue to a head and the company would undergo the appropriate internal debate. But instead, the security guards passed the word that this person was to quietly be allowed to go out without the check.

I thought that was a fascinating insight into the effectiveness of the whole scheme, but it was not helping me. I did not want special treatment, I just wanted the whole thing to go away.

Then I visited Intel Israel. The first time I left the plant in Haifa, I put my bag up on the counter and waited, as I had been trained to do over the years. The security guard looked at me strangely and shrugged his shoulders. They didn't do exit bag checks in Israel! (Years later, I was told that they used to do them there but stopped for some reason.)

When I got back home, I fired off another e-mail to the security policy folks, in which I wrote, "I think it's important that the general engineering population in the U.S. be notified that American engineers are, by official corporate policy, much less trustworthy than their Israeli counterparts. I bet they don't know that, and they have a right to know." Evidently, the policy makers did not agree with my proposal, because no such memo was issued, but they uncharacteristically did not try to refute my point in private, either.

The entire matter came to a head months later, when I was in the exit line behind an Intel VP carrying a large legal briefcase stuffed with documents of all colors and sizes. I sighed; this search was going to take 5 minutes all by itself. But to my astonishment, the VP put the bag down, flashed something in his hand and immediately went on his way. I asked the guard what he had shown to avoid the bag search. The guard refused to answer the question, but I was determined. "Is there some secret pass? How does one qualify? Do you have to take a lie-detector test, or get special ethical training? Would a note from my mother suffice?" The guard looked very uncomfortable, but would not talk. Now I was really intrigued—after all the e-mail I had traded with the security officials, nobody had ever even hinted at special secret passes.

So that night I sent an e-mail message to my general manager, who, as it turned out, also had a secret pass. When he offered to get me one, I refused and said that I preferred to fix the whole stupid system instead. I again appealed to the policy makers, writing, "Well, it turns out that the U.S. engineers not only are less trustworthy than the Israelis, they're also less trustworthy than people above grade 11, because that's the threshold for applying for the secret pass. Our employees have a right to know these rules."

The policy makers responded that upper executives had begun finding it embarrassing to have their non-Intel guests searched on the way out. I wrote back, "Then those executives now know exactly how annoying, condescending, frivolous, intrusive, and embarrassing those same checks are to the people who actually work here, except that we have this done to us each and every day."

I got back an odd response that essentially said, "This problem is going to go away." A week later, the exit bag checks were gone. I don't know if I should get the credit for this, but I certainly lobbied tirelessly to make it happen.

Sailboats and Ditches

Many management books recommend "team-building exercises," in which groups of people who normally work together professionally get to interact with their peers in new ways, while climbing a mountain, playing paintball, and engaging in other activities not normally found in their job descriptions. Intel provides many such opportunities, but when these activities are executed from within the normal hypercompetitive Intel culture, they do not always have the desired effect.

I once attended an off-site meeting in Monterey, California, for the leaders of all microprocessor development activities within Intel. The concept was that we would split into groups of six, and each group would take a sailboat out to a designated figure-eight racecourse. The first one back to the docks won.

As my boat left the docks, its owner asked if any of us had sailed before. I'm no expert, but I have had a sailboat for many years, so I raised my hand. No one else did. But someone else immediately leaped up and said "How hard can it be?" and took over. Within a couple of minutes, we were becalmed, watching the rest of the boats sailing serenely out to the racecourse. Judging from everyone else's sails, there was not a surplus of wind anywhere on that course, but at least they were *moving*. Now that we were in irons, sailing ability did not matter much, so everyone took a turn at pretending they were Captain Ahab, looked enviously at the sailboats in the distance, and muttered about the would-be captain who had got us into this predicament. Never mind that any of the others would probably have accomplished the same outcome. Finally, one VP had an inspiration, "The rules are that we were to leave the docks, sail around, and the first one back wins, right? So let's wait until the right moment, start up the motor, and cruise into the harbor just ahead of the otherwise-fastest boat. We will have met all of the requirements." We thought he was kidding, but I really do not think he was. Nobody else had any better idea, so that is what we did, or rather what we *tried* to do. The event's organizer knew his staff too well, had anticipated shady maneuvers, and had provided a spotter on the pier, who ruined the plan. How this kind of behavior was going to meld us into one high-output team was a little hazy, but nobody seemed surprised or at all worried about the idea of putting winning ahead of competing fairly.

Not that I am immune to ignoble competition. At another off-site meeting, we rented 12 full-motion flight simulators and flew two teams against each other. If you were shot down, you would be reincarnated a minute later, often in the same spot, about 2000 feet above your aircraft carrier. One of my counterparts within Intel, a guy whom I routinely found on the opposite side of whatever I thought was right, was flying for the other team and had shot me down at least twice. He would anticipate where I would be reincarnated, wait there until it happened, and then shoot me down again before I had a chance. This was infuriating, so I devoted the rest of the evening to finding that guy and shooting him down. I beat him, but not overwhelmingly.

The only way to restore the cosmic balance was to completely annihilate him, so the next several times I happened to be in Santa Clara, I went back to that flight simulator facility and practiced, for hours. A few months later, we had another off-site meeting at the same place. The same guy showed up on the other team, and I waxed him to my heart's content. I also felt good about having learned Intel's team-building methods so thoroughly.

The paintball exercises were probably the least successful and shortest lived team-building experience. It became abundantly clear that not only were they failing to achieve any higher goal, but they were positively counterproductive. In Israel, everyone gets military training, and the Israelis on staff were joining the same team, and applying that training with relish. One exercise ended with a VP cowering in a ditch, while several members of the other team blasted away at him. Even worse, when Intel people heard of this incident, they were first appalled, but once they learned the name of the VP in question, they thought that, overall, justice had been done.

I learned two valuable lessons from these team-building exercises. It can be very hard to turn off competitiveness, and payback is, well, you know what they say about that.

Orbiting the Bathrooms

Intel has a formal policy called "Copy Exactly," which led to such great results in the chip fabrication plants that the company tried it in many other corporate areas.

One such area was building design. Intel's Ronler Acres buildings in Oregon have the same floorplan as those in Jones Farm or the Folsom site in Sacramento. When you travel, this homogeneity is great, because it is easy to get your bearings in a strange building.

The trouble is that one size seldom fits all, no matter what the little tag on your T-shirt says. After we had moved into the Ronler Acres buildings while designing Pentium 4, the male engineers discovered a problem, one that many women will recognize, having endured it much more frequently: not enough bathroom capacity. The building's bathrooms were designed to handle a 50/50 mix of men and women on a fully populated floor, but they most emphatically could not accommodate a design team that was 80% male and that had compressed their offices, thereby boosting "fully populated floor" to well beyond expectation.

This mismatch of capacity and demand led to a daily ritual, wherein the male design engineers would go into one bathroom, find a line of men waiting, and head out to the other bathroom. What they did not yet know was that the same scene was playing out at the other bathroom, generating a similar line of unhappy engineers heading toward the bathroom they themselves had just left. In effect, there was a continuous loop of uncomfortable engineers orbiting the two bathrooms instead of designing silicon.

As a project leader, it seemed obvious to me that this was a tragic waste of human potential, stemming from a really stupid source—that all buildings had to be designed the same way regardless of intended use. I brought this issue up at a divisional staff meeting, but got surprisingly little support. In fact, the finance guy, the person you would think would be most annoyed at hearing how highly paid engineers were spending substantial fractions of their day, thought the whole thing was so funny that he bought a toilet seat, spray-painted it gold, and installed it on the chair in my cubicle. I was seriously tempted to go buy the rest of the commode, install it in his cube some weekend, and put the golden toilet seat on as a finishing touch. The problem eventually seemed to subside, but I never knew why. Perhaps everyone stopped drinking caffeinated soda after the project taped out.

MANAGEMENT BY OBJECTIVE

From ten thousand feet up, the overall flow of a chip development project (even those as massive as Intel's) and the technology it is developing are reasonably clear. You form a team, acquire or develop the necessary tools, conceive a design, implement it, and validate the result.

But you cannot run a project from ten thousand feet. Projects have to be executed from the trenches because only from there can you see the myriad details the team must resolve. For this reason, and to strike a reasonable compromise between overhead and benefit, Intel mandates the use of iMBO (Intel Management By Objective). Andy Grove described the genesis of this idea in *High Output Management* [16], in which he points to two key questions that any management planning effort must address: What is the right target, and how can I measure my progress toward that target?

> *You cannot run a project from ten thousand feet.*

iMBO's basic idea is to list a set of objectives the team must accomplish over a quarter. These are things that if left undone might jeopardize the project's overall schedule. Typically, a manager identifies four to eight objectives, some carried over from the previous quarter, especially if they were on the previous quarter's list, but are still not complete. The manager also identifies a set of activities by which to judge that objective's completion.

What I found worked best was to "seed" the next quarter's tentative iMBO list with my own ideas, and then spend 30 minutes of staff time discussing them. Almost always, the team had valuable inputs on which objectives were the best ones for the next quarter, and how those objectives could be achieved and measured. This discussion was often the most valuable aspect of the whole iMBO method.

The other very valuable fallout of using iMBOs came during the quarterly review of how last quarter's results should be judged. Each quarter, the team that had taken the objective assesses how well they have accomplished it, essentially "grading the quarterly sheet." A graded quarterly key results sheet might look partially like this:

Graded Q4/92 Objectives/Key Results, P6 Architecture

Objective: Complete BRTL development, AMB:
  1   1. Run 95% of all Real Mode tests on BRTL, except for BBL, EBL, DCU, and MOB.
  0   2. Run BenchmarkA and BenchmarkB on full model.
  1   3. Resolve all SRTL gating issues.
  1   4. Resolve 15 simplification issues.

And so on, for typically 4–6 objectives and 4–6 examples under each.

<u>Figure 6.1.</u> Dilbert's coworker gets his iMBOs wrong. Reprinted by permission of United Media.

AMB stands for "As Measured By," and the list of activities corresponds to the judging criteria.

Each objective must be concrete, specific, and meaningful, and the team must be honest in judging its state of completeness at the quarter's end. In the sample above, the team felt it had accomplished tasks 1, 3, and 4 for the first objective, but had not completed task 2. We certainly had done better than Dilbert's coworker in Figure 6.1.

It probably seems as though having a team grade its own accomplishments might yield "perfect" results, quarter after quarter. That can sometimes be a problem; managing with iMBOs can be tricky because, although they are an extremely effective tool when used properly, they are also very easy to subvert. A sure way to destroy the iMBO's effectiveness, for example, is to tie compensation to the iMBO grading. A great deal of judgment is required to select the right objectives and the best metrics by which to measure them. Any unnatural pressure to score well on iMBOs, meaning any pressure other than having the project turn out as desired, would subvert the process by grade inflation. When every group gets a perfect score every quarter, the iMBOs are no longer filling their role as a planning procedure. And if a manager chooses to be honest even though all the other managers around her are rounding their numbers up, few employees will want to work for her, since it would, in effect, cost them compensation.

I was blessed at Intel with excellent managers—Fred Pollack, Pat Gelsinger, Dadi Perlmutter, Will Swope, Randy Steck, and Mike Fister—all of whom felt that a perfect score on a quarterly key results sheet might mean your group had an excellent quarter, but it might also mean you were not aggressive enough three months ago when you planned this quarter's activities or that your ability to fairly score your group's results was suspect.

Subversion aside, the iMBO process is a valuable tool. As Andy Grove mentions in his book [16], the act of identifying what you believe are the highest-priority tasks for your group in the next three months is also the act of ruling out certain other tasks. If they are worth doing, include them, and if they are not on the list, do not do them. Writing tasks down in this way has the salutary effect of forcing a team to be honest about what they think is really important, as opposed to what is simply interesting or fun.

The list of intentions also drives out miscommunication among cooperating design groups. If I receive your list of proposed iMBO objectives for next quarter, and I do not see the completion of some task I was relying on you to accomplish, I will assume the worst and go talk to you about it. It is better to find out now that we have our metaphorical wires crossed, rather than three months from now.

WE ARE SO RICH, WE MUST BE GOOD

The 1990s belonged to Intel (and Microsoft and Dell and many other computer-related companies, except for any of Intel's competitors). Intel began that decade as a 22,000 person, $2 billion enterprise, and ended it as an 80,000 person, $28 billion behemoth, with large profit margins on parts selling in burgeoning markets for which it held 80%+ market share. Intel even benefited from the "irrational exuberance" of the Internet-boom stock market, when price-to-earnings ratios were considered declassé and high-tech portfolios were de rigeur. Life was good.

The trouble is that, even at a place famous for its paranoia [14], human nature prevails. And it prevails with a vengeance whenever really smart, aggressive people are involved.

Approach any failed start-up and ask the principals what went wrong. You may get conflicting stories, but you will have no trouble engaging them on the subject, and you will find them very forthright, humble, and open to other ideas. They know beyond a doubt that their best-laid plans did not work out, and this knowledge seems to help the rational mind push the ego aside and focus on reality. Some may unjustifiably blame others, but few will start singing "Oh, the Cleverness of Me."

Now approach highly successful corporate executives and try to get an honest appraisal of their efforts over the same period. With very, very few exceptions, you will find that they believe they succeeded because their plans were brilliant, and success was inevitable when a talent as huge as theirs was applied to a problem. Virtually none of them will ever admit that luck might have been a nontrivial component.

I recall feeling the discomfort of that reality in the late 1990s, when I was participating in a high-level staff discussion on strategies and tactics for Intel's microprocessor development road map. Exuberance was the order of the day. The various staff members got up, one after another, and reminded the audience of what their groups' plans had been and how incredibly wonderfully those plans were turning out. Nobody questioned anyone else's plans. All was peace and mutual admiration, like Woodstock without the mud.

But that was not the talk I had prepared. My talk pointed out that for three successive years, our chief competitor (AMD) had not fielded a credible threat to any of our products. I likened it to showing up for the Superbowl or the World Cup and finding that the other team had not appeared, and had forfeited the game. Yes, that means you win, but it does not mean you are good. I gingerly pointed out some of our own execution errors, holes in our overall product road map, and places where we were not cooperating well between projects. My theme was that we were getting away with these errors, but should not count on continuing to do so in the future.

As I waited for the audience reaction, I was reminded of the phrase, "well received." Although I never quite knew what it meant, it seemed to me that its semantic range must have complete adoring acceptance at one extreme and hostility verging on lynching at the other.

For any reasonable meaning of that phrase, my remarks that day were not well received. The dominant reaction was laughter. Many people thought I was kidding; others thought I was just deluded, somehow blind to the obvious—that it was our corporate birthright for things to go extremely well all of the time. I kept hearing the phrases "Chicken Little" and "sky is falling" at lunch that day.

I had not seen this reaction coming. I likened my job as the company's chief architect of what was (and is) by far Intel's most valuable product line to that of an army scout. My unique contribution would be to conceptually roam several years into the future and watch how the coming technology might intersect with how the buying public might use it. When I applied that thinking to IA-32 and reported my results to this august group of technologists and managers, they heard only that I was proposing to sell the cash cow and start raising goats.

To be fair, they were not entirely wrong. It was a trivial exercise in the 1990s to graph the worst-case thermal dissipation of each successive microprocessor generation and extrapolate into the future. Depending on your assumptions about new cooling solutions and the effectiveness of yet-to-be-developed, low-power implementation techniques, you could adjust the year at which the curve would become ludicrous. Until that happened, there was still a lot of money to be made doing what we had been doing all along. But there was no mistaking the overall pattern—thermal dissipation was going to lead our industry right over a cliff.

If user demand for faster microprocessors could be counted on to remain unsated through this period, then the additional expense and noise of higher-power processors might not upset the apple cart quite yet. But I was also worried about the speed demand aspect. Historically, computers had never been fast enough; they had enough performance to be useful, but not enough to completely satisfy their users, so each new generation of faster machines was greeted with open arms and wallets.

As Clayton Christenson reminds us, however [17], all technologies climb similar maturation curves and eventually reach a point where their basic performance becomes satisfactory. By "satisfactory," he means that more performance is not valued enough to remain a viable differentiating sales factor. And as his book clearly shows in example after example, the progenitors of the technology in question are often the very last to realize that the performance horse they have ridden to market for so many years has gone lame.

My remarks stemmed from my concern that many signs of this particular end game were on the horizon and that corporate product development and research, and planning as well, should be taking this contingency explicitly into account.

As the laughter died out, it dawned on me for the first time that my career at Intel might not be of life-spanning duration. The culture had entrenched certain trends, influences, and attitudes that I simply could not alter, no matter how well I structured my argument or how carefully I crafted the data in my foils. I suddenly had a much better understanding of why big, successful companies are so seldom still big and successful after technology makes a sharp right turn.

BURNOUT

During P6's crunch phase, I sometimes heard executives worry that we were pushing the team too hard, that we did not know how to conserve our energy, that our good results to date were because we had got the best out of the team and that they were going to burn out. We managers worried about burnout, too, but we also knew stress levels are affected by more than simply working too much.

Burnout occurs when the employee just does not care about the product any more. The surest way to that outcome is if they do not believe in it in the first place; they must buy into the project's premise. For the P6 project, this was relatively easy. We all knew the company's fortunes would directly rise or fall on our product and its children. We also be-

> *We believed that an x86 microprocessor could be a legitimate contender for a performance leader.*

lieved (despite serious doubts both within Intel and the RISC community in general) that an x86 microprocessor could be a legitimate contender for a performance leader, and that demonstrating such a thing would have earth-shaking implications for the entire industry. We were believers on a *mission.*

Burnout also follows if engineers lose faith in their management. Engineers will do what it takes to succeed, but nobody likes to feel exploited. They want to know that while they have their heads down, getting the technology right, their teammates in marketing are getting the sales messages down and that management is making the right connections to get this new chip into successful volume production. They also need to believe that their own careers will trend in line with their contributions, sacrifices, and successful results.

Our engineers were not burned out. They were tired, and the cure for that was rest, upper management's acknowledgment of their incredible work, and immersion in the flow of accolades that follow a successful product. The worried executives were overlooking that key factor—our engineers *wanted* to succeed. Feeling like all their work was not in vain was the essential balm for these tired souls.

7

INQUIRING MINDS LIKE YOURS

Critics can't even make music by rubbing their back legs together.
—*Mel Brooks*

Over the years, I have received hundreds of e-mails and unsolicited inquiries in airplanes, dimly lit restaurants, online forums, parties, and street corners. It seemed fitting that I devote some part of this book to the more thought-provoking of these questions.

What was Intel *thinking* with that chip ID tag, which caused such a public uproar?

What was Ford thinking when they designed the Edsel? Or Coca-Cola when they did the New Coke? Beforehand, they thought "This is going to be great!" and afterwards they thought "Whoops! Whose stupid idea was *that*?"

To see how Intel started down this particular garden path, we must start with Intel's motivation and the chip feature that started all the trouble.

The yield[1] that a silicon manufacturer attains is an extremely important factor in determining a company's profitability and the final chip's price. To help track some of the variables related to yield, Intel's manufacturing engineers had long ago inserted dozens of fuses, which could be selectively blown during manufacture, to help mark individual silicon die as to XY position on the wafer, wafer lot, fab number, date, time, and other infor-

---

[1]Yield is the ratio of final working parts to the total number built, usually expressed as a percentage. Because of the tremendous complexities of the silicon manufacturing process, there are many ways for any given die on a wafer to become defective and, therefore, unshippable as product.

The Pentium Chronicles. By Robert P. Colwell
© 2006 IEEE Computer Society

mation. With cumbersome test procedures available only to Intel technicians, these fuses could later be read and correlations drawn.

In 1998, an Intel marketing person had what they thought was a great idea. Many software vendors, most notably Microsoft, had long been asking for a hardware mechanism by which they could permanently and irrevocably tie their software to a specific hardware platform to help combat software piracy. The marketer knew about Intel's manufacturing fuses and proposed that we incorporate those fuses into a new product feature called "Unique ID."

I objected, on the grounds that Intel manufacturing was not set up to coordinate unique fuse settings on a worldwide basis. Nor was there evidence that, if the fuses happened to be blown incorrectly as a result of a fab error, Intel would be willing to trash the entire wafer. The feature would have had to be a very valuable one to make that a viable proposition.

The marketer proposed that we simply rename the feature as "processor ID" to get around the uniqueness concern, and Microsoft agreed that in the unlikely event that two microprocessors were made with the same ID, that alone did not fatally compromise whatever antipiracy measures they were thinking of.

At the time, Intel marketing was looking for additional ways to increase the appeal of the new Pentium III microprocessors. They came up with a marketing campaign that was to be kicked off in a January 1999 Superbowl TV ad. The ad's message was that listeners should go buy a Pentium III system, because only those systems would have this ID scheme. If any Web denizens tried to access the new Web site without a Pentium III, they would be turned away, but Pentium III owners would be recognized (by dint of their CPUID, automatically read by the Web site) and given some series of incentives once inside the Web site.

In only a few weeks, once it became known that the Pentium III had an internal ID tag, visible from the outside, there were picketers in the streets. Foreign governments were passing formal resolutions to prevent the use of Pentium III's in their countries. Customers were up in arms at what they perceived to be Intel's attempt to force (Intel's idea of) morality on them. Only a few days before the Superbowl ad was to have aired, a shocked Intel sold that time to someone else and pulled the plug on the Processor ID feature as a way to attract new customers. Intel issued new driver software to turn the feature off by default and the uproar gradually subsided.

This was the second time I had seen the surprising interactions between a high-tech product and the buying public. The FDIV bug episode had occurred a few years earlier, but it was not my chip's bug, so I was more insulated from the issue. The same pattern of quasi-irrationality was present, however—we would ask the very people who said they were most upset about this perceived invasion of their privacy, "Why have you not been equally concerned about the unique ID of your Ethernet adapter, which is also visible from the Web?" but get no useful answer. They had simply accepted that, but they were not going to accept this, and either did not feel the need to explain, or did not understand the irony.

Was the P6 project affected by the Pentium's floating point divider bug?

In summer 1994, the chief P6 floating-point architect, Patrice Roussel, walked into my office and whispered "There's a bug in the Pentium chip." I said "I sure hope you're wrong. Show me."

Patrice reached over to my keyboard and quickly brought up three windows side by side on my workstation. The leftmost window was a 486-based computer, the middle was a Pentium machine, and the rightmost window was a simulation of the P6 chip we would be taping out only a few months later. I looked at all three windows and observed the obvious: "The 486 and the P6 agree, but the Pentium says something slightly different." Patrice whispered, "Yes, I know, that's the point. The Pentium is wrong." I asked Patrice who knew about this; he said so far it was just him and me. I said "Then I'll tell you what you have already figured out: Problems like this can have serious corporate consequences and have to be handled carefully by our executives, so tell the Pentium design team what they need to reproduce the problem and debug it, and don't tell anyone else. Let the executives handle this."

The reason for this secrecy was to minimize the problem of "insider trading." Trading securities on the basis of information that is not generally known to the buying public is illegal and unethical. Patrice had just come across information that (as far as he and I knew) could affect the stock price, so we had both just become "insiders," no longer able to trade any of our stock until the situation had been publically resolved. The point of the secrecy was to keep our fellow engineers from joining us in this predicament.

About three months later, a college professor stumbled across the same bug, failed to get satisfaction from Intel, and went to the brand-new WorldWide Web with his story. The press picked up the story of how Intel's chips did not work, Jay Leno made fun of it, and Pentium jokes became all the rage:

Q: What's another name for the "Intel Inside" sticker on a Pentium chip?
A: A warning label.

Q: What do you call a series of FDIV instructions on a Pentium?
A: Successive approximation.

And on and on. I happened to be traveling from Oregon to Boston in the second week that this story was hot. I got into a Boston cab and the driver asked me where I worked. "Intel," I said. "Whoa! How about that Pentium bug?" he said. I thought it was weird that even the cab drivers knew about an obscure floating-point CPU bug. He dropped me off at the hotel and as I checked in, the clerk noticed my affiliation and said, "Hey, I heard about that Pentium bug!" I was starting to wonder if the whole thing was an elaborate set-up, like *Candid Camera*. But when I got to my room, I decided to call my mother and (I am not making this up) she said, "Hi. Hey, your chip doesn't have that Pentium flaw I've been hearing about, does it?"

Then one night, while patrolling an Internet news group for P6-related questions, I noticed a post that really set me back on my heels. The poster said that he didn't blame the engineers for having designed the FDIV bug into the chip, nor did he blame validation for not having caught it. He opined that the person most culpable in the whole affair was the Intel manager who first knew of the errata but did not post it immediately to the Web so the Pentium users would know of it. He argued strongly that said manager should go to jail over this egregious failure of public responsibility.

Considering that the manager in question was me, I had a decidedly different viewpoint on the whole affair and reached a substantially different conclusion. First of all, it was not *my* product, it was the Santa Clara x86 team's chip, and it was now their management's responsibility for dealing with it. Second, whether this Net denizen knew it or not, all technical products (not just Intel's and not just Pentium) embody errors, inadvertent deviations from the published specifications. There has to be a formal communication channel between manufacturers and their customers in order to disseminate new information about product errata, and it cannot possibly be based on random Intel employees posting whatever they want.

This incident proved to Intel that the rules had somehow changed. In the past, people did not really know what a computer did, what it was good for, or why they should care about the answers to those questions. But now, even an obscure design erratum like FDIV had become cocktail party knowledge. Microprocessors had entered the popular culture. I was sure this was an important change in the rules, but as yet had no idea of what the new rules were.

Neither did Intel's corporate management. For a few months, they pursued a rational approach to the problem that had historically worked very well: Commission an internal technical team to assess the problem, reassure Intel's customers that we were looking into it, and if we concluded that there was a real problem, we would get back to them with our plan. After all, this is what the company had done for design errata on previous chips and this process had worked fairly well overall.

What nobody noticed was that the rules really *had* changed. Until the early 1990s, computer users tended to be relatively technically sophisticated, using the machines to pursue science, engineering, or dedicated tasks such as running spreadsheets or doing documentation. The microprocessors were much, much simpler, as was the software running on them. And if there were bugs, resolving them was an issue between the microprocessor vendor and that particular customer.

As Intel's tech teams investigated the source and implications of the bug, Pentium system users found themselves, for the first time in history, with the ability to easily compare notes with each other. Somebody wrote a short application that could be easily downloaded and run that tested the floating point unit of the chip. If the program found a Pentium with the errata, it informed the user that she had a defective microprocessor and should contact Intel for a replacement. Very few of those users could have written that test, but they could now all get a copy and run it.

From Intel's perspective, this erratum was not all that serious. Most users did not use much floating point, the bug was very sporadic and manifested very infrequently, and a substantial amount of floating point code tended to be of the convergent kind (which could still be expected to reach a correct answer even if the bug did manifest; it just might take a few iterations longer to get there).

The buying public was having none of it. In effect, they were holding Intel to the same standard as they had held the makers of Tylenol or packaged chicken in the supermarket: If the product isn't perfect, *as judged by the buyers, not by the producers,* then the product should be replaced at the manufacturer's expense. Intel was horrified by this prospect, because they knew that no high-tech products (or for that matter, any products of any kind) were perfect, and the vast majority of buyers lacked the necessary technical skill to differentiate bugs from normal design compromises, or to judge which bugs were of recall severity and which could simply be worked around.

Eventually, Intel's chief marketing VP had an epiphany. He told Andy Grove, "We have been going about this all wrong. The rules really have changed, and here's how. Suppose you went to the car dealership to pick up your new Mercedes Benz SLE500 sedan. The car's up on a pedestal, rotating around, and you perform your final inspection before driving away in it. To your horror, you see a big scratch on the driver's door. The engineer in you realizes that the cargo capacity is unchanged, the fuel economy is as before, the number of passengers is the same, the engine horsepower is undiminished, and so on. But do you drive the car away? No, you do not. Instead, you tell the dealer that you paid for a perfect car and that is all you'll accept. That's essentially what Intel's customers are now telling us. They now set the rules." Within a week the company had an-nounced a formal recall program, with all of its design engineers assigned to phone banks to reach all 5,000,000 Pentium customers and arrange a replacement for their chips.

Ironically, the entire episode may have been a net benefit to Intel, even with the $475,000,000 price tag. After all, Intel often spends more than that on marketing cam-paigns. And in the end, just as celebrities and politicians sometimes request, "Say what you want about me, but spell my name right," when the FDIV issue finally subsided, the Pentium name had achieved a remarkable recognition rate among the general population worldwide. It had provided an opportunity for Intel to demonstrate its willingness to back up that brand name, and it taught Intel an extremely valuable lesson about how the rules had changed, and who now owned the job of making those rules.

Why did Pentium have a flawed floating point divider, when its predecessor, the i486, did not?

For most of the Pentium design project, the floating point divider was exactly the same as the 486's. But late in the Pentium project, upper management requested that the entire project search for ways to make the die smaller. (Smaller is always better in silicon chips, because you can cram more chips onto each wafer and the odds of each one working after fabrication go up as well.) Not all designers took this request very seriously, but the engi-neers working on the floating point divider did. They came up with an idea to save some space in a lookup table and one of them performed an analytical proof that the idea was sound. That proof turned out to be flawed, but the insidious side effect of having per-formed a "proof" was that it misled the Pentium validation team into thinking there was no real threat of new bugs due to the late change to the FP divider. (Normally, validators get very suspicious about late changes, because they know that where they see human fin-gerprints they will find design errata, and they have learned from harsh experience that late changes are the most dangerous of all.) So the bug came from the die size reduction effort, and it got past validation due to the flawed proof, which seems not to have been checked by anyone. (This was not surprising, because validation in 1993 did not general-ly have to check formal proofs.)

Here is the punch line: The smaller FP divider unit did not make the Pentium chip any smaller. Why? For the same reason that if you somehow removed Kansas from the United States, it would not make Canada and Mexico any closer together (see Figure 7.1). To

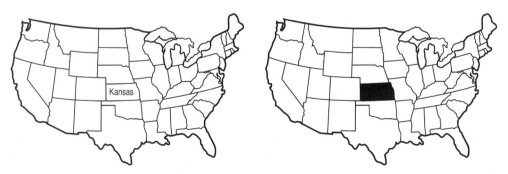

Figure 7.1. Removing the state of Kansas does not make the perimeter of the United States any smaller.

make a chip smaller, you would have to save area across the entire X dimension, or across the entire Y dimension, or both. Saving a little in the X dimension, when a neighboring unit is the same size as before, simply makes no difference to the overall size of the die.

So FDIV was not just a design error. It was not just a design error plus a broken formal proof. It was not even just a design error plus a bad proof plus a validation oversight. It was, first and foremost, a conceptual error at the project management level, because one simply must not take chances like this late in a project, unless one's back truly is against the wall. Such changes should not be allowed, much less encouraged, when there is no possibility of payback from it; it is all risk and no reward.

How would you respond to the claim that the P6 is built on ideas stolen from Digital Equipment Corp.?

It still rankles me that some people in my field think P6 was a great success mostly because we stole the good stuff from others. As far as I can tell, this idea got its start in 1997, when some Intel executives gave interviews introducing Intel's new internal research groups. Unfortunately, the Intel executives were quoted [26] as having said the new research groups were an appropriate investment, because "we have to stop borrowing all our ideas from other people." I was outraged at this mischaracterization of my design team's creativity by my own management, and I stormed into my boss's office and demanded that the next time these executives were in town for a review, I get the first 10 minutes of the meeting to redress this grievance.

Digital Equipment Corp. (DEC) officials had also read that interview, and they were apparently just as angry as I was, but for a different reason: They thought *they* were the ones getting ripped off. So they sued. Intel eventually settled the suit for $600,000,000, which convinced some people that we really *had* stolen DEC's best ideas and that is why P6 was so good.

I did eventually get my chance to present my point of view on this to the executive in question, and I made it as clear as the English language and professional deportment allowed that P6 was a creation of Intel's Oregon design team. For the same reasons that every new design incorporates the best of the art, there were features in the P6 for which one could trace a plausible ancestry. An example of this is a paper published by Yale Patt and Tse-Yu Yeh in 1991 on two-level adaptive branch predictors [35]. This paper appeared exactly when we had just realized that we needed a much better predictor than anything currently known. The general direction proposed by this paper helped us refine what eventually became our own branch predictor design. Likewise, certain functional blocks in the P6 were (purposely) named similarly to those in the original out-of-order design by Tomasulo at IBM in the 1960s, as a way of honoring the field's pioneers.[2] And as Prof. Wen-mei Hwu described in the foreword to this book, the rough outline of how one might go about designing a viable out-of-order engine had been trailblazed in the 1980s. This kind of idea sharing represents the best of what our academia/industry arrangement can achieve and I think both groups can be proud of their achievements. But in no case did we ever look at DEC patents or borrow any ideas from them or their products.

A similar case arose when Professor H. C. Torng of Cornell University somehow concluded that the P6 must have borrowed some of his patented ideas, and Cornell began sending annual licensing letters to Intel's legal department. Every year, I would explain

---

[2]Our functional blocks did not perform exactly as Tomasulo's, however, which has sometimes caused consternation among some computer architecture historians.

the situation: None of the P6 engineers had ever read the patents in question,[3] so literally borrowing anything from them was impossible. True, since we had not read the patents, none of us could be sure what was in them, but I had read all of Prof. Torng's publications while in graduate school (and I was the only one on the team who had). While his ideas were novel at the time they were published, they were clearly not relevant to what we were implementing on P6, and at no point were they even under active consideration for inclusion.

After several years of this ritual sword-rattling, imagine my astonishment when a colleague e-mailed me a URL that showed a smiling Prof. Torng holding a plaque and a check to Cornell for $2,000,000, awarded to him by an Intel VP and an Intel Fellow. The plaque said, "Thank you for your fundamental contributions to the P6 microprocessor." I was nearly apoplectic at the thought that not only had my company failed to stand up for my design team, not only had people been awarded $2,000,000 for work that had nothing whatever to do with P6, but Intel's legal department and upper management had not even bothered to inform us that they had found it more expedient to buy Cornell off than to fight the issue in court. We had to find out in the newspapers that we had once again been implicitly accused (by our own company) of illicitly appropriating other people's ideas.

Having helped Intel deal with several lawsuits over the years, I do understand that the U.S. court system has a very difficult task in terms of providing justice in high-tech, complex cases in which a jury of one's peers really lacks the background for grasping the necessary subtleties, and that situations sometimes dictate that a company occasionally has to treat such cases as business decisions, independent of what is truly right or wrong. There is a time and a place for business expediency. But there is never an excuse for treating one's own design team this shabbily. It felt like we were stabbed in the back by members of our own team.

I eventually sent a very surly note to our executives along the lines of "If you intend to award two million dollars to every person on earth who did *not* contribute to the P6, the total is going to come to approximately twelve trillion dollars." I never got a reply to that e-mail.

Whenever I hear an innocent athlete being accused of having succeeded only because he cheated by using steroids, I remember the DEC and Cornell incidents and I think I know exactly how he feels.

What did the P6 team think about Intel's Itanium Processor Family?

When I joined Intel in 1990 to start a new design team in Oregon, I was prepared to contend with some understandable hostility from the existing x86 team in Santa Clara. After all, that team *built* Intel; they did the 286, the 386, and were finishing the 486. They were the chip design authorities in the company and if they had wanted to pick on the new kid on the block, they would have been within their rights.

But they didn't. Every time I called or visited the P5/Pentium team, they were the very model of professionalism: helpful, engaged, interested, and forthcoming. Superb engineers such as Robert Dreyer, Jack Mills, Ed Grochowski, Don Alpert, Gary Hammond, John Crawford, Ken Shoemaker, and Ken Arora were not only knowledgeable, but a genuine pleasure to work with. If we needed advice or information about x86 compatibility,

---

[3]It is common practice in the industry to instruct engineers never to read the patents of other companies, a direction they universally comply with most happily. This helps avoid possible triple damages for "willful infringement" if one's company is ever found to be infringing on another's patent.

or design tools, we got it. The relationship between these (almost-rival) teams could hardly have been better.

Unfortunately, things always change, and if they are already good, there are few ways for them to get better and many ways for them to get worse. Intel found one of the many ways when it commissioned the Santa Clara team to conceive and implement a new 64-bit instruction set architecture, eventually known as the Itanium Processor Family (IPF), and then gave them (what I believe were) confused and conflicting project goals.

The first problem stemmed from the decision to form a partnership with Hewlett-Packard to jointly conceive and specify the new architecture. Understandably, HP wanted to contribute their best technical ideas to this new architecture, but also wanted to make sure that in no case would they end up competing against any of them. So an intercompany firewall was required as part of the deal between the IPF team and the IA32 team in Oregon. We in the Oregon design team did not care about whatever HP technology was being protected thereby, but we did care about the fact that this firewall had a strong tendency to compartmentalize the Santa Clara team from the rest of the Intel design community. Us-versus-them psychology creeps into such situations by default, but this firewall requirement made it much worse. In cases of profound disagreement, we could no longer mutually revert to data and simulations to resolve the issue.

The second problem was, I believe, intrinsic to the charter required of the Intel IPF team. In essence, they were told that their mission was to jointly conceive the world's greatest instruction set architecture with HP, and then realize that architecture in a chip called Merced by 1997, with performance second to no other processor, for any benchmark you like. The justification for this blanket performance requirement was that if a new architecture was not faster than its predecessors, then why bother with it? Besides, HP's studies had indicated that the new architecture was so much faster than any other, that even if some performance was lost to initial implementation naiveté, Merced would still be so fast that it would easily establish the new Itanium Processor Family.

This plan did not go over well with the Oregon design team. At one point, I objected to the executive VP in charge that no company had ever achieved anything like what he was blithely insisting on for Merced. No matter how advanced an architecture, the implementation artifacts of an actual chip would offset them until the design team learned the proper balances between features, design effort, compiler techniques, and so on. Moreover, there are always uncertainties in complex designs and new designs most of all. The one thing you do not do with uncertainties is to stack them all end to end and judge them all toward the hoped-for end of the range. With any one issue, you can make an argument that it is likely to turn out at the high end of the desirability range, but you must not do that with every issue simultaneously. Nature does not work that way but, in effect, that is what Merced was assuming.

> *The one thing you do not do with uncertainties is to stack them all end to end and judge them all toward the hoped-for end of the range.*

My criticisms were not accepted on a technical or rational level. Instead, I was accused of criticizing another project just to make my own look better. I said, "I would say exactly the same thing even if it were my own team designing Merced. You cannot expect any design team in the world to get so many things right on their first try. And with the number of new ideas in IPF, what Intel *should* be doing is designing Merced as a research chip, not to be sold or advertised. Take the silicon back to the lab and experiment with it for 18 months. At the end of those 18 months, you'll know what new ideas worked and which ones weren't worth the cost of implementation. *Then* design a follow-on, keeping the good ideas and tossing out the rest, and that second chip and its follow-ons have a chance to be great. It's worth investing a year or two at the beginning of a new instruction set architecture that you hope will last for 25 years." The response: "I hope you're wrong. I cannot afford to design a chip that I cannot sell upon completion." I said, "Then we have no business trying to design a new instruction set architecture." The result was a stalemate.

The Oregon team also did not like the idea that with P6, we had opened the server markets for Intel and now were being told "Oregon is not even allowed to say the *word* server" for fear of too much internal competition. Given our concerns about the viability of any first-time chip like Merced, we felt Intel was unnecessarily risking its presence in the server space, since it was relatively easy to continue designing variations of our x86 desktop chips for servers for as long as necessary until IPF was ready to take over.

So the two teams ended up at odds with each other, partly because the usual communications paths had been intentionally severed by management. But we also mutually suffered because (it seemed to me) Intel had just plain never figured out what strategy it was attempting to follow with IPF and IA32.

Early in the IPF development, around 1994, we were told that the 32-bit x86 line would be superseded by the 64-bit chips by 1999. Our management may have believed this because HP told them so, or maybe the Santa Clara team told them, or maybe it came from their own intuitions, but we didn't see it that way from Oregon at all. The P6 team believed we could follow the P6 with another 32-bit machine and that prematurely switching to 64 bits would simply cede the increasingly lucrative x86 market to our competition. We saw no real draw for 64 bits prior to 2006 or beyond, so we believed it was ill-advised in the extreme to consider hampering our 32-bit efforts in the desktop or the server markets.

Within a couple of years, the Merced development effort had had enough trouble, with still no 64-bit killer application in sight, that the idea of migrating Intel's user base en masse to 64 bits by 1999 was no longer mentioned. Also, we had begun designing what eventually became the Pentium 4, and earlier claims from some quarters that it was impossible to improve on the P6's performance were being steadily refuted. So the corporate strategy for pushing both product lines mutated into something more like "let the world sort it all out." Toward the year 2000, the strategy mutated even more, to essentially what it is today: 64 bits for servers and 32 bits for everything else.

One subtlety that caused a lot of trouble was the insistence that the new 64-bit engine be "fully compatible" with the 32-bit engines being developed. Since we were actively adding instructions to these new 32-bit chips, the Merced project had a moving target to hit and began to feel they could never catch up. So they tried to halt further innovation in IA32, insisting that we stop changing, since their chip was the future anyway.

This proposal did not go over well in Oregon. We pointed out that the IPF road map was not aimed at desktops, and even if it had been, it would have been too dangerous to risk the company's major revenue stream on a hope that (a) Merced would be compellingly fast and (b) the world would switch its software from the x86 standard to the new IPF standard fast enough to drive high-volume demand. Meanwhile, our competition would continue to innovate in approximately the same way we would have had we not been stopped, and neither our 32-bit chips (lacking the new address extension features) nor our 64-bit chips (for lack of new software, and because IPF chips were being designed to server economics, not desktop) would be able to counter them.

I also argued that one of our focus areas with the Pentium 4 was real-time, human-interface applications, such as audio decoding or DVD playback. If the CPU falls behind, the sound crackles or the screen loses a frame and looks jerky. Historically, to say two processors were object-code compatible simply implied that in finite time, both processors arrived at the same outputs. The faster one would get there first, but both would get there eventually, and for applications such as e-mail, word processing, and so on, that was all users required. Human interface applications were a different breed. Eventually getting a particular video frame of a movie right is not good enough; the processor has to get it right by a certain deadline to satisfy the user. Many of the new IA32 instructions that Merced was struggling to include were aimed at these new real-time applications, and it did not appear that Merced would run those fast enough. So then why was it so important to have those new instructions in the chip? Beyond all that, why would someone buy an expensive new Itanium Processor Family workstation just to run DVD movies on it, in an IA32 format?[4] No matter how you looked at it, the strategy did not appear to be self-consistent.

Essentially, the company's lack of a coherent strategy forced the Santa Clara and Oregon teams into technology and product road map disputes that we had no viable means for resolving. This soured the relationship between the teams, to both teams' detriment, and I was sad to have witnessed this firsthand. It did not have to be this way.

Is Intel the sweatshop some people say it is?

No. And maybe a little bit yes. I'll explain what I mean, but first, a story.

In 1984, I was still working on my PhD at Carnegie-Mellon University, and a large part of my thesis [31] was a deconstruction of Intel's 432 chip. I had some ideas about why that chip was having trouble getting any traction in the industry, but I needed real data. Fortunately for me, George Cox was Intel's technical representative to Carnegie-Mellon, had worked on the i432, and offered to bring me out to Intel's Jones Farm site in Oregon for a summer to work with the 432 simulators and designers. I did, and the much-appreciated cooperation from company experts such as Konrad Lai and William Bain went a long way to providing me with the data I needed to finish my thesis.

But Intel in 1984 was a company in trouble [14]. The stock price was depressed, employee stock options were "underwater" and not perceived as very promising, and the overall corporate sales trends were in a free fall. The 432 was not selling well; actually, it was generally regarded as a disaster in the industry [32]. So even though I was pursuing my own work, not immersed in the general design activities around me, there was no mistaking the overall air of gloom.

But worse than that, there were aspects of the company that made me just shake my head. For example, there was a sign-in sheet if you arrived to work late. The idea was that the company's workday started officially at 8 A.M. and all employees were expected to be at their desks by then. If an employee arrived at work after 8 A.M., he or she would be requested by the security guard at the front desk to sign a list, documenting the fact that they had arrived late. This list would be stowed after 9 A.M., so anyone who was *really* late would not have to sign the list. It was not uncommon to see people at 8:45 A.M. sitting in their cars in the parking lot waiting for the list to go away. It was also not uncommon for people to sign the list with alter egos such as Donald Duck, Mickey Mouse, and other names that were probably not in the corporate phone directory. The names on the late list

---

[4]They could, after all, have run those DVD movies in the native IPF format at higher performance levels.

would then be distributed to the slackers' managers for whatever corporate discipline was deemed appropriate.

It took only one incident for me to tell my boss I would no longer attempt to honor the late-list scheme. In 1984, the highway intersection with the road to Intel's Jones Farm plant was not a full interchange. You had to wait in a central turn lane, between the four lanes of highway, for your chance to cross directly in front of speeding vehicles. One morning early in that summer, I was third in line for making that turn when the first car's driver misjudged the speed of an oncoming Maserati, and clipped its back end. This caused the Maserati to veer toward those of us waiting in line, and when the car entered the median area, it went down into the center ditch, then back up our side of it, became airborne, and crushed the car in back of me. That driver was an Intel employee, as was the person who made the initial error. I told my boss that the only time of day when there was a line waiting at that intersection was just before 8 A.M., because of Intel's late list, and I would no longer contribute to that problem. He said fine, as he never cared about that stupid late list anyway.

There were other aspects of Intel in 1984 that were unappealing. For example, there were no bike racks outside, in case you might want to ride your bicycle to work. But that was at least consistent, because there were no showers inside either. Andy Grove used to say he wasn't running a country club, and that the company owed its employees whatever they needed to get their jobs done, but not more than that. Nowadays, there are exercise rooms, showers, and ping-pong tables. I don't know if Andy changed his mind about such things, but I do remember unfavorably comparing Intel to other companies at which I had worked. I also distinctly remember driving away from Jones Farm in late August 1984, seeing it in the rear-view mirror and muttering "Thank God I'll never have to work *there* again."

Fast forward to 1990. Intel still had the exit bag-checks, but the late list was gone, and there were arrangements with local health clubs for showers and exercise. Things were looking up.

I have worked at startups and they are immersion experiences. You sign on for the ride, and all you can do is hang on as the roller coaster careens madly around the track for a few years. Your work is your life, and there is not much time left for anything beyond it.

My experiences at Intel were very intense at times, such as the 3-month push to get the initial P6 behavioral model running, and the 7-month tapeout crunch at the end of the project. But was it a "sweatshop"?

Intel rewards results. Its corporate structure is arranged in such a way as to identify its top producers and reward them. Native ability, education, attitude, opportunity, experience, and motivation all play roles in how productive a given person can be. But sheer hard work does the rest. If a company has a working performance recognition structure in place, then it logically follows that for any two people with roughly equivalent backgrounds, the one who works harder is likely to be the one who gets the most done, gets promoted soonest, and collects the bigger raises and stock option grants. In that sense, it sometimes seems to people that Intel disproportionately weights time spent working. But for the part of Intel that I knew well, that is a misconception—as managers we worked very hard to recognize results, not hard work per se. Employees who spent a lot of time at their desks but did not accomplish as much as their peers would generally not find themselves on the fast track. So in that sense, Intel did not qualify as a sweatshop.

In a more subtle way, though, it can feel to many employees as though they are on an invisible treadmill, running about as fast as they can go, when one day their boss sidles up to them and whispers "Great news! You've been promoted to Grade 6!" Their immediate reaction is generally joy at this confirmation that their hard work has been noticed, with rewards to follow. But then they realize that more is *expected* of a grade 6; they have just been put into a new peer group of people who have been operating at a grade 6 level, some of them for years, and their own output will now be compared to this group's, not the group they had grown comfortable with.

Some engineers find they either cannot or do not want to operate at this higher level, and trouble may eventually follow in the form of demotions or other disciplinary actions. But most find that the same technical moxie and ability to work hard that got them this far can be expanded and will work again at this new level. All they have to do is apply themselves even harder.

Little wonder then, that after several years of this, employees may get the feeling that the main reward for success is to be asked for even more output. The company really does operate this way. But thinking in "sweatshop" terms misses the point. The point is that the company continually selects for its highest producers and strives to put those producers into positions of highest output. Personally, I consider this a good thing, but there were times when I could empathize with those who quailed at the long-term pattern this performance evaluation process sometimes evoked.

How can I become the chief architect of a company such as Intel?

Part of any manager's job is to counsel his or her employees in planning their careers. Some employees take career planning very seriously—they know where they want to be and how long they think is reasonable to get there. Most are more like I was. Give me interesting work, creating products that are meaningful, and I will do my best to contribute to them. And if I succeed, my career will take care of itself. At least, I hoped it would.

I was often asked the question "What must I do if I want to end up with your job?" I used to answer "It's too late. You had to have been really bad when you were little to deserve this punishment." (I was just joking; I loved that job during the P6 project.)

The interesting thing to me was that the questioner was almost always someone quite young, either just out of school or in her early twenties. I no longer remember quite how the world looked from that vantage point, but I know it was much different from how I was seeing things from a 40-something's perspective. Often, the questioner wanted me to condense the random walk of my own career into a list of just those items that turned out to have been important to my ending up with the chief architect's job, so that they could then go about collecting those same items on their own resume (and far more efficiently than I). When the last item had been checked off, all they would have to do was wait and an equivalent job would fall into their laps.

I do not see it that way. If there is one thing I know about the chief architect job, it is that I could not have done it successfully when I was in my twenties. Nearly all of the things I have ever done, including writing code, writing microcode, designing ECL hardware, designing TTL, designing custom CMOS, writing validation suites, debugging hardware in the lab, doing performance analysis, doing technical documentation and presentations, reading magazines and talking to people at conferences, as well as the voluminous nontechnical reading I do, informed the decisions I would make or help make, the directions in which I wanted to take the team or the product, and how I would go about leading the organization. Experience matters, and it cannot be substituted for by intelligence, political acumen, or marrying the boss's daughter (not that I've ever tried that one).

> *Find something you are passionate about, and go after it with everything you have.*

In the end, the pattern that makes the most sense to me is this: Find something you are passionate about, and go after it with everything you have. Really apply yourself, holding nothing back, with the aim of achieving excellence, no matter the task, no matter how menial it feels or may seem to others. It may turn out that your real passion lies in designing phase-locked loop circuits, not project management, and if you excel at everything you are assigned, sooner or later you will find that task and end up owning it. The really cool part of doing excellent work is that it catapults you (over time) into the company of people just like you—people intensely committed to success, people you can rely on to routinely turn up brilliant insights, and who will occasionally save your bacon in a most gratifying way. It just does not get any better than that. Do excellent work, and you can write your own ticket regarding what work you would like to be doing.

Some of you are thinking that "Do excellent work always" is near-vacuous advice; something from *Bill and Ted's Excellent Adventure.* I mean something quite specific, though. I mean that no matter what task you have been assigned, take it upon yourself to learn the context for that task. Why was it assigned? Where does it fit in the bigger picture? Why were you asked for a certain result? Is there a better way to achieve what your supervisor was really after? Give her back more than she expected, every single time.[5] Sometimes, merely stepping back from the details of the task is all it takes to see a much better course of action. Other times, you just have to slog through the task. No matter what, give every task your entire focus and approach it as though you intend to knock it out of the park. When your management realizes you are reliable in the small things, they will start trusting you on bigger things and your career will jump to a higher energy state.

Working hard is essential. So is a real commitment to a lifetime of learning, because the field changes so fast that most of what you know is going to be either obsolete or wrong within just a few years. No one can coast and stay at the leading edge.

But an ability to communicate comes in a close second, in my estimation. If you have a gift for managing people, great—that will be very useful to you and much revered by your future bosses. If you are like most engineers, though, you will learn on the job, by trying things and making mistakes. You can rely on good communication skills to pull you through—they will help you see when things are not going well, and will help you extract the signal from the noise when your bosses are trying to tell you why.

Earlier, I argued that Intel's Operational Excellence iniative was wrong-headed for putting the emphasis on how a product is to be designed, instead of on the product itself. Yet here, I have exhorted you to do excellent work as your ticket to your dream career. I am not being inconsistent; if your task is to paint a building, then you will have produced excellent work when the building looks fantastic upon the job's completion. OpX would draw your attention to the scaffolding you used.

Why did you leave Intel?

I left the company mostly because I was frustrated. I felt that as one of the principals who had led the company to a high-clock-rate x86 strategy, I should have been able to lead it

---

[5]I am indebted for this advice to my uncle, Joseph Malingowski. Most of what I know about how to look at technology, I learned from him.

away from that strategy when that became necessary (and we knew from the beginning that it eventually would). But it seemed to me that that time came around 1998, and over the next two years I was unable to even make a dent in the product road maps, all of which called for linear continuation of the various chips we had already designed or which were in the works.

I was also chagrined that in a company in which everyone was assumed to have read Clayton Christenson's book on disruptive technology and how successful companies so often keep plying a previously successful strategy well past the point of efficacy, we were doing (in my view) exactly the same thing. And nothing I said to anyone seemed to have any effect.

I felt that we had hit a home run with the P6 project, and that it was (and is) successful far beyond what anyone had a right to expect. That project was just plain fun, working so closely with so many incredible engineers.

But the Willamette project was not fun. Part of the problem for me was the design manager, Randy Steck's successor, with whom I had serious differences of opinion about the chip development process. But an even bigger problem was the corporate interference I have detailed elsewhere in this book. And while I was off trying to keep the company from destructively interfering with Pentium 4 (through quantum entanglement with the Itanium Processor Family) the chip itself was sailing into complexity waters that seem, in retrospect, far too deep for what they were worth. Beyond all of that, however, was a looming thermal power wall that was no longer off in the distance, as in P6, but instead was casting its long, ugly shadow directly over everything we did. That experience was primarily why I was so sure I did not want to work on any high-clock-rate chips beyond Willamette. I just did not think there would be enough end-user performance payoff to justify the nightmarish complexity incurred in a power-dominated, high-performance design.

I think the future is mobile. In particular, I think the future is battery- or fuel-cell-operated and that what will be valued in the mainstream a decade or two from now will be *sufficient* performance to accomplish some desired end goal (like HDTV playback or GPS reception) at very long battery life. This is a daunting goal, and so far removed from historical CPU design goals (especially the highest possible performance at all costs) that it will take a minor miracle to get existing teams to achieve it. Without inspired direction from corporate leadership, it is not going to happen. Business as usual is no longer going to work. I left Intel because I did not want to be the one who proved that.

AND IN CLOSING I'D JUST LIKE TO SAY . . .

You can spend your entire life as a design engineer and never have the good fortune to find yourself on a team of incredible people like I did on the P6 project, but I hope you do. It is an experience that will elevate your own abilities, give you a feeling of intense acceleration, like a roller coaster heading over the steepest drop, and the incredible sensation of having your own intellect amplified beyond reason by proximity to so many brilliant people. Engineering is fun, but engineering in a project like P6 is sublime.

Years later, when you think back over the project and the great products it created, there will be a feeling of immense satisfaction combined with awe at the sheer talent and dedication that were there in such abundance. In all your design projects, do your part to arrive at such a happy circumstance: Hold every project you find yourself in to the highest standards. Expect your team to attain greatness and never settle for less. If a particular project does not turn out the way you wanted, remember that mistakes are the learning curves with the steepest slopes, and redouble your commitment to the next project. As Goethe said, "Whatever you can do, or dream you can, begin it. Boldness has genius, power, and magic in it."

BIBLIOGRAPHY

[1] Y. N. Patt, W. W. Hwu, and M. C. Shebanow, HPS, a New Microarchitecture: Rationale and Introduction, in *Proceedings of the 18th International Microprogramming Workshop,* Asilomar, Dec. 1985.

[2] Y. N. Patt, S. W. Melvin, W. W. Hwu, and M. C. Shebanow, Critical Issues Regarding HPS, a High Performance Microarchitecture, in *Proceedings of the 18th International Microprogramming Workshop,* Asilomar, Dec. 1985.

[3] D. Patterson, Reduced Instruction Set Computers, *Comm. ACM 28:1,* 189.

[4] D. Phillips and R. O'Bryan, *It Sounded Good When We Started,* Wiley, 2004.

[5] S. Shem, *The House of God,* Putnam, 1978.

[6] H. Petroski, *Small Things Considered,* Knopf, 2003.

[7] H. Petroski, *Design Paradigms,* Cambridge University Press, 1994.

[8] http://www.snopes.com/critters/wild/frogboil.htm

[9] http://inventors.about.com/library/inventors/bledisonpatents.htm

[10] http://plus.maths.org/issue10/news/mars/

[11] J. Weissman, *Presenting To Win: The Art Of Telling Your Story,* Prentice-Hall, 2003.

[12] D. Kushner, *Masters of Doom,* Random House, 2003.

[13] R. Turnill, *The Moonlandings,* Cambridge University Press, 2003.

[14] A. S. Grove, *Only the Paranoid Survive,* Currency Doubleday, 1996.

[15] A. Mishkin, *Sojourner,* Berkeley, 2003.

[16] A. S. Grove, *High Output Management,* Random House, 1983.

[17] C. Christensen, *The Innovator's Dilemma,* Harvard Business School Press, 1997.

[18] R. Feynman, *Surely You're Joking, Mr. Feynman!* Norton, 1985.

The Pentium Chronicles. By Robert P. Colwell
© 2006 IEEE Computer Society

[19] D. Vaughan, *The Challenger Launch Decision: Risky Technology, Culture, and Deviance at NASA,* University of Chicago Press, 1996.

[20] R. Feynman, *What Do You Care What Other People Think?,* Norton, 1988.

[21] G. B. Shaw, *Man and Superman,* Epistle Dedicatory, 1903.

[22] R. P. Colwell, Latent Design Faults in the Development of Multiflow's TRACE/200, in *22nd Annual International Symposium on Fault-Tolerant Computing,* Boston MA, July 1992.

[23] K. Beck, *Extreme Programming Explained: Embrace Change,* Addison-Wesley, 2000.

[24] K. Sabbagh, *Skyscraper, The Making of a Building,* Penguin Books, 1989.

[25] R. P. Colwell, G. Brown, and F. See, Intel's College Hiring Methods and Recent Results, in *Microelectronics Systems Education Conference,* 1999.

[26] L. Zuckerman, Suit by Digital Says Intel Stole Pentium Design, *NY Times,* May 14, 1997.

[27] B. Colwell, Employee Performance Reviews, *IEEE Computer,* September 2002.

[28] B. Colwell, Design Reviews, *IEEE Computer,* October 2003.

[29] T. Gilb and D. Graham, *Software Inspection,* Addison-Wesley, 1993.

[30] B. W. Kernighan and D. M. Ritchie, *The C Programming Language,* Prentice-Hall, 1978.

[31] R. P. Colwell, *The Performance Effects of Functional Migration and Architectural Complexity in Object-Oriented Systems,* PhD thesis, Carnegie-Mellon University, 1985.

[32] P. M. Hansen, M. A. Linton, R. N. Mayo, M. Murphy, and D. A. Patterson, A Performance Evaluation of the Intel iAPX 432, *ACM SIGARCH Computer Architecture News, 10,* 4, June 1982.

[33] S. Covey, *The 7 Habits of Highly Effective People,* Fireside, 1989.

[34] J. Shen and M. Lipasti, *Modern Processor Design: Fundamentals of Superscalar Processors,* McGraw-Hill, 2005.

[35] T. Y. Yeh and Y. N. Patt, Two-level Adaptive Branch Prediction, in *24th Annual Symposium on Microarchitecture,* 1991.

[36] Sanders Shoots for the Body, *PC Week,* November 6, 1995, p. 149.

APPENDIX

OUT-OF-ORDER, SUPERSCALAR MICROARCHITECTURE: A PRIMER

Assume that you are a programmer and your job is to write an assembly program that will cause the computer to calculate the sum of the integers 2 and 3.[1] You fire up your text editor, and you type in something like this:

```
Program 1:
I1: Load R0, mem[0x20]  ; get the first number to be added, put in R0
I2: Load R1, mem[0x24]  ; get the other number, put in R1
I3: Add R2, R1, R0      ; add them together, result in R2
I4: Output R2           ; tell user the result
```

Clearly, if these four instructions execute in the order specified {I1, I2, I3, I4} the correct answer will appear on the output. It is also clear that if I1 and I2 are done in the reverse order, the program still gets the right answer. The Add in I3 does not care which value, 2 or 3, was loaded into its register first.

But instructions 3 and 4 cannot be done in any order other than that shown. If the Add occurs before both values have been loaded into their registers, then it will add whatever happens to be in those registers and cheerfully write that sum into R2. Likewise, if I4 occurs before I3 has executed, I4 will report whatever happened to be in R2 before this pro-

---

[1]Why use assembly code, instead of C or Java? Assembly code semantics are direct; the programmer has the right to assume that the computer will execute the first instruction first, then the second, and so on. Higher-level languages often have compilers that might reorder the programmer's instructions before generating the final assembly code.

The Pentium Chronicles. By Robert P. Colwell
© 2005 IEEE Computer Society

173

gram even ran. There is a dependency chain here: I4 depends on the result of I3; I3 depends on the results from both I2 and I1. Therefore, I4 cannot execute until all three prior instructions have produced their results. There is no dependency between I1 and I2; they are completely independent instructions and, therefore, can execute in any order desired.

An out-of-order microarchitecture like the P6 is designed in such a way that it can detect instructions that must execute in program order (because of true data dependencies, like the one between I4 and I3 in the example). There is no magic here; if instructions must execute in a particular order to get the correct result, then the P6 carefully observes that order. But if (as often happens) instructions do not have to execute in the order they happened to be listed in in the program, the P6 will execute them in whatever order it deems best.

P6's microarchitecture is also superscalar. This means that it has enough hardware resources to execute multiple instructions at the same time, a potentially very large performance gain, if those resources can be kept usefully busy. For Program 1, the two load instructions can run at the same time, because neither depends on the other. But I3 and I4 must wait until both loads have completed, and I4 must wait until I3 has completed. True data dependencies prevent out-of-order execution, as well as simultaneous superscalar execution.

Running Program 1 out of order probably does not seem like a very promising performance win, although shrinking a four-cycle program to three by performing the two loads in parallel actually is a significant gain. But consider a slightly more complicated example. Suppose your task is to sum the numbers from 1 to 10. Ignore Gauss's theorem for solving this immediately; think about a straightforward extension of the code in Program 1. Program 2 has to do ten loads to get the numbers being summed. Our computer can do only pairwise additions, so five adds produce five intermediate results, and four more adds complete the calculation.

```
Program 2:
I1: Load R0, mem[0x20]    ; get the 1st number to be added, put in R0
I2: Load R1, mem[0x24]    ; get the other number, put in R1
I3: Add R2, R1, R0        ; add them together, result in R2
I4: Load R3, mem[0x28]    ;
I5: Load R4, mem[0x2c]    ;
I6: Add R5, R4, R3        ;
I7: Load R6, mem[0x30]    ;
I8: Load R7, mem[0x34]    ;
I9: Add R8, R7, R6        ;
I10: Load R9, mem[0x38]   ;
I11: Load R10, mem[0x3c]  ;
I12: Add R11, R10, R9     ;
I13: Load R12, mem[0x40]  ;
I14: Load R13, mem[0x44]  ;
I15: Add R14, R13, R12    ;
I16: Add R15, R2, R5      ;
I17: Add R16, R8, R11     ;
I18: Add R17, R16, R15    ;
I19: Add R18, R17, R14    ;
I20: Output R18           ;
```

Program 2 thus has considerably more leeway for executing out of order or concurrently. In this example, I have assumed a microarchitecture with at least 18 registers, and I have not reused any of them, to make the example easier to understand. Program 2 needs to do ten loads, which are independent of each other. Assume that the out-of-order machine can identify those and run them two at a time, and to keep things simple, that all instructions take one clock cycle to complete. The loads in I1 and I2 will execute in clock cycle 1 and therefore, I3 can execute in clock cycle 2 (both of its operands being ready). The loads in I4 and I5 can execute as a pair in clock cycle 3, followed by I6's add in clock 4, and so on, down to the series of adds starting with I13.

There are some data dependencies in I13–I16. I16 needs the result of I15 before I16 can execute. I15 needs I14's result. I13 needs I2's and I6's results.

```
Clock
Cycle
   Program 2:
1  I1: Load R0, mem[0x20]    ; I2: Load R1, mem[0x24] ;
2  I4: Load R3, mem[0x28]    ; I5: Load R4, mem[0x2c] ;
3  I3: Add R2, R1, R0        ; I6: Add R5, R4, R3 ;
4  I7: Load R6, mem[0x30]    ; I8: Load R7, mem[0x34] ;
5  I10: Load R9, mem[0x38]   ; I11: Load R10, mem[0x3c] ;
6  I9: Add R8, R7, R6        ; I12: Add R11, R10, R9 ;
7  I13: Load R12, mem[0x40]  ; I14: Load R13, mem[0x44] ;
8  I17: Add R16, R8, R11     ; I15: Add R14, R13, R12 ;
9  I16: Add R15, R2, R5      ;
10 I18: Add R17, R16, R15    ;
11 I19: Add R18, R17, R14    ;
12 I20: Output R18           ;
```

With this judicious code rearrangement, the program still gets the correct result but takes 12 clock cycles instead of the original 20.

Part of the motivation for designing an out-of-order, superscalar engine is to exploit these opportunities for concurrent instruction execution. Equally important is the out-of-order engine's tolerance of cache latency. Caches are fast, physically local hardware structures that maintain copies of what is in main memory. When the processor executes a memory load to an address for which the cache happens to have a copy, that load is said to hit the cache and might take only one or two clock cycles. If the cache does not have a copy, the load misses the cache, and the load instruction incurring the miss must now wait until the hardware contacts main memory and transfers a copy of the missing data into the cache.

In P6's era, cache misses required a few dozen clock cycles to service. With the Pentium 4 generation, a cache miss could take several hundred clock cycles, and the general trend is worsening with each new process generation. As in Program 2, most code must perform a series of loads to get data, then operate on that data, and, finally, send out the data just created. Until the loads have completed, nothing else can happen; the program stalls for the duration of a cache miss.

An out-of-order engine partially circumvents this limitation: If one load misses the cache, all instructions that have a true data dependency on that load must themselves wait. But any instructions that are not data-dependent on that load, including other loads, can "go around" the stalled load and try their luck.

PLAUSIBILITY CHECKING

Initially, we intended the P6 DFA to answer one simple question: Did the published performance results for out-of-order engines apply to an Intel Architecture design? Was it at all plausible that an out-of-order design would speed up x86 code execution?

We had grounds to worry that it wouldn't. All modern instruction-set architectures have reasonable numbers of registers, fast temporary storage that instructions access directly. The Intel Architecture has only four general registers, EAX, EBX, ECX, and EDX, plus three others that can sometimes be used. When these are not enough to support a given computation, the rest of the storage must reside in main memory, increasing the load on the caches, bus, and memory. Before we bet the company's future on an out-of-order microarchitecture, we wanted some evidence that it would work.

The best model for an out-of-order microarchitecture would be a program that includes all the relevant structures, programmatically interconnected the same way they would be in the actual design. All unit interfaces would be present just as in the actual design, and units would interact (logically) exactly as their silicon counterparts would.

The trouble with this kind of model is that you have to design the machine before you can model it. By the time you have finished writing the model, a year has gone by, and you are committed to the design before you have ever really used the model to verify the approach. This is not project risk mitigation; it is prototyping.

We needed a way to evaluate design choices that did not require completing the entire design before obtaining useful results. To illustrate my point, consider real code (which is exactly what we did in the P6 project, although it was a bit more complex). This C code is for a slightly modified "hello world," with some extraneous integer manipulations thrown in to make things more interesting:

```
main() {
 int i, j;
 for (i=j=0; i<25; i++) j += i;
 printf("hello world, j=%d.\n",j);
}
```

The resulting assembly code is

```
    .file "hello_world.c"
    .version" GNU C 1.37.1"
    .optim
gcc_compiled.:
    .text
.LC0:
    .byte 0x68,0x65,0x6c,0x6c,0x6f,0x20,0x77,0x6f,0x72,0x6c
    .byte 0x64,0x2c,0x20,0x6a,0x3d,0x25,0x64,0x2e,0xa,0x0
    .align 4
    .globl
main:
    pushl %ebp
    movl %esp,%ebp
    xorl %eax,%eax
    xorl %edx,%edx
.L5:
    leal (%eax,%edx),%edx
    incl %eax
    cmpl $24,%eax
    jle .L5
    pushl %edx
    pushl $.LC0
    call printf
```

Main initializes the registers, then we enter the loop at .L5, corresponding to for (i=j=0; i<25; i++) j += i; in the C program. The leal instruction uses registers eax and edx as inputs, and writes edx with its output. leal is an Intel Architecture artifact that requires some extremely complicated addressing modes. Implementers are thus forced to provide address generation units that are so capable that they can be used as general-purpose integer computation functional units in some cases. This is one of those cases.

The incl instruction increments register eax, which implies that eax is both an input and an output for this instruction. The cmpl instruction compares the value in eax to the constant 24, and (implicitly) writes the flags register, which the conditional branch jle .L5 then checks.

Even this small code slice contains multiple chains of dependencies, which are the first-order determinant for the question, "If you had infinite hardware, what is the upper limit on code speedup you could get?" If you know the answer, you can then ask corollary questions such as, "What if the hardware weren't infinite; instead of 3,000 integer ALUs, what if I only had four, but all else was as before?" It was DFA's job to traverse a "trace" of the program execution, observe all true data dependencies, and then move all instructions to the earliest clock cycle possible with the specified hardware constraints.

For example, the first instruction in this program is pushl %ebp. This x86 instruction is actually a sequence of two operations, one to copy the value of ebp onto the program stack, and the other to adjust the top-of-stack (TOS) pointer appropriately. Copying ebp to the right place on the stack requires the value of the top-of-stack pointer so, clearly, that copy must precede the TOS pointer adjustment. But the next two instructions do not depend on either of the two operations from the pushl instruction; both can proceed in parallel with the ebp copy in clock cycle 0, if the hardware configuration is sufficiently robust, as specified on the command line to DFA.

What do you get when you xor a register with itself, as in xor eax, eax? You get a zeroed register. If the goal was to clear a register, why would you use this convoluted method instead of simply moving a constant 0 into the register? Because xor eax, eax happens to be more efficient object code, and became popular in the Intel 486 era, when disk and memory were extremely limited. In our out-of-order world, however, this construct could be problematical; it appears that this instruction cannot execute until the most recent instruction preceding it that wrote eax has completed. We eventually put hardware in the P6 decoder to notice this special construct and allow this instruction to proceed without (pointlessly) waiting for any previous register writers.

The output of early DFA runs looked like the following:

```
( 0)000014e8: pushw BP <TOS fbfffc48>
( 1)000014e9: movw EA,R ESP EBP
( 0)000014eb: xorw EA,R EAX EAX
( 0)000014ed: xorw EA,R EDX EDX
( 1)000014ef: leaw EA,R EDX <MEM 00000000>
( 1)000014f2: incw AX
( 2)000014f3: cmpw Iw,AX <IMM 00000018>
( 3)000014f8: jle Ib <IMM f5> <INST 000014ef> taken
( 3)000014ef: leaw EA,R EDX <MEM 00000001>
( 3)000014f2: incw AX
( 4)000014f3: cmpw Iw,AX <IMM 00000018>
( 5)000014f8: jle Ib <IMM f5> <INST 000014ef> taken
( 4)000014ef: leaw EA,R EDX <MEM 00000003>
( 4)000014f2: incw AX
( 5)000014f3: cmpw Iw,AX <IMM 00000018>
```

```
( 6)000014f8: jle Ib <IMM f5> <INST 000014ef> taken
( 5)000014ef: leaw EA,R EDX <MEM 00000006>
```

The first number (in parentheses) is the earliest clock cycle that DFA believes (subject to hardware constraints such as the number of ALUs) a given instruction could be executed while still observing true data dependencies. The first instruction seen is assigned clock cycle 0. The next one, the mov at 0x14e9, has an input that depends on the outcome of the push (through the ebp register). So DFA schedules the mov for cycle 1. The xors at 0x14eb and 0x14ed don't depend on any previous instruction (being an x86ism for clearing the registers), so they are scheduled as early as possible, during clock cycle 0. The leaw at 0x14ef requires register edx as an input, so it must be scheduled after the previous write to edx has completed; that would be the xor edx that was just scheduled for clock cycle 0, so this leaw is scheduled for clock cycle 1, and so on.

With its ability to show how existing x86 traces would map onto a wide range of theoretical out-of-order engines, DFA showed us what microarchitectural features were important. It helped us decide the sizes of temporary staging areas and predicted the resulting performance. This support helped establish that the project performance goals were reachable in the silicon die area constraint we had.

GLOSSARY

AMB	As Measured By. Intel "Management By Objectives" places a heavy emphasis on quantifying what is to be accomplished in the upcoming quarter.
AIX	IBM's Unix for their RS6000 workstations.
BRTL	Behavioral Register-Transfer Language. RTL is a kind of programming language intended for chip design. The BRTL was the precursor model to the Structured (SRTL) chip functional specification that would ultimately determine the actual product features.
Bug	Design erratum, an error in the logic implementing the chip.
C	High-level computer programming language.
Cache	A fast local on-die copy of a subset of main memory contents.
Chip set	It takes more than just the Pentium chip to make a computer system work. A set of smaller chips handle interfacing of the system to various input/output standards such as USB, PCI, and networks. These other chips are collectively known as the chip set.
CISC	Complex Instruction Set Computer. A style of computer instruction set architecture design, exemplified by Intel's Pentium chips, characterized by a relatively large (hundreds) number of instructions of substantial intrinsic semantic content.
CMOS	Complementary Metal-Oxide Semiconductor. Refers to the type of transistors and circuits used in a silicon chip.
CPU	Central Processing Unit. The term is a holdover from decades ago, when computers filled whole rooms. CPU has come to mean the

The Pentium Chronicles. By Robert P. Colwell
© 2006 IEEE Computer Society

	microprocessor (as distinct from the chip set), and can also refer to the individual processors on a multicore chip.
CPUID	Identification facility built into Intel microprocessors starting with the Pentium III in 1999, consisting of a set of software-readable fuses which are set to a unique value at manufacturing time.
Debug	The act of finding design errata or other anomalous behavior and tracing it to its root causes.
DFA	Data Flow Analyzer. This is a computer program written during the P6 project to find out if there was enough intrinsic parallelism in normal x86 code to justify the complexity of an out-of-order microarchitecture.
DRAM	Dynamic Random Access Memory. A computer system's main memory is built with DRAMs.
EAX	One of the paltry few registers specified by the Intel Architecture (IA32).
ECL	Emitter-Coupled Logic. A transistor circuit technology precursor to CMOS.
ECO	Engineering Change Order. A formal order to change something in the project POR (Plan of Record).
Errata	Design flaw or error. See Bug.
FDIV	Floating Point Divide. This is the x86 instruction whose implementation had a design erratum in the original Pentium chip.
FIB	Focussed Ion Beam. This is a special tool that permits certain post-fabrication edits to be made to silicon chips, greatly facilitating post-silicon functional debug.
FPLCU	Floating Point Load Converter Unit. The Intel Architecture (IA32) requires that floating point numbers be in one format when stored in memory, and another format when operated on by the floating execution units. The FPLCU performs the necessary conversion between the two formats.
Frontside bus	The P6 CPU had a bus to its L2 cache, and another bus to the rest of the system. For drawing convenience, the L2 was drawn on the P6's "backside" in block diagrams. The bus connecting P6 to other P6's and the chip set became known as the "frontside" bus to distinguish it from the L2 cache bus.
GPA	Grade Point Average.
GPS	Global Positioning System.
HDTV	High Definition Television.
HOTM	Health Of The Model, our attempt to combine several validation indicators into one overall metric for RTL health.
HPS	High Performance Substrate, the name given to the out-of-order computer architecture research performed at the University of Michigan in the 1980s.
IA-32	IA stands for Intel Architecture, and the "-32" indicates the 32-bit version of that architecture, also known as x86.
IAA	Intel Achievement Award.
IEEE	Institute of Electrical and Electronics Engineers, a professional society.
IHDL	Intel Hardware Description Language, an Intel equivalent to industry standard languages such as VHDL and Verilog.

iMBO	Intel Management By Objective.
In-order	A style of microarchitecture design wherein the program instructions are executed in precisely the order specified by the code.
IP	Intellectual Property. Trade secrets, best-known methods, internal rules of thumb, source code, confidential documents, and patents are all examples of IP.
IPF	Itanium Processor Family, once known as IA-64. A native 64-bit instruction set architecture, co-developed by Intel and Hewlett-Packard in the 1990s.
ISA	Instruction Set Architecture, the collection of instructions, addressing modes, registers, and other artifacts with which an assembly language programmer must contend.
I/O	Input/Output. The essential computer system consists of a CPU and a memory; bits flowing into or out of that computer system (from, say, a hard drive or a network) are known as I/O.
K	Kilo, but with a minor twist. Normally kilo means 1,000. But in computer parlance kilo means 1024 (2 raised to the 10th power).
L2	Level-2, as in Level-2 cache. This tends to be the CPU's largest cache. The Pentium Pro implemented its L2 cache as a separate silicon die installed into the same package as the P6 CPU.
MAS	MicroArchitectural Specification. This is the document by which a designer captures all of the essential elements of their design: block diagram, theory of operation, comer cases, timing diagrams, and communications protocols.
Mbyte	Megabyte. "Mega" means million, except that the same power-of-two distortion as with kilo applies. Normally, mega means 1,000,000, but in computer system usage it literally means 2 raised to the twentieth power, or 1,048,576.
MESI	Modified, Exclusive, Shared, Invalid. Caches are great performance boosters, but care must be taken to avoid having inconsistent versions of memory data lying around the system. The obvious way to prevent such inconsistency is to change all copies whenever any copy is altered, but that degrades overall performance substantially. The MESI "protocol" is a good compromise between performance, cost, and complexity, and gives the programmer the illusion that all copies are always synchronized.
Microarchitecture	Microarchitecture refers to the functional structure of a CPU. The original Pentium, the P6, and the Pentium 4 are three different microarchitectural implementations of the same basic instruction set architecture (IA-32).
Microcode	Some complex instruction set computer (CISC) instructions are so complicated that implementing them directly in hardware is difficult. Worse, for performance enhancement or feature revision, the designer may want to make late changes to the functioning of a particular instruction, and if that function has been implemented in hardware, change may no longer be feasible. Microcode is a way of providing the functionality required in a programmable format. The microcode "program" is usually stored on the CPU chip in a read-only memory.
Micro-op	Intel Architecture instructions are complicated. Instruction de-

coders translate the x86 instructions into sequences of simpler operations with more regular formats. These simpler operations were called "micro-operations," or micro-ops. These micro-ops carry along with them all of the information needed for them to find their way through the machine autonomously; there is no central traffic controller in P6 to direct micro-ops.

MMX
MMX refers to a new set of instructions that were added to the IA-32 instruction set with the original Pentium processor.

MP
Multiprocessor. MP systems have more than one CPU. Multicore chips are chips with multiple CPUs on-die—"MP on a chip."

MSEE
Master of Science in Electrical Engineering.

NDFA
"New" DFA, a version of the P6 DFA program, updated to model the Willamette (Pentium 4) microarchitecture.

OpX
Operational Excellence, an Intel initiative intended to improve the execution performance of designers and design teams.

P6
P6 was the code name of the chip development project that eventually produced the Pentium Pro microprocessor. It also became the name for the essential microarchitecture from that microprocessor, reused in the Pentium II, Pentium III, and (in modified form) Centrino products.

PCI
Peripheral Component Interconnect, a standard computer system interconnect for I/O.

Pentium
The next chip after the 486, designed by the 486 Santa Clara team.

Pentium Pro
The first product based on the P6 microarchitecture, introduced in 1995.

POR
Plan Of Record. A design team's intentions affect a great many groups, and it is essential that those intentions be visible and if necessary, modifiable. The team's POR is their current understanding of what they are designing.

Postsilicon
After the design effort has finished, and the fabrication plant has made the chips per the design team's specifications, the project is said to be "postsilicon."

Presilicon
During the design of a chip that hasn't yet taped out, the project is said to be "presilicon."

R&R
Ranking and Rating. (Sometimes also known as "Ranting and Raving.") The procedure by which Intel attempts to make an ordered list of its employees, sorted by relative contributions to the company over the period. An essential part of the company's intended technical meritocracy.

RCG
Recent College Graduate.

Register
A register is a fast temporary storage device in a microarchitecture.

RISC
Reduced Instruction Set Computer.

ROM
Read-Only Memory. Software can read it, but can't write it. Its contents are permanently determined during manufacturing.

RTL
Register-Transfer Language. RTLs include Intel's iHDL, and industry standards such as Verilog and VHDL.

Simulator
Simulators are computer programs that accurately mimic what the RTL code specifies. Many designers spend much of their project time in front of simulators, trying to figure out why the simulated machine isn't doing what was intended. (See "Bug.")

SRTL	Structured Register Transfer Language. SRTL is the gold standard for a chip development—it completely specifies exactly what the final silicon chip will do. Many design tools are keyed to the SRTL.
SSE, SSE-II	Streaming SIMD Extensions, an instruction set addition to IA-32, similar to MMX. What MMX did for integers, SSE does for single-precision floating point, and SSE-II does for double-precision floating point.
TTL	Transistor-transistor logic, an older silicon circuit/process technology largely supplanted by CMOS.
Unix	Unix is an operating system developed by Bell Labs in the 1970's.
URL	Uniform Resource Locator, a global address for Web sites on the Internet.
USB	Universal Serial Bus, an interconnect standard for computer systems.
VLIW	Very Long Instruction Word, a way of designing computers where one instruction word (containing hundreds or even thousands of bits) directly controls the operation of multiple functional units. Josh Fisher and Multiflow Computer Inc. pioneered this style of design; Intel's Itanium Processor Family is a descendant.
VTUNE	VTUNE is a software program that works with Intel microprocessors to collect and display performance-related statistics.
Willamette	Code name for the chip development that eventually became the Pentium 4 processor.
Willy	Mike Haertel's Willamette simulator.
x86	Synonym for Intel's 32-bit architecture, IA-32.

INDEX

The Pentium Chronicles. By Robert P. Colwell
© 2006 IEEE Computer Society